Awakening

Awakening is not what you think

Nevşah

BALBOA
PRESS
A DIVISION OF HAY HOUSE

Copyright © 2019 Nevşah.

All rights reserved. No part of this book may be used or reproduced by any means, graphic, electronic, or mechanical, including photocopying, recording, taping or by any information storage retrieval system without the written permission of the author except in the case of brief quotations embodied in critical articles and reviews.

Balboa Press books may be ordered through booksellers or by contacting:

Balboa Press
A Division of Hay House
1663 Liberty Drive
Bloomington, IN 47403
www.balboapress.com
1 (877) 407-4847

Because of the dynamic nature of the Internet, any web addresses or links contained in this book may have changed since publication and may no longer be valid. The views expressed in this work are solely those of the author and do not necessarily reflect the views of the publisher, and the publisher hereby disclaims any responsibility for them.

The author of this book does not dispense medical advice or prescribe the use of any technique as a form of treatment for physical, emotional, or medical problems without the advice of a physician, either directly or indirectly. The intent of the author is only to offer information of a general nature to help you in your quest for emotional and spiritual well-being. In the event you use any of the information in this book for yourself, which is your constitutional right, the author and the publisher assume no responsibility for your actions.

Any people depicted in stock imagery provided by Getty Images are models, and such images are being used for illustrative purposes only.
Certain stock imagery © Getty Images.

Printed in the United States of America.

ISBN: 978-1-9822-2969-6 (sc)
ISBN: 978-1-9822-2971-9 (hc)
ISBN: 978-1-9822-2970-2 (e)

Library of Congress Control Number: 2019908087

Balboa Press rev. date: 07/16/2019

Contents

Introduction vii
1 The Information of Truth 1
2 Awakening 51
3 Breath 77
4 Final Messages 213
5 What Have We Learned? 214

Epilogue 221
Final Test 223

Introduction

I do not have any words to describe what Awakening is.

Therefore, I let go and I let God.

Thank you for reading.

1

THE INFORMATION OF TRUTH

There Is Nobody Out There

Awakening starts when you stop dealing with life itself and accept that all the experience you have is a reflection of your consciousness.

"I am responsible for my life" is the first awakened sentence you will form.

Every experience you have is under the influence of your consciousness. There is nobody out there. Everything you do you do to yourself.

Everything you see in a person you perceive as the other is a reflection of your own accusations, interpretations, and beliefs. This world you think you are in and perceive as reality is a reflection of your own judgments of and guilt about yourself.

Everywhere you look, you see your relationship with yourself. The news you watch, the people you meet while walking on the street, your reflection in the mirror, your best friend, your boss, your colleagues, your spouse—all these show you your judgments about yourself. Remember that whomever you judge reflects the features you accuse yourself of. Therefore, whatever you do you do to yourself—and actually, you do in fact do it to yourself first—is reflected in others.

Try it! Write down the features, behaviors, and events you judge or do not like in people. Write, write, write.

Write at length. Then read what you have written from the beginning. You will see that they all are circumstances, events, and behaviors you judge in yourself and accuse yourself of.

There is nobody out there.

Even the corporate existences you call "people" do not exist. They never did. This information has been hidden from you for centuries on many levels. On the other hand, it has been expressed on many levels.

Albert Einstein proved that the universe is composed of atoms and that 99 percent of an atom is void. Yet, knowing all this, you think there is something material outside. This is really surprising!

The place you call Earth is nothing but a cloud of dust—nothing but the thoughts you have believed in for years and continued for centuries. Do you not believe?

Your world is exactly however you believe the world to be.

You believe that the world exists on its own and separate from you, but actually, the thing you call "world" is a holographic image under the influence of your thoughts and reflects your thoughts. If that were not the case, 99 percent of the atom would not be void.

The place you call Earth does not really exist. This information was hidden from you for years. Maybe it is not hidden; maybe everybody tries to reveal it. But even if it is hidden, the truth comes out eventually.

The truth cannot be hidden forever.

Remember the movie *The Matrix*. Examine the theories of Einstein and the universal laws. Look at your thoughts, make some trials, change those thoughts, and watch how your life changes.

Every moment, you think you're making a decision with your own will. In fact, you play your part in the movie contained in a chip placed in your brain. The irony is, you think that a life formed by a cloud of dust that does not even exist is meaningful because it stimulates your five senses.

We have made a mistake.

We have believed that we are separated from God, and we have come into this psychopathic world. We have believed that this world is real and was really created. We did not just believe it; we invested too much time into the tiny brains we have owned for thousands of years to prove that the world is real.

This mistake can only be made in one way: only a consciousness that doesn't know true life can think this life is real.

We have confused truth with illusion because we do not know the truth. Therefore, we must remember again.

We should question our thoughts, the lives we live, and whether this life is real. We should look for the truth; try to get to know God; and find out the creative energy of Him, His creation, and what He has chosen to create. We should find this out so we can say that things that actually do not exist do not exist and stop saying, "It was created," about a world that was not actually created.

All religious books have contained the same information for centuries. This world is only a split second and a single thought in the presence of God.

The Creator is one. He is the only creator. Only God can create.

Anything not created by God is not actually created.

If this world is composed of a single thought, a single idea, is this thought really created?

Created things own all the features of their creator. If God created a mortal body, then isn't God also mortal? Can someone who never experienced death create death? If God created pain, then doesn't this mean that God also suffers? How can someone who does not know pain create pain? God knows it all.

If He knows it all, how could He create coincidences?

Is anything in this world created if He did not create it?

Look at the world, at your surroundings. Really look. See the features of your world. Let's look around together. From the earthly window, there is death and pain in this world; kids get sick, die, and suffer; blood flows in this world; and bodies chop up other bodies. It is a world full of wars, a place full of diseases. Nothing in this world is permanent. Everything in this world is temporary. Happiness is temporary, peace is temporary, calmness is temporary, pain is temporary—everything is mortal. We all end up with death.

The unity, integrity, and wholeness in this world can be found nowhere else.

Doesn't saying God created such a psychopathic world mean He is psychopathic? How can people have lived with such a delusion for centuries?

So you say that immortal and infinite God created a mortal world?

If He did not, then this world does not exist. Because God is the only creator, anything not created by Him is not created. He is the Creator.

Of course, ego has a counterthesis to all the things I have written. Ego will say to you, "God knows everything. He can create death even if He never experienced it. He cannot experience pain, but He knows." He does not experience but knows? What a grave contradiction these beliefs have!

God is the Creator of all; if we experience the world, then He is also created.

Sister, does this world definitely exist just because you experience it with your five senses? How can you decide that? Who has proven this to you, other than your five senses? Are your five senses real? Are your feelings true? Are your thoughts true?

Ninety-nine percent of the material you touch is void. It does not really exist; it is a cloud of dust. Is this the life you think is real?

Let's look at this from a different perspective.

All religions tell us about the love of God. Despite this, you believe that God has created a psychopathic world, but on the other hand, you believe that He loves you. Does love kill? Does love make you suffer? Does love make you sick? How can God, with infinite love and light, hurt you?

I am sure the ego will answer this. It will say this world is a test, a journey of learning.

Yeah, of course. God separated you from Himself and sent you to this psychopathic world to suffer, shed blood, see wars, attack, and die. He loves you so much that He gave you all these experiences to help you mature and grow up.

He kills you, but He loves you; He makes you sick, but He also loves you—how can you believe all that?

It is not possible for you to be one with God unless you understand that this world is an illusion, a dream, and does not exist.

Why? Because a consciousness thinking that it is created by God cannot surrender to a God taking its life. It can only be intimidated by Him, fear Him, and even hate and resent Him if He takes its loved ones away.

Unless you stop attributing all the disgraces in this world to God, you cannot feel or know the love of God.

Awakening

You have to understand that everything in this world—deaths, wars, diseases, orphaned children, people dying at young ages—is just a thought and not real, and you have to wake up.

Half the people thinking that the world is real secretly resent God and have become atheists, and the other half worship God by fearing Him. The purpose of worshipping should be to be one with God. What you do because you fear Him is not worshipping.

Let me ask you this: Have you ever hugged someone you fear? Have you ever gotten close to that person willingly, despite this feeling?

You haven't, right? You cannot get close to someone like that. On the contrary, you escape from such people.

If God gives you a body and then takes it away—in other words, if God kills you—can you reach Him? Is it possible? Can you get close to Him? Can you surrender yourself to Him? Can you love Him? Can you really, from the depths of your heart, thank Him?

If you believe that this world is real and think that everything in it is created and even created by the Creator, how can you be thankful toward Him? I really wonder.

What are you saying? "My God, thank you for the disaster of soma you have given us. Thank you for the illness and dying children. Thank you for all these diseases"? Can you say this from your heart?

Real thankfulness is only possible by understanding the truth.

There is no world. There never was. It was never created. The world is just a thought, an idea in the presence of God. If a thing not created by God was created, how would it look? It would look like nothing but an idea. You can be thankful for this.

"God, I am thankful that I was mistaken. You did not create such a psychopathic universe; therefore, it was never created. Because something you have not created cannot be created. An idea was not created; actually, it stayed just as an idea. Everything in this world was a temporary dream, even a nightmare. So thank you!"

Communication Is Not Limited as Perceived by the World

There is no limit, shape, system, way, or method of real communication and real connection. God can manifest Himself in many ways. He is everywhere in every second. Thanks to Him, we can communicate with each other anywhere, and we cannot change this fact. We do not need to touch or be near someone or something to communicate. We are constantly communicating.

Quantum physics says that a star millions of kilometers away from us changes when we look at it. Since science and spirituality have not fully met yet, there has not been any explanation comparable to "The consciousness created everything in the cycle of time. There is nobody out there. There is only me." Yet it is pleasing that many scientists are stepping into spirituality. It is time that the information of truth be spread to wider masses on the earth. If not, this book would not exist, and I would not be alive.

Do you know why a star millions of kilometers away changes when we look at it or even think about it? Because that star is in our mind. That is why we are constantly communicating with our surroundings—because we are in communication with the collective consciousness.

Contact is constant. Universal vibration is constant. Life is constant.

We communicate with millions of living creatures we see and don't see around us when we sit somewhere, whether we realize it or not.

Our consciousness is such a bottomless well that most of the time, we do not even realize what we create. It does not matter. The truth is everywhere and constant. Love is everywhere and constant. Real communication, real love, real flow, and infinite vibration are always everywhere. Remember that we only think there is a miscommunication or a distance between ourselves and our loved ones when we are angry with them when we argue with them. This is not possible.

Love is constant. Love is the only truth, and it is constant.

The truth is constant everywhere. There is no way, shape, or method.

If you want to get away from the dark and from mistakes, get away from the dark and from mistakes Stop looking there, and get away from the thought that darkness may exist.

AWAKENING

There is no darkness. There never was.

There is actually nothing to get close to or away from. When we feel ourselves in darkness, when we think we are all alone without anyone, we fool ourselves. All these thoughts are meaningless illusions created by the slightly slipped side of our consciousness, the ego. They have never actually existed—never.

You can relax. There is nobody to get away or hide from.

The thought that we are separated from each other is an illusion.

There is nothing out there.

There is only one truth: self. And self is everywhere.

Illusions can only exist within the cycle of time, and the cycle of time itself is an illusion. Pure love that thinks it is lost within an illusion of time and has never actually left its home—that is us!

It is crazy that we think we can change life.

Anything not created by God is not actually created. He can only create love and heaven. He cannot create anything but total love.

Total perfection cannot create anything else. Total light does not create darkness.

Everything we experience other than these is just a dream, a fabrication. It was never created.

The mortal world is just a split second and idea in the presence of God.

What is submission? Surrendering to God? It is nothing but remembering the truth; staying in the presence; and being connected to God, His breath, and His self. Can someone who has surrendered to Him and to the self, who thinks with Him and lives in line in the presence of Him, dream? Can such a person create illusions?

No.

Submission is not letting go of yourself and doing nothing; it is ensuring you are with Him consciously. It is being conscious and aware and staying in the moment and in connection with Him. It is surrendering to yourself; to what you do, will do, say, and will say; and to the power that controls you and being with Him no matter what.

Truth is always under the protection of God in this moment.
There is only one reason, one source of truth: God.
But there are thousands of reasons for and sources of illusions.

Every time we judge someone, we cause the message "We care about the illusion" in deep parts of our consciousness. But why would we care and judge something that does not exist?

Judging is actually a war declared by the ego against the consciousness. Judging harms our awareness because it causes us to have the feeling that something other than God's will may exist. It causes us to forget Him.

Anything created by Him is total and perfect.

You believe that the brain in your body can think, right?

Actually, what helps us think is the mind—His mind. The organ called the brain in our body has nothing to do with this.

We can think using His mind.

What good is a brain without life energy?

Think about people in a vegetative state. The brains of those people stay where they are, right? But since they do not work, maybe because the connection required in the mind for them to think and work is severed, they go into a vegetative state. It's not because the brain is not going somewhere or is disappearing; it's because its connection with the mind is severed.

When I was a kid, the brother of one of my friends had brain damage. His brain had many diseases. In other words, it was incompatible, or its connection was severed. At that age, it was impossible for me to understand what that brain damage was. Apparently, he had a body and brain just like mine. However, despite the fact that he was much older than I was, he seemed not to know what to do with his hands and feet. He made weird noises and uncontrollably made seemingly meaningless things with his hands and feet.

All meaningless things can exist when the meaning ends. When the connection with the truth that brings meaning to our lives is severed, not only do true and unnatural things start to happen in our lives, but also, we start to experience pain, remorse, and problems not compatible with our lives.

Actually, there is only one reason for all: incompetence or disconnection. For a person disconnected from the source, the meaning, and the truth, it is natural to appear in an inhuman situation.

The human, who is created by God, the perfect existence, can incorporate health, happiness, joy, satisfaction, love, and intelligence in its own nature and essence. When all these are disconnected from the source and mind, then they are impossible to continue.

We have the power to make truth, excellence, and perfect possibilities in human nature the truth of this world. Of course, it is not possible to change that truth. The truth always exists, and it always will. It does not change. It does not decrease or increase. Nothing happens to it. Our human truth is just like that.

A human is an excellent existence with perfect possibilities within its form. This existence can pour love, light, mercy, joy, and health into its life through His mind.

Divided, Separated Truth

The truth created by brain-body relation exists in the possibility (i.e., assumption or thought) that the human being is inherently separated from the Creator's one mind. Since there is truth where there is no separation and since the truth is one, an unreal creator—an artificial god or the ego—can only exist where that singularity, infinity, perfection, and truth is distorted or seems to be distorted. As-ifs happens like that. People seem as if they are sick or as if they are sad, for example.

What is the same cannot be different. What is one cannot have separate components or bodies.

Well, what is more natural than this? There is one infinite, unlimited, perfect Creator. However, a mock creator tries to be His competitor and creates illusions because it cannot create the truth—because truth has only one Creator. These two naturally and inherently cannot be together; one comes from eternity and goes to eternity, and the other creates a reality with an ending. One comes from love and goes to love, and the other creates weird energies, such as love, anger, and pain. One is the God of infinite beauties, and the other creates ugliness along with the things it calls beauty. In this case, the beauty or goodness created is not, of course, real; it is just a form of beautiful, infinite goodness that can end or turn bad.

I have to ask: Can beauty with an end, a light that goes off, or goodness that can go bad come from infinity? Can something be infinite and at the same time have an ending? Can something be continuous and at the same time noncontinuous?

We have been deceived, haven't we? This is called the ego trap.

The ego can do nothing but try to trap us and deceive us, right?

It is only possible with a deception to hide a truth that does not change and always infinitely continues and to make it seem as if it is not real. It is possible only with a simple spell. That is the game of ego.

I am sure you have heard the phrase "detaching from earthly pleasures" many times. We live on this earth, but we are not earthlings.

Islam and many other religions tell you to prepare for the other world, not this one, and not to be too detached from this world. What they mean by "this world" is actually the world that does not exist—in other words, the illusion in which agonies, sadness, diseases, mistakes, sins, and evil can exist. Why would we deal with a dream, an illusion, or an unnatural thing? Why would we spend time on it?

When some part of your body aches, does the pain go away when you dwell on it, or does it disappear when you forget about it?

The energy goes wherever our awareness goes. The thing we pour our energy to grows.

If we did not dwell on diseases, mistakes, problems, and agonies as much and if we could say, "This is not even real!" then it would all be good. Because they never existed; they just seem to exist with our energy.

Imagine that time is a line, and the time from our birth to our death is marked on this line. You are born, and you live for seventy, eighty, or a hundred years. The life starts with birth at one point and ends with death at another point. It is a journey we can show on a line.

Now imagine that time does not really exist. Everything happens in this moment. Connect the points where the line starts and ends. This is real life.

Awakening

The life-and-death cycle you think you are living, the dream, happens between these two points. However, in reality, there is nothing now.

Nothing.

And everything.

Real life happens now. The heaven you created with God. We are the creators, directors, and audience of this life-and-death cycle.

We are hand in hand with God now.

Other than this moment, we think that we can create something without Him and that there are things we have created without Him. We are becoming detached from ourselves and from Him.

Whatever He creates, we act as if He created the opposite, something He cannot have created with the thought that there are certain things He cannot create. We believe He created pain, sadness, mistakes, sin, crime, torture, failure, death, and diseases. The moment when we believe all these might exist is the moment we are detached from the now.

We, by ourselves, did not create anything. We cannot.

The cycle of time and the things inside, past and present, were never created.

All that lives can only exist within Him.

The mortal world and the real world are not the same.

When we let ourselves be deceived by the illusion of time, we live the same experiences again and again. Just like repeating dreams.

The only way to connect with this truth and wake up is to go deep into this repetition. We must breathe again and again, constantly, to wake up to the cycle, wake up from the cycle, and be free in the cycle.

This is only possible through connected breaths while living in the cycle.

If we can stay connected to ourselves, to our breathing, we can realize that all the pain, sadness, disappointment, and diseases are products of imagination and were actually never created. We only experience them until we see the truth and wake up completely.

We can wake up to the fact that the cycle of time is the repetition of the same movie, and we can be freed from its spell.

This place is a spell. It's an unreal place where the ego tries to deceive us by using our senses.

Turn to God. Just look at Him, remember Him, and be in connection with Him.

Just hold on to Him, to the real life.

Create only with Him, and serve just Him.

Because nothing different is possible. As we think it is possible, as we think the negativities, pains, wars, fights, anger, and badness that were not created and could not have been created by God are real, then we create nightmares for ourselves that are never actually created. We might we think we can create something alone, but we cannot do this. However, we can throw ourselves into illusions and stories that never existed and never will.

Wake up!

Stop dealing with diseases, pains, and problems that are not even real, and turn to God.

Leave the mortal world and the meaningless stories you fictionalize by yourself, and accept what He created, His words, His eternity, His beauty, and the infinite life.

It is crazy not to be able to do such a simple thing and to constantly, pertinaciously, and willingly create pains, fears, torture, wars, fights, and diseases.

In fact, the only sick part of us is our mind.

The only real disease is thinking that anything other than perfection, integrity, magnitude, love, infinite grace, blessing, health, joy, happiness, peace, and energy may exist.

The part of us that thinks that anything other than the ones created by God and the heaven created by Him might exist and that this life can turn into a nightmare is the only part that is broken and needs to be fixed.

Everything can be made right in the truth and light of God. Anything that does not go right and does not flow is the reflection of our part—the ego—that tries to get away and stay away from Him.

Awakening to truth is nothing but being one with His mind, the mind of the Creator to whom all of us are connected.

When this connection is formed, all the illusions, pains, anger, conflicts, and feelings of being lost or stuck created by the brain-body relation go away. When we leave the ego system, the mechanism that makes the illusion all unreal nonsense seems to exist or to have been created. When we leave the ego and turn to the one mind, the words end. Then only a deep quietness, creativity, and He exist.

You just need to turn to Him, look at Him, and not deal with the other nonsense. God will do the rest.

It does not matter how we turn. You can perform the salat, meditate, or fast. You can pray in Turkish, English, Arabic, or Persian. It does not matter.

God is the Creator of all, and He listens to us all the time.

The Eyes of the Body Can Only See Fear

Maybe you believe that you can be full of only bodily pleasure. Maybe you perceive the world as a place that can give you peace, happiness, and satisfaction.

Whatever your dreams, desires, and hopes are, the result is always a disappointment, isn't it? And there is no discrimination here; all within the reality of life live the same things. Don't they?

What if this is not the case? What if it is you who creates the pains, diseases, and negativities you live? What if God only created the beauties, wealth, health, and happiness, and we cannot see this truth because we do not intermediate for Him?

It is possible to live in heaven.

It is also possible to create heaven.

And to remind heaven.

It is also possible to watch heaven.

There are people who know, see, and currently live the infinite heaven in the background of this world.

The pain and nonsense you experience is not there; it is not created.

There are people who do not live any of that other nonsense because they turn to God and choose God. It is possible.

It is possible to wake up and maintain that awakening.

How? By remembering that the mortal life is an empty dream and has no meaning within itself and by saying, "I am fictionalizing it all within this dream, the cycle of time, under constant influence of my consciousness. And I can create everything again hand in hand with God, with the same thoughts, with His light!"

We must remember that the real creative power belongs only to Him. The illusions are not created by Him and, therefore, do not have sources. They are purposeless and not created.

We cannot create anything without Him. We might think we do; we might think the illusions are real. But anything not created by Him was never created. The energy of creation was not included in our illusions. Therefore, none of them are eternal. The dream is bound to end at some point because it has never actually existed. It was never created.

Let's give up on chasing empty dreams. Let's choose to create with God so that we can create happiness, peace, and love and live in heaven.

Let's be free from the illusion and awake to the truth.

When we wake up to the fact that the nightmares we experience are temporary dreams we create, none of the things we have lived with will matter anymore. When we give up on ascribing meaning to meaningless things, real liberation begins—because we wake up.

There is nothing to forgive, because the things to be forgiven never actually existed. They were never created.

The duality, distinction, crowd, and distinctness we see when we look at the world on our own with our own will and awareness, our consciousness—created by disturbing our breathing—may scare us, confuse us, and disturb us. However, when we look at it by remembering who we are in the world and remembering that God is always by our side and that this world is a simple design, a dream, and when we beautify everything with the light of the truth by including His holiness, the duality, crowd, and distinctness may be seen as reflections of the eternal love, light, happiness, and peace.

When we live our lives by remembering that we live the truth at every moment, this place turns into heaven.

You can change your whole life with a single choice. We can change, beautify, and heal this dream we are having by choosing to live lives remembering God. Healing is nothing but remembering the truth. We can reflect His light, love, beauty, and holiness here to this world, and we can create with Him, with our healed mind, every day.

And of course, everything we see now is a reflection of Him. This is the only way to be liberated from all the nonsense we have experienced and to completely heal.

The only way we can stay comfortable, peaceful, happy, healthy, and sane in this world is to carry God's holiness to the world. Then you can feel at home, get comfortable, and be safe. We can find the trust He gave us in our friends and our family. We can feel His love in everyone everywhere. We can see Him in the eyes of everyone we meet, in all living creatures.

God is everywhere.

We can explain the illusion we live as follows: The Holy Spirit, which cannot leave the side of God, has never left it, and never will, saw a dream. It saw a tiny dream as short as a split second: "What if there is a world in which God is not by my side, a world I created myself? What if this world is the opposite of everything I know and everything that belongs to Him?" Then an infinite possibility was born. Bodies, lives, experiences—none of them were lived. None of them exist; they are all products of imagination. The Holy Spirit realizes that it is aware of everything. It remembers the truth, so to feel the dream more, to absorb it and live it as if it were real, it adds consciousness into the dream and makes that consciousness aware only of the things happening in the dream. It creates that consciousness in such a way that it will not remember the truth, so it will forget where it is, get caught in the dream, and live everything in it as if it were real.

Think of a 3-D movie. When the required tools—suitable glasses and a sound system—are given to us, we think we are actually in that movie. We get so caught up that we feel as if we are experiencing everything happening in the movie. We react, scream, fear, and move. Actually, we never leave the seat during the time we watch the movie. Our reality does not change during the movie; we sit there and watch. There are moments during the movie when we forget where we are and get lost in the movie. We think we are really in it, but actually, one part of us always knows the truth.

Based on what does the consciousness create? We create what we want to live. We create based on the status of our consciousness.

A restricted consciousness that is only aware of this world has no other awareness. It will never understand the truth and does not know the creative power, infinity, wholeness, and integrity that we, as holy spirits, own. It tries to restrict us. But we constantly overcome ourselves—that is, our restricted consciousness—and create totally different situations. Actually, it is also surprised. He cannot fully understand the truth because its capacity is limited. Therefore, all wise people say, "The truth is not something we can understand with our mind." A restricted consciousness—in other words, a consciousness whose awareness is restricted to understanding the mortal world and dream—cannot understand the truth of our soul. Circumstances in which we exceed ourselves; don't care what our minds tell us; and overcome all the limits and rules, the system of the mind, and this world are called miracles.

We are a miracle. We are much more than what the rules, laws, and systems of this world can understand.

The restricted consciousness and mind cannot even imagine our real identity and the wisdom, wealth, infinity, and wholeness of the Holy Spirit, which are parts of God, and only busy themselves with creating this world and being aware of what is going on here. The conscious mind does not know the truth; it thinks we should develop constantly. Since it thinks that an unreal dream is real, it thinks there should be a reason for our existence here. Are there any reasons for the dreams? Can any dream that does not exist have any purpose or reason?

No, but the restricted consciousness, mind, and ego think so.

The restricted mind thinks we came here to develop, move forward, and mature. It has a magnificent system to ensure this: pain. It think the more pain there is, the more progress there is. This consciousness thinks the nightmare it saw in bed is real and that struggles like little children tossing around. Its motto is "Feel the pain. Pain is what makes you feel you exist and what makes you remember that you are alive. Feel it."

Actually, the restricted consciousness does a good job. Yes, this is its job: to ensure you sink into the event. Ego, thinking that the best thing to do is go through pain, gives us this product to do its job in the best way.

The ego believes that it matures us with pain. Only our mind can have such a thought; the Holy Spirit always remembers the truth.

The only way to enlightenment is to connect with our spirit through our breath.

Only our Holy Spirit can remind us of the truth.

Since we use a restricted mind and consciousness in this dream, everything in this dream is created with the same system. All movies, experiences, images, dreams, and imaginations have the same system. As we dream, the consciousness creating this life works.

In our consciousness, the part of us that thinks we are separate from God—the ego—starts to fear and panic. It creates nightmares when it believes in this thought and feels alone and desperate. These are just like the nightmares in our sleep. The same part of our consciousness creates both. Imagine your child having a nightmare. He makes weird noises, yells, fears, and becomes angry; it is obvious he is under the influence of the nightmare. Look at his movements and reactions—he thinks the nightmare is real. We react because we think the things we live are real.

Your little child has not woken up; he is stuck in the nightmare. It is obvious he is scared; he sweats, and he is bothered. Even though he is sleeping in his room, in his bed safely, he thinks what he sees is real at that moment, just as we think the nightmares we create are real. However, you know that what your child sees and lives is just a dream.

We cannot go into another person's dream. Why? Because it is not real. It belongs to the person dreaming. It is an illusion. God cannot enter the illusions we create. He does not know what we live in our nightmare. How can He know? It is all a product of imagination.

But what happens when the child wakes up from the dream? Nothing. Where does the dream go? Nowhere, because it has never existed, and anything that has not existed cannot go anywhere.

What happens when we create while remembering this life and truth all the time? Everything we create is a reflection of God and His holiness, infinity, wealth, beauty, and health. How limited our consciousness is. The holiness of God can reflect everywhere and exist everywhere through us. There is no power enough to limit His infinity.

How does life turn out to be when we start to live our lives with Him? It is filled with the Holy Spirit, divine love, and thousands of successive miracles. It is filled with magnificent, magical experiences that we cannot understand with our restricted mind. It's the reflection of the perfect, the form of heaven descended in the world!

You Cannot Suffer Enough

Previously, I stated that God cannot enter our dreams. But we all hear Him when He says, "Do not worry. I am always by your side. It is all just a dream. It is temporary."

What do you do if you see your child having a nightmare, being scared, screaming, and believing it is real? Don't you slowly wake him and say, "You are safe; it is just a dream"? God does the same to us.

God did not create the mortal truth. An infinite thing does not know what *end* means, and it cannot want or create it. Therefore, death was never created. What we call "death" is nothing but a product of our imagination, an illusion.

We create all the pain, sadness, negativity, wars, and fights we live, and we think this illusion can be different.

God is always with us. He never left us. It is impossible for all these negativities that we believe we can create by ourselves to exist, because it is impossible for us to be alone.

When will you stop believing that we can be separated from God? That we can stay away from Him? That anything not created by Him can exist? How long will you continue to see the flowers, trees, and angels created by God in this heaven as toxic materials, as monsters?

It is hopeless to search for hope in a place where hope does not exist. It is absurd to search for love in a place where we shut ourselves off to God, the only true love. It is unreasonable to expect peace from moments when we turn down peace.

The thing we are looking for, the truth, is not within the illusion we created. Turn to God. Everything you search for is with Him.

When we forget who we really are and think this illusion is real, we ascribe too much meaning to our bodies, material things, events, and places. We babble when we forget that the true meaning is not within life but within ourselves. Just like the child who forgets he is actually sleeping comfortably in his room and sinks into the dream he is having, when we forget who we actually are, whom we are with, and our real home and think that what we see is real, we panic, fear, and stumble. We start to ascribe value and meaning to tiny, meaningless things—a body, a house, a car, and the world of things we've created. Then everything starts to be meaningless, and we feel lost.

No matter how far away we feel ourselves to be from God, this separation never occurs.

Going home—awakening—is inevitable because what we see in our sleep has never existed.

If you have woken up from the dream, if you are aware of who you are, if you know the greatness of the core of yourself and others, this body; this life; and the experiences, events, people, and reality of the material world seem small.

We are part of the infinite, limitless, and perpetual truth. Nothing in this world can be compared to this truth.

When these tiny hands touch others, they cannot satisfy the giant core within us. When these two tiny bodies stand side by side, the love searched for by that giant spirit cannot be experienced.

Humans make the biggest mistake by thinking that they are only composed of a body and that the truth is only composed of an illusion created.

When we think we are separate from God and think this dream to be true, then fear and panic start. This thought becomes inevitable.

Fear causes people to defend themselves. Fear is the only reason for a fight or war. The person who remembers that God is always by his side and knows that God has unlimited potential, power, abundance, mercy, belief, love, and trust never attacks and never defends himself. When we wake up from the dream, we know that whatever happens in a simple dream cannot harm us.

Whatever life you are living, whatever the conditions and circumstances are, the truth is only composed of an illusion created. We can hear God whenever we want, and we can connect with Him whenever we want. We can hear His breath and His voice, and we can feel His presence.

We can turn this dream into heaven with His trust, support, love, grace, and blessing and with Him always by our side.

There is only one purpose, one way in truth, because there is only one truth. Our purpose is to turn toward God again, because we actually never left Him. Since the only purpose is to turn to Him, other purposes or targets in life never satisfy us.

As you know, natural breathing is the most natural form of our breath; the breath given to us by God is also the path taking us to Him, the sound reminding us of Him, and the guide ensuring we can connect with His presence, our Holy Spirit. Most of us—statistics tell us 90 percent—start to disturb this breath when we are at the age of two or three. You will remember this information from my books titled *Nefes (Breath)* and *Yansımalar (Reflections)*.

With the development of ego, we see that around the time when all fears start to manifest themselves, as well as thoughts of being separated from God and being able to create without Him, we disturb our breathing.

Breathing is the path to God. The Holy Spirit ensures that God is connected to us and that He can remind us of Himself.

When we start to twist our natural, holy breath given to us by God, we feel separated from Him, and we feel unprotected, loveless, missing, limited, and mortal. The fear of death starts in our hearts. The fear of failure, lovelessness, worries, uneasiness, problems, and diseases occur.

The fastest way for a person to make himself sick is by disturbing his breath. When we disturb our breath, our connection with God—the only place we belong to; our only home; and our eternity, grace, love, and understanding—severs. We forget who we are, and we feel lost.

Our first duty is to be one with God, walk with Him, talk to Him, and create our lives with Him.

Our second duty is to bring everyone together with Him and thank God that it is happening.

Life continues as life, as a simple dream, and our core is aware that it seems to be living here, but it actually is not here; it is resting by the side of God. The Holy Spirit, filled with rest, peace, and silence, is actually the sole truth of all of us. What we live does not actually matter. When we are able to remember this, we are saved.

Everyone will devote him- or herself to God one day because there is no other truth. We are already one with Him. There is no other choice we can make.

We can pretend to be separated from Him, as if we have other targets and other purposes, for some time, but it does not matter. Eventually, everyone will turn to Him because we never left Him.

All diseases and problems start with a single twisted thought: *I can be separate from God.*

Thoughts of *I can think without Him. I can do or create something without Him. I can have a separate will and desire* continue with this twist. All these thoughts arise from not making a distinction between illusion and the truth.

Disease is inevitable for the mind that assumes illusion is real.

The ego continuously tries to draw us into the illusion and make us forget the truth. It looks for ways to make us believe that unreal things can exist. It struggles to prove all these are real. It believes that if enough evidence is found and enough studies are made, someday we can be fooled forever. It tries to make us believe that our perfection can be disturbed and that we can get sick, get hurt, and be unhappy with justified reasons, necessities, and circumstances.

It constantly creates reasons for this. They should be proven.

You have justified reasons and justifications to get sick, don't you?

What about age? It has been proven that our cells age over the years, hasn't it?

There are many reasons to die, aren't there? When someone gets sick or dies, the doctor can list the causes.

Every problem seems to have a reason, doesn't it? Your sadness? Your pain? Your disappointments? They all have reasons.

The window is open; you get cold. That is why you become sick. If your beloved cheats on you, you can be sad. You have a justified reason to be sad. He slapped you. You are hurt. He hurt you. What he said wore you down, made you sad, and disappointed you. Don't you feel how your heart aches? The things he said caused this. You have a fever; you are sick. Your blood showed this. You are sick. That happened to you. Go right to the hospital. Have tests and workups. The evidence proving your sickness has been collected.

The weirdest part is that we really believe all these to be real! We believe we can die, get old, get sick, get tired, and get sad; we believe the imaginary events of this world can really affect us.

During breathing sessions, there are people—if people get caught up in the dream too much—who think something is happening to them, even though all they do is breathe. They lie down comfortably in the session, they just inhale and exhale, and they get up, saying "I am having a heart attack! I am going to faint!" Can you believe that? When God's breath—our life, which is pure, living energy—starts to fill us, sometimes we think even that can hurt us!

When I ask these people, they all have some justified reasons they learned. She felt her heart tighten or her head ache. If there had been someone around saying, "This could be the symptom of a disease," or if she had read in the newspaper that tightening of the heart meant a heart attack, she would probably have had an infarction then.

Ego has a mechanism to prove with a reference to past events that is so stereotyped and so embedded in the subconscious that we can make even the healthiest baby have serious diseases in a couple of hours just because it has dust in its nose and sneezed.

If there is even one person believing in diseases around us, we have the potential to get sick, because this is a reflection of the belief in our consciousness that we can get sick.

Ego is continuously trying to prove unreal things so that it can create and so that they can appear as if they exist.

If there is a reason, we can get sick. If there is a reason, we can die.

God is outside, in front of, behind, and beyond this whole cause-and-effect system. His holy and unlimited power is outside the system created by restricted minds needing proof.

God's reflection in this life appears as a miracle. A miracle is beyond all evidence, theories, and laws. Miracles are gifts given to us. They are gifts of God. They do not work with the system of this world.

I have seen people whose cancer, panic attacks, and intestinal failures were cured just because their breath was opened as they remembered the truth and accepted God's gifts. People who recovered had sane minds because they remembered who they were and woke up from the dream. People healed themselves when they were schizophrenic, did not hear, or stuttered. Today there are thousands of people who've had successive miracles after participating in miracle courses and opening their breath.

They do not need to prove their miracles because the miracle is the answer of all.

Only illusions need proof or evidence.

The truth does not need to prove itself. When we wake up to the truth, there can be miracles beyond the whole system—all the rules, medicine, and science we know and learn in this world. It is super that science is starting to deal with spirituality, even slowly. Scientists are realizing that they cannot get anywhere by determining and proving problems and diseases. I am sure humans will do much more. Scientists aware of the spiritual truth have started to realize that they make a disease exist when they confirm it.

Awakening

God is the only Creator; anything not created by Him is not created. The truth is not open for discussion. It does not change. It does not develop, exist, disappear, start, or end. It is eternal and infinite. It is the same for everyone, and it is indisputably accurate and true. In truth, in the point of truth, there is only one purpose, one idea, and one truth.

But ego is different for everyone. It serves different ideas, purposes, and truths. Every consciousness that has chosen ego has its own reasons and proving mechanisms. Those minds try to prove themselves. They try to make unreal things real, and this makes people sick. It is a waste of effort.

Ego has different perspectives, perceptions, and idols it serves. Millions of possibilities we believe were created after billions of different perceptions are illusions.

It is variable, it is plural, and it is disputable; its truth can never be proven. It just confuses, makes people uneasy, and brings sadness and pain. It is the perfect mechanism for creating pain.

The only way out is to turn to God and remember the truth. There is no other way.

We must turn to the mind as it was created by God in the purest, cleanest form. When we make this turn choice, illusions automatically end. Unity and oneness are chosen. Everything is plural, driving us to different ends. The truth is chosen, and all arguments are finished. All arguments, wars, errors, and perspectives come to an end when we make this choice.

We then experience a single existence, the same information, the same light, and the same truth. Only truth enlightens when everyone makes the same choice. There is nothing to be afraid of because light does not seem different to anyone. The truth is the same for everyone; it never deceives. It does not flow less to one person and more to another. The light, truth, and true love embrace everyone the same. With the same unification and oneness, the light unconditionally flows to everyone.

There is nothing to fear from this equality. This order is perfect and eternal.

All fears end at the point of truth. All fears end when we take shelter in God. Only by His side and under His protection, not before or after, do we find truth.

All arguments, judgments, and proof exist in the point of distinction. The only truth felt, known by everyone, does not need any proof, because the ones who know and realize choose silence. Silence is the expression of truth.

Forgiveness is one of the most important steps to enlightenment.

Getting away from the dream, the illusion, and the mechanism that makes us believe that anything other than truth can exist—getting away from ego—is the only possible way to leave the whole illusion behind—in other words, by forgiving.

Forgiving means letting all the experiences go to the illusion, to the place where they belong, so they can go back outside existence and truth.

Forgiving means remembering that we are in a dream, and everything happening here does not really matter; all experiences, emotions, and feelings are games to keep us in the illusion we created and to make us believe the reality of the illusion by letting the game go on.

Ego Has Its Plan of Forgiveness

When we think the events of this world are real, we can make our ego mind believe this. In this case, first we accuse the people across from us and humiliate them, and then we forgive. Our message is clear: "You are disgusting. You are a tiny, miserable rat. You are wrong. You are evil. You are stupid. But since I am a supreme creature and am superior to you, I am forgiving you."

There is nobody out there. We are the ones who create all the experiences we live. Everything we live is a reflection of the status of our consciousness.

Every time we accuse someone or judge someone, deep down in our consciousness, we say, "You deserve to be accused."

When we do not see the people across from us as part of us and define them as others, we give away some part of our consciousness.

Every time we hide ourselves by saying the word *others* and every time we are not honest, we create hidden components that are pushed deep down until we cannot reach them anymore.

Every time we see ourselves as different from others, we move away from ourselves.

There is nobody out there. Everything out there is a reflection of our consciousness. Everyone we call "someone else" is the diseased place inside us, which we alienate.

Health is only possible with awakening to the truth.

When we wake up to the truth, remember we are whole and one, and remember our eternity and who we really are, the illusions will not mean anything anymore.

Then the journey to the truth starts.

When we remember the truth inside, the absolute and final journey to God starts. We start to see the circumstances that our consciousness has split from the one as our own circumstances, we start to help and support everyone who is lost and thinks the illusion is real, and we begin to forgive everything for ourselves.

We know. The truth has always been and always will be. There is nothing untrue and never will be. Truth can only be created by God. Anything not created by Him is not actually created. All these illusions the ego thinks it can create without God (i.e., create by itself) never existed. Therefore, real forgiveness is waking up to truth.

Real forgiveness is understanding that there is nothing to forgive.

The illusion we live when we believe that we can create without God and that we have free will when we choose ego is doomed to end someday. When we try to change, improve, or correct meaningless things in the illusion, which is not even remotely connected to true creation, all these efforts are meaningless. Real creation already makes this change. It is impossible for the illusions to exist or continue for long within real existence. He is the one erasing the illusions. Anything untrue has never existed and will never exist.

The acceptance that illusions do not exist is the only forgiveness and only cure.

How many times do we need to live the same things again and again to be liberated from the nightmare that we think we created but that actually never existed to accept that it is not real and leave it behind?

We were in a nightmare we created, a nightmare that did not exist, and now we have woken up.

All we need to do to be liberated from all this unreal nonsense and wake from this bad dream is to surrender to God.

Know that we are equipped with all the tools required for our salvation.

All words end with God. Sentences stop, and lips get sealed. At this point, words, information, and beliefs are all insufficient and unnecessary. They all lose their meaning; only holiness stays.

Do you want to remember peace, unity, oneness, and real peace? Forgive. Forgive yourself and everyone. Forgive unconditionally and unlimitedly.

We are the ones who will forgive ourselves because we are the ones who pretend to create all these bad experiences we live.

Asking for forgiveness from God would be possible only if He had had something to do with this illusion.

God can only create oneness, eternity, wealth, mercy, love, expansion, growth, development, infinity, and definitiveness as Himself. The Holy Spirit does not know what a condition is, what crime is, what death is, or what lovelessness is, and He does not create such things.

God only creates happiness, true love, wealth, unity, and peace, embodiments of Himself.

God is love; He does not accuse, and He does not forgive, as He does not accuse. He loves, loves, and loves all His subjects and the whole of creation unconditionally. He embraces and caresses all of existence.

God created all His subjects in the same way—with the same breath and the same beautiful, pure thoughts—so they can get His beauties. We are the ones who disturb the breath, its will, its balance, and its mind; we are the ones disturbing its natural form.

When we remember the truth and create this dream with Him, everything will be beautiful, healed, and united.

If we experience ourselves as defective, missing, or erroneous; if our lives are filled with mistakes, defects, and problems; or if there are diseases, pains, and sadness, it is because we sailed away from Him. We did not choose Him and only Him. We disturbed and twisted our natural form, natural breath, and natural mind structure created by Him. It does not actually happen; it just seems to.

God loves us unconditionally. He does not punish. He does not get mad.

God has never accused us. We are the ones accusing ourselves and feeling guilty. Actually, there is only one reason for this: we created this illusion, thinking we can create something without Him, and we are living silly circumstances that do not really exist. Every time we experience these circumstances, we feel guilty because even if our mind is not aware, our soul is aware of what we are doing: we are fooling ourselves by trying to create illusions that do not exist.

God will wake us from the nightmare we are living and remind us that all these illusions do not actually exist.

His side is the place where we all want to be. In real terms, everyone, every soul, is searching for this. This is an option we all want to choose.

When we do not face God, a natural crime mechanism within us starts to operate. That is inevitable because we only want the things He has given us, the things coming from Him. We wish for happiness, peace, love, wealth, comfort, and health. When we believe we can create other possibilities and cannot have the others as we experience, we blame ourselves because we cannot face God. We blame ourselves because instead of the most beautiful and perfect experiences created, we are in an unreal act every moment we dive into the illusion we created. We have forgotten our power, our integrity, whom we really belong to, and who we really are; we have our way—and, of course, we feel guilty for doing this.

Forgive. Forgiveness is the path that takes us to the truth, our home. As you forgive, you go back from the place you have gone, from the illusion you are lost in, to your home. You will wake up. When you forgive all the choices you have made without knowing yourself and others and all wanderings and unreal acts, when you do this completely and for eternity, you will come back home.

Forgive. Remember that today, yesterday, and even tomorrow and all the experiences that may happen in the illusion never existed, and forgive completely now.

Accept and forgive yourself and the subjects of God. Forgive all tricky irregularities seeming to be created. Do this because they never existed.

Teaching Is Setting an Example

The only true teacher is God, and He teaches with His infinite love, acceptance, embrace, wealth, holiness, and eternal power of forgiveness.

There was an old and angry farmer. He was rich and had thousands of hectares of land and hundreds of workers. Everyone knew him for his cruelty, and they were all afraid of him. One day a poor man came to the lands of the farmer. He stole a few fruits from the garden for himself and his hungry children. But he was caught before he could get away. The workers took him to the farmer and explained what had happened. The farmer said in anger, "Hang him right away as an example to the others!"

Another day, a poor couple entered the farmer's garden to take food for their family, and they were caught. The workers took them to their boss. The farmer said again, "Hang them right away as an example to the others!"

Years passed, and many were hanged because they entered the farmer's garden similarly. The farmer got older, and one day he died. Feeling guilty about the things he had done in the world, he walked to the doors of heaven. He tried to sneak in without being seen. He walked and walked until one of God's angels stopped him. In regret, the man told what he had done in the world, and the angel ordered the officers, "Forgive as an example to him!"

Don't you know that the universe and creative power stand at attention for our desires? The universe and the energy of creation are looking forward to fulfilling our desires because our desires are their desires. But as long as we do not fulfill them, as long as we do not live our core, He does not support us. He cannot get to us because of all the fear and pain we produce. It is not surprising that the desires of people are not fulfilled when there are so many fear mechanisms and so many people fooled by them in this world.

Life is actually an easy, beautiful order. Everything happens automatically and easily when we are faithful to ourselves and do not think, *What would others say? What would happen then?* When our own balance and own order of life start to serve us and the events that nobody can understand or believe start to happen successively, all of a sudden, we reach our target.

A man serving his core; being completely faithful to himself; and living with surprising determination, power, and obstinacy taught me true love, commitment, devotion, and faithfulness. He was so connected to his core and had such a huge power to do the things we wanted to do that he became a true teacher for everyone around him. His freedom and courage were an example for everyone and encouraged those around him to live for themselves. This man changed my life. I, who has been a teacher for years and also is still a student, changed everything in my life in a couple of months thanks to him. He stood as a good example for me, as well as others, and he showed things I needed to see so beautifully that it was impossible for me not to change. I looked at my life and asked myself the following questions: "Is this the place I want to live in? Is this the person I want to be with? Do I want such a life?"

Maybe they were tiny details that caught my eye, but each was important. I did not have to live anything my core did not come to live or anything I did not deserve or want. Whatever situation I was in and whatever I was doing, whatever people around me said, myself and my desires were more important. It was as if the universe were looking forward to carrying my life to a better, more beautiful level. "Decide!" it was saying to me. "Just decide. I will handle the rest for you."

And it happened just like that. The day I decided, my life started to flow at a different pace. It was as if everything and everyone were supporting me. When I decided to leave my second husband and step into the life I really wanted to live, I was pregnant with my second child. Can you believe that? I was pregnant, and I decided to leave my husband. Although many could not understand that, people who knew me and knew I had become more and more devoted to myself and was progressing determinedly in that path thought it was normal. In that situation seen as incomprehensible, weird, and even insensitive or impudent from a social-consciousness level, all I saw was a woman running to her faith. A woman running to herself. A woman faithful to her core. It required a huge amount of courage, determination, and belief because I had no reason to divorce in the level of world consciousness. My inner voice answered the question "But why?" with "Because." Because I felt so, I knew it should happen, I was sure about what I wanted, I was determined, and I was going forward. It was hard to explain, but everyone seemed to understand. I started to talk to people from a different level, from a different dimension.

Everyone easily and rapidly adapted to my decision I made to be faithful to my soul, my core, even if it seemed contradictory to everyone and everything. It was as if the universe were working for me, spending all its energy for me, and celebrating me because I held myself before everything, was faithful to myself, and did everything I wanted. My gift became the biggest gift in the world. I met the person I had spent years looking for. I felt deep inside me a perfectness I could not have even imagined as a gift of God to me, with divine, infinite, constantly increasing love and commitment. He was like a gift sent to me by God. The day I embraced Him and accepted Him with all my existence, I realized I actually accepted myself, my biggest gift in life, and my destiny. This was just His reflection.

I promised that day that throughout my life, whatever happened, I would be faithful to myself first and only. I would do what I wanted. I would not change for anybody or anything. I would do this like a prayer, remembering how divine and incredible a choice it was.

My whole life changed after meeting and feeling a true teacher and after seeing his commitment to himself and his courage. His connection to his truth affected and even blessed me. I cannot thank him enough.

I gave up being a teacher. At least I am not giving any education on life. I do and live only the things I want to. I know that this will first surprise and even shake those watching from their perspectives, and then it will make them do the same.

There Must Be Another Way

This is the first mindscape in the path to enlightenment: thinking there must be another way. There must be a way to live life without pain and fear, to live freely without any limitation and happily.

There is another way. There is a way to be happy with everything and every moment experienced in this world and to live in love and joy freely and be courageous. Entering this path is possible with a choice made at the mind level. We may need to train our mind for a long time for this. We need a good education and lots of exercises to allow our mind to let go of the ego consciousness we are used to, which judges, diminishes, intimidates, and twists the truth by drawing a veil of gray clouds over our eyes, and choose the miracle consciousness. Most importantly, we have to remember that there is another way even if we cannot find it right away, and we have to pray God to show us another way is enough.

AWAKENING

What is miracle consciousness? True consciousness.

If we divide our mind in half, the ego consciousness creates illusions, shows life in gray, causes us to perceive with a critical perspective based on past experiences, and causes us to suffer all the time, whereas the miracle consciousness knows the truth and remembers and reminds us who we are and what our core is. Miracle consciousness, because it is the true consciousness, is something we all have. It is a true miracle with our limitlessness, infinite power, creativity, and possibility to step into infinite joy and happiness because of our core and creation.

The word *miracle* might sound a little shocking at first. Many people react when they hear it; they find this word a little exaggerated. We named the last stage of our breathing seminars—which will allow us to discover the miracle within us, our truth, who we are, and the fact that we are all miracles—the miracles course. This name was not just perceived as an exaggeration by the people who heard it; it even got a warning from the authorities.

The more you underestimate yourself and the more you try to cover the truth, the more exaggerated the word *miracle* will seem.

The sentences "You are a miracle" and "I am a miracle" might even seem scary to minds that are used to covering the truth and underestimating themselves and humanity.

But what if it is true? What if I am a miracle? What if we are all miracles and all have unlimited potential that can do whatever we want, create whatever we want, and take control of our lives?

Do you know what happens when you realize this? First, you become silent. You are afraid to express this awareness because you are surrounded by ego minds that are prepared to suppress the true power, true creativity, and true miracle. You think, *I must shut up and say the truth to only those who want to hear it. I should say it to nobody else, only the ones who want to hear it and know themselves.* Then information is exchanged around the world behind closed doors in a confidentiality network.

The notes of truth written on the walls of historic buildings, the sides of old pictures, and the edges of ancient books are only for the ones who know how to see and want to hear.

Time has changed. The world is in such chaos and desperation that the number of people saying, "There must be another way," is increasing day by day. That's the reason why the number of people participating in my seminars also increased. Now people want to know the truth. There is a saying in English: "Enough of this bullshit!" That is right.

For thousands of years, humanity tried everything to be happy and joyful, find peace, fall in love, feel true love, and be enlightened. People looked everywhere but within themselves.

Humanity built houses for happiness and satisfaction; bought and sold houses; built cities; got married; started families; got divorced, remarried, and redivorced; bought new houses; established new businesses; and moved to new cities. It did not help. To be happy, they drank, ate different foods, traveled, did sports, chatted, went to the movies, read books, created millions of different hobbies, established clubs and houses for these hobbies, earned money, spent money, distributed, and collected. It did not help. They dressed up, put on makeup, created brands, created fashion, and created new values to fall in love, be loved, be liked, and feel beautiful and valuable. They bought new places, yachts, apartments, purses, and shoes and went to luxury holiday resorts and nightclubs. It did not help. They drank; danced; and created motorcycles, convertible cars, loneliness, polygamy, and white slavery to feel free. It did not help.

It did not help.

Whatever they did, humanity could not find what they were looking for. It did not help. They were worthless. They needed value. They bought expensive clothes, purses, houses, and cars to feel valuable and to love and like themselves again. They found titles to feel valuable. They created so-called luxury. It did not help.

It did not help because their consciousness always knew the truth. Their hearts never left them. The miracle inside never left humanity and continued to remind them of the truth silently. Everything you search for is within you because you are the only true miracle. As long as you continue to search outside, you will only find despair, hopelessness, weariness, anger, and fear because the thing you are looking for is not outside. As long as you do not find it, you will think you will never find it, and you will fear.

One day humanity said, "There must be another way." That day, everything started to change. The miracle showed humanity the path, and it increased its voice every day. It continued to shout and make humanity busy until humanity saw and remembered. It reminded them again and again as long as humanity underestimated themselves and the others: "All of you are true miracles because you all are the children of God!"

Remembering this truth might not always be easy. The ego consciousness part of our mind is so slippery, vague, and unstable that it can activate in the least expected time and make us believe that something that hurt us or made us mad is real. It is filled with millions of sentences that will make us think the solution is outside, disregard our power, and postpone our happiness: "If something else had happened, if he had said something else, if he had done something else, then I could have been happy. Then I could have loved myself, and everything could have been perfect." Okay, what about this? What if everything is complete and perfect as it is? What if life has a perfect balance and order, and it has nothing to do with us? What if happiness, peace, and love are not connected to external factors?

Ego is ready to do all it can to show us the opposite and even to prove the opposite, and it will continue to do it. Every time we let our guard down, like an impatient enemy ready to attack, it will try to make us believe that something other than us—in other words, the events of life—can affect us, make us sad, and disturb our balance or, on the contrary, make us happy, give us peace, and comfort us. If you have failed for a long time while being fooled by the ego, if you could not find what you were looking for, you are in luck. If you say to yourself, "There is nothing that gives me happiness in this life," you will fall into depression and start to think that this life is a disgusting place (which is right!). Then, if you do not commit suicide, the light within you will find and capture you eventually. This is called enlightenment. Some people are enlightened in one night, some in a couple of days, and some in a few hours. But I assure you, everyone will be enlightened and say, "Nothing I am looking for is here."

The choice of miracle consciousness is the wisest choice you can make at the first moment you understand that life is not satisfying you. This choice is, in a sense, saying, "This part of my mind does not satisfy me. I want to use the other part." Or we can say, "This life does not satisfy me because it is not real. I want to see the truth. The momentary satisfactions, happiness, and coming and going peace and joy I live here are not enough for me. I am looking for something more real. I want a happiness that lasts forever. I want a love that lasts forever. I want such satisfaction that I will not have any hunger or need any temporary sedative for sale in the outside world."

Let me introduce you to the only sane and balanced part, the center of light, infinity, and truth, the miracle consciousness. The miracle consciousness exists and will exist for eternity within us with the choice of truth, which can only be made at the level of mind, independent of everything in this world, under the protection of God and angels for eternity. It is the only consciousness we all belong to, all have, and are all connected to. It is the only source of infinite happiness, health, peace, love, satisfaction, creativity, light, wealth, and unlimited miracles.

Imagine a fountain—a spring of happiness and satisfaction affluent within ourselves. It is constant and unlimited, giving us wealth, lightness, relief, peace, and comfort. This is the miracle consciousness.

There is no mistake in the journey to awakening.

There is no mistake in the journey to true learning, true awakening.

We all live what we need to live all the time, as we deserve. Nothing we do not deserve is happening, and it cannot happen. The universe presents us a magnificent journey to show us and destroy the nonsense we've ascribed meaning to and the mindscapes that are not real.

If you have a single thought of *I do not deserve …* look at what you are thinking about that person, situation, or event. Do the other party deserve it?

The Reality We Live in Is Not His Reality

Form, shape, body, and distinction cannot be His truth; it never was. The part of our consciousness that is connected to Him knows this.

He is unlimited power that is infinite, holy, single, whole, continuous, everywhere, and always. He cannot turn into a form, shape, or body. He never did.

Infinity cannot be limited.

Holiness cannot be simplified.

What is continuous cannot have an end.

Awakening

What is constant cannot end.

Single cannot be plural.

What is everywhere at all times cannot be destroyed.

He cannot have anything to do with mortal life.

Humanity has a single problem: we think that this mortal, finite, limited reality is true. There is no other problem.

We are so busy with the outside world and so lost that most of the time, we do not have time to sit and think or to question life.

Almost everyone is waiting for a disaster to start to question life.

People start questioning after a breakup, death, or sadness.

I think everyone should continue questioning. There is only one answer we all know and share: His voice. Of course you hear His voice because there is no other voice.

Everyone will awaken. Everything unreal will, of course, be destroyed before the infinite one truth because nothing else ever existed.

If you had known and remembered that the mortal reality never existed, would your life be like this?

Would you deal with the realities you ruminate on?

Would you take life, people, and events so seriously?

Isn't it funny that you take this unreal, limited dream—this artificial and even fake life we think we have been living for a while, a dream we have when we feel asleep—so seriously?

We understand how meaningless many of the things we ascribe meaning to actually are when they are taken away from us. This is called maturity and true learning.

In the mortal reality that has no importance or value compared to the immensity, infinity, wholeness, and perfection of the truth, we all ascribe meaning to certain things, give them too much value, and make them important for ourselves. Our soul, which wants to show us how worthless they really are, takes each of them away from us within a perfect plan. Is youth, beauty, energy, or health too important to us? It takes that away first.

Money? It should take all of it away so we can see that we can stand on our feet without a penny in our pocket and can be liberated from this value.

A spouse, partner, or friend must go at some point, until the meaning we ascribe disappears completely, we can still be happy by ourselves, and we destroy the meaning of having someone by our side.

We ascribe such meaning and put ourselves in such miserable situations that our soul has to take all that away from us and destroy it all to remind us what we actually are, who we are, and whom we are connected to.

Does the truth—the infinite, perfect whole—need a spouse, a lover, or a friend?

All searches are toward the things we believe we do not have.

The person who remembers that he has everything; that the mortal, temporary reality is not real; and that he is connected to eternity will search for nothing. He awakens.

We are all His extension. We never left Him; we cannot. All failures, unrest, and wars are situations that arise because of the assumption that we are alone here and can have a will independent from God. If we could wake up to the fact that nothing other than God's will can exist and that all the problems, pain, wars, and fights are meaningless illusions, all these situations would disappear. They do not exist; we just perceive them as if they exist.

We think that yelling at someone or hitting someone can hurt that person. We think we can hurt someone with our behaviors or words. We even think we can kill creatures that have a soul that will exist forever and are experiencing a body only for a while. How crazy is that?

If we remembered that all creatures and life are under the protection of God forever, would we spend energy on those meaningless things? Wars, murders, diseases—what is the point? This nonsense that cannot really hurt you or me or injure any of us is nothing but wasted energy.

The world is full of little children who created an illusionary world for themselves based on nightmares, and as a result, they bicker, wage wars, act superior, and pick fights. They do not know what they are doing. If they realized how stupid they were acting, they would not do it.

We are wealthy. We will be in the kingdom of God for eternity. This is the case, was the case, and will be the case.

We established weird orders to prove the contrary, didn't we? There are even people starving to death. Human kind can be absurd.

The world is full of people who forgot how wealthy the world is. It actually has enough of everything, and we are equals. People who have forgotten try to reach upper levels with what they have in this world and become so stupid and self-alienated that they waste all their energy in that pursuit.

A human can spend all his or her energy and power to be different from others—on something that will not and cannot happen, on an empty dream. How stupid can we get?

The Only Lesson to Be Learned

There is only one lesson humans will learn in this world: this world is an illusion, a dream. Since it is an unreal design and we see and perceive only the reflections of our mind, we do everything we do in this world to ourselves.

A human will be enlightened when he or she truly understands this information on every level.

Whatever you do, you do it to yourself.

The hand you reach out to a person you perceive as an other is a hand you reach out to yourself. When you refuse him, you refuse yourself. If you can embrace the world, it means you are embracing yourself; if you change, your world will also change.

Everything you live in your inner world is reflected on the empty screen you call the outside world. Therefore, whatever your relationship with yourself is, that is your relationship with the world.

Angry people are angry because they are angry at themselves, and gruff people are gruff because they are gruff and unmerciful toward themselves. A murderer is a person who has killed himself, his core, thousands of times.

However we treat ourselves, we treat everyone that way. We perceive life as a place outside us; however, the world is within us, even in our heads. Write down every idea you have about the world on a piece of paper, and then read them out loud. You will see that you have written your life scenario.

There is nothing out there. Here right now, there is only one self. There is nothing other than it; there never was.

Therefore, we are both alone and together. If you perceive that you are a body, you will feel alone; if you remember the truth that this world and everything in it are just a dream and that everything you see and experience is the dream of a single mind, you will not feel alone. We are in it all together, and we are part of one self.

Therefore, whatever you do, you do it to yourself. Whatever you say, you say it to yourself.

Therefore, giving is also receiving.

The person who is ready to give everything, is ready to share himself with the whole world, and is hiding nothing from anybody is the owner of the world. The world is his, and he experiences this.

Everything you hide from the person you perceive as an other will be hidden from you. Everything you want him not to know will be hidden from you. Everything you run away from will follow you, and everything you push will come back to you.

Whatever you do, you do it to yourself.

When you understand this truth and adopt it in your life on every level, you will be liberated.

What happens when we do not remember the truth and do not understand the reality of this world? While everything is going well, a problem occurs. Actually, problems, or things not going well, are reflections of the first thought of separation. When we think we were separated from God and came to another world, we experience a great disappointment, a great feeling of separation. All problems in the world are actually a reflection of this main problem. The thing we believe becomes a problem.

Awakening starts when we show the courage to question the thoughts we learn from our childhood and the thoughts imposed on us by the collective consciousness, the ego. When you start to question the reality of this world, you take the first step toward awakening.

If you really believe in this world and believe that it is real and that you came to this hell after leaving your home with God, your life will be made up of problems and disappointments. This is inevitable.

All the disappointments and problems you live are actually reflections of a single thought you have produced that creates the main disappointment: *I am separated from God, and I have come into this world.* That is crazy!

It is impossible for such a person not to fear, feel alone, be restless, panic, and get sick. Therefore, all diseases come from the thought that we came to this world and can exist separately from God.

Awakening

I have seen that 100 percent of people living in the world and thinking the word is real have resentment and reaction toward God. They do not express this so as not to sin, because they are scared, but they are angry at God.

There are people whose children die at the age of twelve or thirteen and who are raped, suffer, or have to endure unbearable agonies. They think God gave these things to them, and they resent Him. I know.

Nobody can be thankful in this world.

Nobody can be thankful for this world.

Nobody says, "Thank God," for the momentary pleasures and satisfactions and the later endless chaos, war, death, torture, pain, and disease. Do not fool yourself!

It is not possible for a person who is not thankful by heart to be happy and healthy.

Everyone will eventually awaken because truth is inevitable. Everyone will wake up to the fact that this world is not real; it is just a dream. Nothing is taught to us. It does not have any meaning or importance. This world has nothing to do with creation or God.

The awakened consciousness is thankful by heart on every level.

This is the only true thanking.

Thank You, God! This world; death; pain; disease; and limited, helpless bodies have nothing to do with creation. Thank You that this silly dream never existed and was never created. Thank You that death never occurred. Thank You that torture and pain never occurred. Thank You that diseases are not real and are just a dream. Thank You that this limited, sick, hurting, crazy, helpless loser body is not me and this body does not really exist; it never did. Thank God. Thank You, God, that I never left You. I never came to this weird, dark, unfamiliar, and unreliable place where a second later is not predictable. Thank You, God, that I am still with You, at home under Your protection. I never changed. I never lost my pureness. I never committed a crime, nor was I accused. Thank You, God, that I own all Your features. I am not a body; I am not limited. I am not a mind; I cannot be twisted. I am not the world; I do not die. I cannot die. Thank You, God, that I am with You, come from eternity, and am going to eternity. I never came to this finite, mortal place.

Only the ones who wake up to truth can be thankful; the rest is all a lie.

In this life, people all think they have thousands of problems, and they cannot see the main problems while dealing with those problems. We all have one main problem: believing that we are separated from God and came to a place called the world. If you fix these problems, all your problems will be solved. If you cannot fix this problem, the problems you have will turn into a ball, and you will not be able to solve anything.

The various problems you have are traps created by the ego to prevent you from seeing the main problem. As you continue to deal with your perceived problems, you take this world more and more seriously, you think this world is more real, and you become a prisoner of this cycle.

Everyone who desires to know the truth will know.

Everyone who desires to awaken will awaken.

All you need to do is let go of this world right now, right here, right at this moment.

When you let the world go, you can see that it is not real. The most efficient method for this is to surrender your breath to the Creator and be liberated from this world with His breath, natural breath. When we surrender our breath to Him, the separation between us ends.

God is the one who gave us the holy breath.

Breath and life belong to Him.

Neither breath nor life is connected to this body; they just enter and exit this body. Every moment, every second, they enter and exit. When you inhale, breath enters the body and sinks into the dream, and when you exhale, it gets out of the dream and wakes up.

Therefore, people who surrender their breath to God will allow His control and connect with Him every time they inhale and exhale. As the breath opens and deepens, as the connection gets stronger, our connection with God and truth also gets stronger. It gets stronger, and we know it. We just know. We know Him, the truth, and who we are. We remember.

All the information in this book was formed thanks to dialogue established with God through the connection of holy breath.

The information of truth is not something you learn; it is something you burn into.

The truth is a rebirth.

AWAKENING

The truth is awakening. Everything is hidden within it.

Natural breath is the only tool that makes us reach the information of truth and God.

Thank You, God, because God gave us a breath that, even though we are in a dream, ensures we see that it is a dream.

Thank God.

Thank You that we can see the truth.

Thank You for all perceptive consciousness.

Thank God.

For centuries, we have been making the same mistake: we think this life has meaning.

As I have mentioned before, the world is only a single split second and only a single thought in the presence of God. This is information you can find in all religious books.

This world—in other words, the mortal illusion—is the reflection of the thought *What would something other than the truth created by God look like if it was possible somewhere within the infinite creation possibilities before the presence of God on the cycle of time?*

God is one.

The Creator is one.

Only God can create.

You can find a few more similar sentences in all religious disciplines. Does a part of our brain believe in the existence of another creator? Is that why religious books remind us "God is one"? Yes. And you are not aware of this fact.

Every moment a person thinks that the illusory world in which he lives for a while within the cycle of time actually exists, every moment he believes that a nonexistent cycle and nonexistent design that are no more than a single second and an idea, he believes he can create a nonexistent world. Therefore, he creates a new god in his mind. Only God can create, and anything not created by Him was never created. If you think that a simple idea, a dream world arising from a void, is real, then there must be a creator of this. Since there is no creator of a noncreated thing, that cannot be God.

41

I must admit it is hard for complicated minds to understand what I have written. Only someone who thinks with God's mind and His judgment can understand the truth.

You can understand the truth only with your heart, not with your mind or logic.

To reach the truth, you should first question the truths you believe in, because the human mind is covered with spider nets, for it has not been questioning for years. You should first remove those nets and do the necessary cleaning.

Right now, start questioning the truths you have believed in blindly like a fanatic without questioning.

Are God and soul infinite?

Does infinite existence know death?

Can infinity have an end within?

If God is infinite, could He create an ending and death?

Is God one?

Does singularity know plurality?

Can singularity have plurality within?

Can one have a difference within?

If God is one, if He does not have differences within, could He create a difference?

Could the difference we perceive in this world have been created if it was not God who created it?

Doesn't everything created come from the Creator? Doesn't the Creator create as Himself?

If the evil we perceive in the world is really created, shouldn't the Creator also be evil?

Is the Creator evil? Does He incorporate evil? Then can everything we believe to be evil come from Him, arise from Him, and be created from Him?

What about sin?

If there is such a thing as sin and if people can commit sin, doesn't that mean their creator must also be a sinner?

If I am a sinner, what is the one who created me?

If I am evil, doesn't that mean the one who created me also has evil within Him?

We have believed in this craziness for years!

The truth is always there and always will be. Illusions never existed and never will. The information of truth is in this reality.

Now you must have this question in mind: "Okay, if what we live—the pain; fear; limited, mortal body; experiences; feelings; problems; and diseases—does not exist, why do we live all of it?"

There is still a part of us thinking that this mortal life, this dream we are having for a while, this situation that does not have any meaning and cannot be anything but a single second and an idea in the presence of God, is life. That part asks this question. The confused and complicated part of our mind that cannot comprehend the truth I have just mentioned asks it. This is the question of the ego that is unable to distinguish the truth from illusion, thinks the experiences we created as just ideas are real, and perceives this universe and everything in it as if it really exists.

Then why does this place exist? Why does the whole universe exist? All those questions have a single answer: the truth has nothing to do with these. All the experiences we have are illusions on the same level.

We have been fooled by the ego for years. We thought the experiences, feelings, emotions, body, universe, and everything in it that have no meaning and do not even exist were real. We believed this lie by using our mind wrong.

We ascribed meaning to the meaningless.

We thought that empty feelings, behaviors, and words were full and that the body was real.

We forgot the truth.

We forgot that we are just a light.

We forgot that only light, love, joy, happiness, and beauties exist.

We were separated from the information of truth.

Now the whole universe has started the journey of return. Humankind is living the biggest and fastest awakening.

Why?

Why? Questions starting with *Why* cause us to get lost in the illusion. Only people in this situation can ask, "Why?" Also, there is a place in the mind that is full of *why* questions and believes that unreal things are real. It deviates from the truth, is severed from its core, is separated from God, and is away from the answer.

A consciousness aware of its core cannot ask, "Why?" Because it knows.

A consciousness knowing God cannot ask, "Why?" It does not deal with the meaningless because it knows the meaningful.

A consciousness that is whole with the answer deals with results, not causes.

Our core existence is the result of God, not the cause. The ego is the one that deals with the question "Why"?" and insists a creation other than God's creation can exist. It argues those situations are real and looks at the cause, not the result.

There is no reason for creation. It just exists, and it will exist forever.

God does not have a reason. He just exists, and He will exist forever.

You do not have a reason, you exist, and you will exist forever.

The one with a reason is the illusion. Emotions all have a reason because they are not real. Problems and diseases all have a reason because they do not come from the Creator; they create their own reasons and their own creators.

The ones who do not know the next page when opening one page are the ones who think they see with the eyes of the body and hear with the ears of the body. The ones living with the information of truth know that every page has the same information of truth.

The truth is the extension of God, and it is everywhere; it is one.

The information of truth does not change or renew, cannot be rewritten, and cannot be reread.

The information of truth is somewhere beyond the illusion of truth, under the protection of God, and since He is one and whole, so is the truth.

Therefore, it is not the first time the things I have written have been written, and it will not be the last. The information of truth is in all the books you have read, on all the pages you have turned, in all the movies you have watched, in all the streets you have walked, and in all the places you have looked.

The information of truth is not in a world with unknowns; it is in wisdom. A place with unknowns was never created. If you stop believing it, you know everything.

If you stop looking at the unknown side, to an unknown illusion, and to your body and the material world and stay in the known side, in the place where all the information and the only information and all the answers and the only answer exist, you will see that knowing and self are the same. You will awaken.

Why do people read so many books?

Because any other situation in a nonexistent illusion based on causes and reasons cannot be imagined.

Would books exist in a reality wherein all consciousness knows everything? Everything in the illusion is the proof that it is not real.

But why do we eat?

Do you—the self that a whole with the main source, an existence that is the expression of the wealth and satisfaction of God—get hungry? The one who gets hungry is not our self but this body, because this body is not real.

Why do we talk?

Would an existence that is the light, the extension of the Creator, try to illuminate the events? Would an existence that is everywhere at all times as a part of the Creator choose to express itself?

All these causes and reasons and all these futilities are the proof telling us that this world and the cycle of time are not real.

Thank God.

The only real relationship is the relationship we have with God. All other relationships we establish in this world are reflections of this relationship. It is either toward Him or from Him toward the world.

When we spiritually, emotionally, or physically feel the lack of anything, it means we are in our journey toward Him.

How? When you expect attention, love, or maybe a warm hug or soft touch from someone or you expect someone to meet your needs, you will not get what you expect. All these are not things you can get from a human or from the world. We cannot meet these desires in the outer world because the world does not have the love, compassion, and attention we search for. The world is just a giant mirror. It reflects us our inner journey. Therefore, when we feel the need for something, if we start to look for it on the outside, the mirror can only reflect to us our search. When we search for what we need in the world, it will not be given to us when we need it.

The world fulfills its duty of reflecting to you what you need.

If what you need is the hug of the person you love, what you search is meeting God, hugging Him, and being one with Him. When you do this, you will not need someone to hug you. Then everyone will always hug you. The world wants to reflect the fact that you are hugging God and yourself.

Is what you need to be loved by someone for someone to be compassionate toward you? Then remember that what you are searching for is the love and compassion of God. The only true love is His love, and the only true relationship is the relationship you establish with God.

You do not want anything from this world.

Anyway, the world, an empty and meaningless mirror, a reflector, cannot give you what you want.

There is only one place where you can find everything you search for and own everything you want: the side of God. Being one with Him and asking from Him is the only way.

The empty and meaningless toys of the world have been stalling all of us for years. Now, with this book, you might end it. You might decide to turn to the true world that is one with God, the place where you can find everything you are searching for, instead of a world in which it is certain that you will not find what you are searching for. You can shut yourself off to this world completely. You can say, "What I want is not in this world," and you can turn to God and the real world you are living with Him.

All religious books tell you this: shut yourself off to this world, and turn to God, the spirit, and your core.

In Islam, this shutting is perceived as physically closing yourself to the world; that is why women cover their hair. In Judaism, this shutting is performed by clerics, men. However, actual shutting or closing is only possible in the mind.

A person who turns to God closes his mind to this world.

A person who turns to God and sees that he can find everything he is searching for in Him will not want anything from this world. Or, on the contrary, a person who has woken up to the fact that he has nothing to want from this world leaves the place where he cannot find what he is looking for and turns to the Creator, the one who will provide everything he is looking for. For him, the search within the illusion has come to an end, and the true journey has started.

All that has happened and all that has lived until the true journey starts are the steps taken to God.

You get heartbroken; get sad; become lonely; blame yourself; get angry; rebel; do not understand; get confused; get no solution; become hopeless, gruff, or rebellious; or lose all your faith and become an atheist. These are all reasons for your return to God. All of these have the same purpose of directing you to the place where you can find what you feel is missing, to the only existence you can truly connect with: the Creator.

The journey toward God is not real; it is an illusion because in reality, a journey toward God is impossible. We never left Him; we just believed for a while that we left Him. That is why the journey toward Him is an illusion and has a search at each level.

We try to return to our source, the fountain of life, our Creator, our core that we think we left. The reflections of this situation in this world are the deficiencies. The world is bound to reflect that we are separated from Him, so it does. We live an illusion apart from Him, and therefore, we live an absence—in other words, without love, attention, or control and with helplessness, anger, darkness, and lost illusion. It is not true, but in our experiences of the world, we see it as true. The most interesting part is that this search occurs in the place where we cannot find what we are looking for. Actually, it is a grand comedy!

We believe we can leave our Creator, the Creator we can never leave, who is full of love, light, compassion, attention, care, respect, happiness, and life. Because of the illusion that we can leave Him, we are separated from all His features and all that He has: love, compassion, light, beauty, joy, and satisfaction.

This world is not the source of joy. It never was, and it never will be. This is the reason for our lack of joy. It never was, and it never will be.

The reason for our disappointments is not this world or the people, events, experiences, writings, or words in this world. It never was. The only reason for your disappointments is the fact that you turned your back on the source of love: God. We refuse to establish a relationship with the source of love. We can find love only in Him and can establish a relationship only with Him. When we do this, the infinite love we feel will not belong to this world. This world cannot be the cause of the lack of love, and it cannot be the source of love.

The only reason for your anger is that you choose something else instead of God.

You need to shut yourself to this world. If you want to find the infinite quietness, peace, happiness, serenity, love, compassion, and light before you, if you want to live with that miraculous, magnificent existence, you need to shut yourself to this world. There is no other way.

Shutting yourself to this world is not covering your hair or cutting your relation with the world. Shutting yourself to this world can only be possible at the level of mind. Choosing God occurs in a place beyond all those levels and everything you know in the physical dimension. It occurs in the heart and consciousness. We can choose to be with God in the deepest point of our core. Anyone really connected to Him cannot continue to take this world as seriously as before.

For a consciousness that discovers His love, the love and compassion of this world loses all meaning.

For a person who meets His light and proceeds with His guidance, no book, guide, teacher, or leader will mean anything. A person who meets the only true teacher and guide and decides to establish a relationship with Him will not accept guidance from anyone or anything else.

For the hearts who know His miracle, nothing in this world—not the Seven Wonders of the World, miraculous events, the birth of a baby, a sunset, good food, or love stories—will mean anything. For the person who knows the miracle itself, everything else is bound to be meaningless.

When a person decides to shut himself to the world, this does not mean he needs to change his life. The place where he lives, his clothing style, and his behaviors can stay the same. This choice is made at the deepest level, in the core, and nobody needs to know this.

A person who completely shuts himself to the world in every sense does not need to isolate himself from the world.

I can explain this in the following way: Get in front of a mirror, and try to take what you think you need from the mirror by domination—for example, love or attention. Look at your reflection in the mirror. What is it doing? That is how your reflection seems when you want love, happiness, joy, lust, or satisfaction from the world. The more you want from the world, the more it wants from you. When you want to get love, it takes love from you. As you stand there to take, the world stands there to take from you.

Therefore, everyone bargaining, saying, "I will give you this much, and you will give me that much," has what he owns taken away eventually.

Let's get back to your decision to shut yourself to the world. When you do not want the world, does the world want you? No. When you choose your core, God, the infinite source, what do you see in your reflection? The whole world chooses its core, God, love, and the infinite source. The world turns into heaven.

We live what we choose to live.

The decision to leave the world behind is the decision to leave everything in this world behind. Look what the people who do not choose the world choose: death, misery, deficiency, diseases, separation, and problems.

Shut yourself to this world, and turn to God. This is what all the religious books mean with their references to closing and introversion.

The place called "the other world" is the true love wherein you are in a relationship with God, and this body does not need to die to be in a relationship with that life. Besides, this body is already dead.

Can your body live without you, without life? Is a body something that can live on its own? If that were the case, should not it continue to breathe and live when life leaves the body?

The body is already dead. It never lived, and it never will live.

When breath—life—enters, the body seems to be living for a while. We give these bodies names, such as Ali, Ayse, Mehmet, and Ahmet, thinking we are creatures. However, the thing that you call Mehmet, Ahmet, or Ayse is actually dead. It does not exist. It does not live.

In reality, this body is just a piece of meat.

Therefore, all religious books tell us to leave the body, as it is not real, and command us to turn to the other world, to the truth.

Then what is the thing that is alive? What is life?

It is certain that it is not in this world. If it were, when I leave this body, my body should continue to live.

But if life is not in this world, then where is it?

Life is in our true world, the other world, as told for centuries in religious books and spiritual disciplines, a place where we are a whole with God. Is that world a physical place? No. Does it look like this place? No. If it looked like this place, this place would need to be true. But we know that this place is not real.

The other world, the true world, the true life we live as one with God, is not like this world because this world is an illusion, and truth never looks like an illusion. The truth is always the opposite of illusion.

Therefore, the other world is the opposite of this world. Good! This is wonderful! I am thankful it is!

There is death in this world, which means death does not exist in truth. Thank God.

There are diseases in this world, which means they do not exist in truth. Thank God.

There are deficiencies, hunger, and pain in this world, which means they do not exist in truth. Thank God.

There is no consistency in this world; everything is temporary. Therefore, in truth, everything is temporary; nothing changes.

And therein rests the peace of God.

The ones thanking God are the ones who know the truth.

This is the truth known and shared by all the enlightened souls, the secret of the peace and happiness of all the enlightened souls.

Now this secret is yours.

Remember it, and share it.

2

Awakening

Choice

The core of all of us is full of love and light; it is whole and perfect. How much we reflect this truth to our mind-body among the mortal-world hype depends on the choices we make in our mind.

The fact that this mind-body is sick, addicted, or rude; is in defense; or has material or moral deficiencies in the mortal life is just an illusion, a dream. When we perceive the truth, we might see it as insignificant. However, when we look from the point of the light of the truth and go beyond the perception regarding the mortal illusion, only the intention known and shared by all the enlightened souls can be chosen, as it is the duty of all us.

The holy mission we all have within as a call is beyond believing in God.

It is bringing His light to this mortal, twisted, fragile, angry, sick, and addicted mind-body illusion to reflect His integrity and perfection here in every moment within this illusion of time.

This is only possible when we make the choice.

The core of us all is the light. Only the mind-body living in this illusion has the possibility of not choosing the light. We all have various choices, such as fighting with the light and thinking we can overcome it. The reality is that you can escape from the light, but you cannot hide because the light of truth is descending in this world as a reflection of the mind-bodies who know Him and surrender to Him and to the holy mission.

How is the choice of miracle consciousness reflected in this mortal illusion, this world?

When the light descends to this mortal illusion, the first thing it does is enlighten the dark choices of mind-bodies—in other words, it surfaces.

By guessing, thinking, and interpreting the choice of miracle consciousness and what the choice would do in the journey of life, you got away from the truth. When the consciousness of miracle descends to the world and is reflected to the illusion by the mind choosing the true light, truth, and love, it connects with the truth, light, and love within every mind-body around it. This natural union and integration enlightens the choices made by the mind-bodies, and the truth becomes visible.

Although we all describe the truth as light, unity, and wholeness, all mind-bodies in this illusion cannot choose this. This choice in the mind-body needs to be made by intending, praying, remembering the truth, and, most importantly, surrendering to God and only to God at every moment, again and again.

When we say, "I have chosen the miracle consciousness in my mind once, so from now on, my mind will be in that consciousness forever," we fall into an illusion. Yes, we are the miracle itself at the point of truth and at the point of the core because of our core, but this mind-body is not. This mind-body, this world, is just a reflector. It reflects us whether we choose the miracle or anything else in our mind.

How? Through the minds containing the true light.

The truth becomes visible through those minds. We (as the mind-body) and these minds that contain the light for a while may escape from the light minds that show us and surface the truth. We may try to protect ourselves from them, but we can never escape the truth. Minds full of light will continue to illuminate the other minds and show the choice if it is not light.

It will show it if the choice made is disease. It will show it if the choice made is addiction. If the choice made is any system other than God's thought system, it will continue to illuminate this choice forever.

How can you escape from the light? How do we escape from the truth and the light in this world?

If we cannot stand the person across from us; feel uncomfortable or nervous; get angry at him; think he is dark, at fault, or trying to limit us or stop us, remember we are running from the light in that person's mind. Diseases, addictions, mistakes, and limits are the signs that our mind made a sick, addicted, mistaken, and limited choice. Our mind did not choose the truth.

If we say, "My freedom is restricted," this means "I did not choose the miracle consciousness; I chose the thoughts that restrict my freedom."

If we say, "I am not comfortable with his presence. He intimidates me. He makes me angry," we actually say, "I made choices that intimidate my core, bother me, and suffocate me in my mind."

When we say, "I want to be free. He [or she, this, that, this person, that system] limits me," this means "I choose the thought system in my mind that limits me, and I do this all the time. I am addicted to egoistic thoughts."

If we say, "I am tired," we say, "For a long time, I have been choosing thoughts that have nothing to do with me. I have been fighting with the truth. I have had thoughts and beliefs against God for a long time now, and I am tired of this."

If we say, "He made a mistake. He is not right. Everyone knows this is not right, but how come he does not? He is a dark human," we say, "Now I am choosing twisted thoughts in my mind, not God's mind and light, and I do these things. I chose the wrong, not the right. I chose the darkness, not the light."

When the mind chooses the light of the truth, when it looks at the world with this choice, it is enlightened, and it enlightens. The mind that chooses light starts to change and improve the mind-body.

With the choice of the truth, love, and light in the mind, integrity is reflected in this world. Therefore, diseases are cured. The minds that choose the disease—in other words, wrong, mistaken, and sick thoughts instead of the right thoughts coming from God—need to escape and stay away from the minds that choose the light.

Freedom is reflected on this world, and addictions end. The minds that choose addiction always escape from the minds choosing light because the light of truth surfaces the addiction to being proven right and the addiction to egoistic thoughts and harmful thoughts. Wholeness is reflected on the world, and the mind-bodies desiring to be different and special try to hide, escape, and leave. These people want to continue their twisted thoughts, such as *I am different from everyone. I am special.* They feel humiliated with the reflection of light.

The light is reflected on the world, and all dark choices are illuminated. The minds choosing darkness, ego, and a limited thought system escape from the light of truth because their darkness is becoming visible, and they do not like that. Generally, they say to the mind reflecting the light, "You are my dark side. I must leave you."

The mind that is filled with light and chooses light, core, and miracle is whole; it is right. It is the light and love. It runs from nobody and nothing. It does not want to leave anyone, be away from anyone, or hide from anyone. It just exists. It is free. It is comfortable. It is bold. It is unlimited, infinite. It continuously illuminates the minds that do not completely choose the truth.

It says, "Your mind chose disease. The fact that you want to leave someone is a reflection of the separate thoughts in your mind." It says, "If you are running from someone, you are running from the truth." It says, "The reason you are tired is because the unreal beliefs and thoughts tire you." It continues to show and reflect the truth for eternity.

Until now, you thought the mind-body was real, and you misunderstood the miracle consciousness, the truth.

When you are told, "I am whole and perfect," you think this is our mind-body. When the light of truth is reflected on this world, it sees that the mortal world is the suitable base for all irregularities, mistakes, errors, and mistaken choices; it is the land of possibilities. It knows that we must constantly make choices so that the light of truth is reflected in our mind.

The reality of the holy self descends to the illusion of world, where errors exist, and fixes it. The people escaping this have to escape all their lives because actually, there is no escape from this.

Peace, happiness, wholeness, rightness, holiness, the only truth that already exists before us—we do not need to do anything for these. It is enough to turn to God and surrender to Him. We need to make the choice so that all these realities are reflected in the mind-body in the illusion. When we do not make any change, we can be addicted, sick, messed up, limited, tired, and worn.

Only one choice is possible in this illusion. We cannot choose both the ego consciousness and the miracle consciousness. Whichever we choose, we turn our back on the other one, and we live the reflections of this choice every moment.

World of Duality

It is not a problem that the world, the dream, has a limited and problem-causing foundation; the problem is that you want to change it.

This choice can only be made in the world.

There is nothing called choice in truth.

The one that is everything cannot choose to be anything. What is immortal cannot choose death. What is single cannot choose to be plural. The truth cannot be lost, disappear, or change. Therefore, variable situations and choices only exist in the untrue, mortal world experience.

The truth has a single consciousness and a single truth: the Creator. There is nothing other than Him.

But there are always two choices in this world. These choices, as I have mentioned before, can only be made at the mind level. We can choose to believe this limited world and the mortal body, or we can choose our eternity and infinity. This choice will change everything in a world in which our consciousness is reflected. If we believe we are a limited body, our life becomes an adventure in which the limits increase every day, and at the end, we feel trapped in a cage. However, if we can remember our truth, the infinity of our soul and core, even if we are in a mortal world experience, this experience can turn into a dream of heaven in which our infinity and holiness are reflected.

When our perception changes, what we see in the dream also changes. Since the mortal world is not real, its nonexistence is finalized by the truth. Therefore, everything planned as the opposite of truth—earthly creation—can only exist as a reflection of the truth with the power to neutralize and destroy it, with the opposite of the design.

In the creation of the mortal world, as soon as Adam exists, Eva appears by his side. Because the design called human disappeared when it was first thought, and it should be with a consciousness that will destroy the men, that will remind him of the truth, and that will prevent the death from being lost in the darkness of the world.

Everything exists in duality in the mortal world because in truth, there is nothing that seems earthly. A nonexistent world design should bring its destroyer along.

Therefore, every mistake in the world exists with its compensation. Whether you focus on the life or not, every mistake will eventually be compensated and remedied.

Every unreal thing we perceive in the system of the world came with compensations and remedies. Disease comes with healing. Disease cannot exist alone because in reality, it does not exist, and for this thought to disappear, the remedy will come right after.

When the idea of the body came to the mind, it disappeared because it has no place in truth. The Holy Spirit destroys it. Even if you try to make the body exist by ascribing meaning by yourself, the Holy Spirit always says to you, "The body is not real," and reminds you of the truth.

The idea of truth has been formed to be destroyed. Therefore, everything happening in this world brings along its destroyer, and the holy trio exists this way.

Spirit is the answer to the body.

The remedy is the answer to the disease.

Light is the answer to the darkness.

Problems exist with the solution because truth does not involve any problem. Since it cannot exist, even if there is a design, it is seen with the solutions that will neutralize it in the world.

Woman is the answer to man.

However, actually, none of these exist but God.

God's truth is reflected in the world as love.

His love is the only truth, and eventually, it will destroy everything, and only it will exist.

His love is experienced between mistake and remedy, problem and solution, disease and remedy, body and soul, man and woman.

His love makes all these dualities one. It does not allow the mistake, disease, problem, and man to be alone, to get lost. He is the one who placed light in the darkness, health in the disease, and woman in the man.

He does not want us to get lost. The unreality of the world is because of Him.

He is the reason of truth, the owner and creator of true love, and nothing but His creation can exist. He is the guarantee that nothing can exist but Him—no illusions can exist. He is the guarantee that the disease will heal, the anger will turn into love, and the mistake will be remedied.

God waits for us at the end of the cycle in which all questions are asked and the answers are provided. He is neither a question nor an answer.

God is at the end where all problems seem to exist for us, and then all problems are solved with the reflection of His truth. He is neither a problem nor a solution. He is everything, and He only exists in the place where the problem is solved and we meet the nothingness in the world with the disappearing of the world, with its staying behind.

Soul Mate and Twin Spirit

The first human, called Adam—actually, the idea of a human—ended within the truth before it even occurred. Adam disappeared before he existed, because he never existed. Eva is the guarantee of his disappearing.

While the man is earthly, connected to the world, and focused on the world, having the purpose of experiencing the world, the woman is the reflection of the true consciousness. The woman is focused on truth. It is the consciousness remembering the afterlife.

The woman breathes to remember and remind of the Creator. The man breathes to create and experience the world.

In other words, the woman represents heaven, and the man represents hell. You may misunderstand the truth because you ascribe too much meaning to the word *hell*; however, what I mean here is not the bad meaning in your perception. The man represents humanity, humanly desires, passions, and fire, and the woman represents the Creator, the true life, holiness, and truth.

Of course, both situations are ideal and at the highest possibilities level. In other words, this happens when man goes after earthly desires, wills, and passions without any fear, hesitation, or limits and almost catches fire and when woman shuts herself to this world and all earthly things.

The man is the burning fire, the hellfire, and the woman is the one who cools him down, comforts, and destroys him.

The man burns, and the woman extinguishes the fire.

The world is the creation of men. The woman comes and destroys the world by reminding man of the truth. She illuminates the darkness, extinguishes the fire, heals the disease, and stands as an example for creation.

The ideal situation happens when the universal feminine and masculine energies we experience as yin and yang exist freely in the bodies of man and woman. Unfortunately, women chose to be earthly instead of shutting themselves to the values of the world and staying in the truth. This delays the descending of truth to the earth. Therefore, women are more interested in the breath, energy, and personal development training, as they need them more.

Ideally, the man is the king of the world. He is passionate, a challenger, hardworking, and productive in the world. He came to this world to create and produce; he is keener on and more compatible with the laws of the world.

The woman is the representative of truth. She is the reminder of the true king. The woman is still and introverted. She knows, remembers, and expresses the truth. She represents God, His holiness, power, infinite freedom, and creativity.

The woman is inherently closed to the world and open to the truth, and the man is inherently closed to the truth and open to the world. They neutralize and destroy each other. That is the purpose. Anything that does not exist cannot exist. Therefore, when the man came to the world, he needed an existence to destroy him, and that was the woman.

When the woman remembers the truth, when she does not value earthly values and becomes the interpreter of God's creative energy and true life, the only thing she expresses will be love, and her only creation will be heaven.

A woman can turn the ground she walks on into heaven when she shuts herself to the world and expresses the truth by turning to the truth. The woman exists to save the man from the darkness he is in, ease the fire burning within him, solve his only problem, take him out of hell, and take him to her heaven (i.e., her womb). If the man did not exist and never came to world, then the woman would not exist either because there would be no need to neutralize the idea of man and no need for the confirmation that the noncreated one is not created.

When a woman knows herself, lives with her core, and lives focused on God and truth, not focused on the world, the area in which she breathes becomes heaven. Since the place she exists in is the area where God is remembered, diseases heal, problems are solved, the man gets comfortable and finds peace, and the woman finds herself.

If a woman is open and explicit, she is a goddess, and her existence can illuminate the whole world.

Breathing grows and expands the woman; it allows her to descend the heaven to the earth.

The saying "Heaven lies at the feet of the mother" is said because of this. The place where a woman remembers the truth is the area where she becomes a mother. When God fills in her womb, she remembers everything again, and at that moment, the earth becomes heaven. It is natural that this does not happen with every woman. Some women are born like this; they start to be enlightened, and everything around them starts to illuminate and beautify.

The woman represents the Creator; therefore, she creates a baby in her stomach.

The man represents the world; therefore, he is always the king of the world.

The woman does not know the world. She cannot comprehend how the world should be, how she should act, or what she should do, because she does not have passions, a never-ending fire, or problems, as men do. The woman knows the truth; she expresses Him.

The man does not know true life. He has forgotten the truth and God to be an earthling, so he needs a woman to remind him.

The love of God is a level we can reach only with the destruction of the world. Therefore, man needs to experience destruction to experience the love of God, true love. We need to stop believing in the world, be freed from our ego, and stop seeing ourselves as a body so that love can exist.

This experience can easily be had between a woman and a man. If they are completely surrendered to love, they can disappear through each other, and only love remains.

The man can only leave the world through a woman. We can see this in every aspect of life. The men who are not strong in life, do not have the truth consciousness, do not remember the core, are not goddesses, and believe the world is mostly real take everything seriously and experience anger, tenseness, worries, and fear since there are no attenuating circumstances. The only thing that can illuminate their world is a woman who has stayed in the truth and remembers who she is and her holy mission. That woman descends the light and love to the earth. She is here to remind of the features of God, His truth, and the afterlife and to be a heaven. She can be the man's heaven. With her presence, she can ease the circumstances he takes seriously in life, the circumstances he thinks to be real, because she remembers love, light, and truth. While the man burns in a pool of passion, desire, lust, and earthly purposes, the woman brings the truth to him and can carry him to the truth by expressing that this is all a dream at every moment, even with her breathing.

Therefore, the relationship of the man and woman allows the world to be made real by the man by caring (Adam) and the experience of destruction by the woman, who remembers that the world is not real and who carries the light, love, and unconditional commitment of God to the earth.

When the man allows and when the woman can be herself, the unity of the two is a destruction, and true love is what remains.

True love is rarely experienced in this world because many of the men will do anything not to give up on the world and what they believe in. They refuse everything that might shake the truths they defend stubbornly and persistently. However, the man must unconditionally surrender to the true love.

He is the one to be destroyed. His ego must be destroyed. The woman, if she knows herself and is one with her core, already knows that she does not exist.

The man must be ready to be destroyed, let go of everything he believes, kill the truths he defends, destroy himself for love, and "burn and melt and be destroyed," as written by Mevlana Jalaluddin Rumi. Only then can the man and woman disappear, when the man unites with a real woman, a goddess, a woman who remembers who she is.

When the man allows and the woman is able to stay in truth, they disappear together, and then only love remains.

Destruction is a must for the experience of divine love.

The light destroys the darkness, and love remains.

Awakening

Healing destroys the disease, and love remains.
The Holy Spirit destroys the body, and love remains.
The woman destroys the man, and love remains.
Divine love is beyond the nonexistent illusions; therefore, illusions are hidden within the possibility of disappearing within duality.

While Adam chose the world, Eva followed him in order to remind him that his choice was not true, and the place he chose did not really exist.

The woman came to the world after the man. In other words, she watched him. As the man followed the darkness and fell into the illusion of the world, the part that would wake him up formed by itself. If Adam had not come to the world, Eva would not have come either. All women and men feel the truth deep down all the time.

Adam was lost in the world; he believed in the world and thought the five senses were real. However, Eva always remembered the truth and stood by it. She came to the world with Adam to remind Adam that the world is not real. Eva was the consciousness that neutralized Adam so we could be sure that God's plan is happening.

The mortal world does not exist. It never did. The mortal world is just a dream that did not happen. However, the man is inherently not aware of the fact that he is the king of the world, and he is not completely aware that this is what it should be, and he will not be just by himself. The woman, on the other hand, is not the king of the world, because inherently, she knows that she is not in the world, and a place called "the world" does not exist. Therefore, while the man does everything he wants in the world, the woman is here to ease him and comfort him. Actually, neither the man nor the woman exists.

The man is the body, and the woman is the Holy Spirit.

The man perceives everything in the physical dimension, and as long as there is not a woman to teach him the truth, everything happens at the physical level for him. On the other hand, the woman perceives everything in the spiritual dimension; everything that happens is a spiritual reflection for her.

Since men perceive everything at the physical level, they can hardly understand a physical sexual relationship and a deep relationship with a soul mate. Only if a man has a true woman across from him will he understand, as that woman can explain this to him with her behavior.

The woman teaches the spirit to the man.

Since the woman perceives everything at the spiritual level, the man she is with is always her soul mate. Everything is a reflection of the spirit. Physical needs, the physical level, and the laws of physics are areas she cannot perceive.

The man teaches the world to the woman.

The man teaches the rules, systems, and ways of the world and the physical level to the woman. Sex, the body, the power and capacity of the body, the lusts and desires of the body are told and taught to the women by the men. Woman does not know or feel any physical lust, desire, or sexuality.

The woman teaches truth, the spirit, love, commitment, holiness, and heaven to the man. The man knows neither truth nor love as long as he does not have a true woman by his side. Neither commitment nor holiness or definitiveness means anything to him. *Miracle* and *heaven* are words that do not fit into the world of men. The man believes in things he holds, sees, and owns. He came to this world to own, and he does not care about anything he does not own.

Woman belongs in truth; she will never belong in the world. She only belongs to God; her breaths bring His light, love, and mercy. What matters for her are the feelings, intuition, and inner world.

I am sure you have read in many books that the Holy Grail is the womb. It is natural that the holy area where the information of truth is located is perceived as a physical organ in the world of men. However, the area where the information of truth and heaven is located is not somewhere in this world. But since a man can only reach this information through a woman, he perceives the area where this information is located as being in the womb. Yes, the womb is one of the places where the information of truth is located in the female body, but it is not the only one.

Actually, the whole woman represents the truth, but the man can only perceive this information at the physical level.

Therefore, Prophet Muhammad is ordered to read, not to write. The woman represents the truth, and the man reads. The woman remembers and reminds of the truth, and the man wakes up and remembers through her. A woman cannot be a prophet; she is already born with the information of truth. She represents the truth, and she knows the truth if her breath is open and her confidence is whole. The need to know the truth belongs to men. It is the man who needs to wake up. It is the woman who wakes the man up. In reality, both are part of the same illusion; neither of them exists.

The woman is the energy that descends the heaven to earth, solves the problems, heals the diseases, and illuminates the darkness. The man is the prince of darkness who chooses the world, creates the problems, and makes the diseases. In truth, neither of them exists. Problem and solution come together; a disease comes with its healing, and the man comes with the woman. The two cannot be separated because in truth, neither of them exists.

The existence of living with God, the spirit, is divided in two as man and woman when they descend to the world. One half of the spirit is in the body of the man, and the other half is in the woman.

The body cannot directly connect to God. But the spirit can.

The man cannot directly connect to God, but the woman can. But only a woman completely free from her body and the world can do this, a woman who is awakened to remember only her spiritual features.

Therefore, if the woman has found the man she will liberate and wake up, her soul mate, if I say, "He's the person you're hung up on almost obsessively, who is always in your mind, and whom you can never let go. The person you cannot stop loving, whatever happens in life. The person you belong to," she will only remember one person. She should never stop loving him and inviting him home because the truth of God is hidden in the unity of twin spirits. When this unity occurs, the whole world will be freed.

We may have hundreds of soul mates; however, we only have one twin spirit among our soul mates.

Soul mates know themselves by the ease, peace, stillness, and freedom they feel. Soul mates support each other. They develop and strengthen. They make each other grow. Soul mates can be wonderful life partners because they proceed together and go through the same paths, and continuing together is safe for them.

Soul mates belong to each other. Because of the millions of lives and dimensions they come and go through together, they feel an endless love, understanding, commitment, and belonging to each other.

If you have found your soul mate in this life, it will not be possible for you to leave the person unless one of you dies.

Soul mates are a reflection of the holy order and plan of God. Soul mates reflect divine unity, endless love, and light to each other.

The minds and life perspectives of soul mates and the experiences they have in the world as humans might be different, but on the spiritual level, they are reflections of each other, the unity of soul in the body. Soul mates resemble each other on the spiritual level, and they even live the same experiences. Their spiritual developments are aligned. Never is one of them behind or in front of the other one.

Soul mates are always at the same level in terms of spiritual awakening. They might see life differently, and their thoughts, beliefs, ages, and expectations from life might be completely different, but it does not matter. They know that they reflect the highest possibilities of each other at the highest possibility level.

I think meeting your soul mate and even living a whole life with him or her is the best and most beautiful thing that can happen to you. In the relationships of soul mates, material and moral awakenings and risings happen at every moment every day and in all senses. Two spirits, reflections of each other, two high possibilities, carry each other to the upper level in every sense constantly and regularly.

I know from experience that this is a huge luxury. Once the connection or unification of the spirits forms in a place beyond the world and the agreement they make, once this true connection descends to this world, it is impossible for these two people to be apart.

Soul mates experience that the word *trust* is not enough in the presence of each other. The experiences they have in all lives and all periods from the moment the world existed, as well as the fact that they are true reflections of each other, carries them to a level of perfect ease, peace, trust, and devotion.

The mess starts here.

Once devotion and reflection at this level happen, this love calls the truth, and it brings the final life along as we make an infinite connection with our spirit and core.

The soul mates who experience the experience of the world together in all lives stay in the experience of being spouses once again in the final life. This experience is a little different from the other ones because both feel this experience without knowing that their twin spirits are called and activated. This time, their relationship will not end as usual with death. This time, the meeting of twin spirits that did not come into the cycle of duality will happen, and it will immortalize each of them.

Twin spirit or twin fire is different from the soul mate. For example, it is impossible for twin spirits to be in the classical spousal relationship, because they exist to destroy the world and the body and go beyond the illusion. The high vibration that occurs when they unite illuminates the world. The human enters heaven. The human stops being a human and becomes a prophet, and the earth becomes heaven.

Their relationship is deeper and more satisfying, developed, and colorful. Love can have different colors and shapes every day or even every moment. At the moment when the soul mates unite, such huge descends in the world that this huge light can be felt in the existence of the man and the woman and the cities they live in.

The word *disaster* becomes meaningful in the presence of twin spirits because it is a disaster for the twin spirits to meet. This limited and mortal body and world will have difficulty in carrying the burning hearts of the twin spirits and the fire in them.

The relationships of twin spirits are lived within the cycle of tides. No unity occurs in the world because the spirits are already a whole. Since a unity at the earthly level is not required, there is not any system suitable for this to occur in the world.

Since soul mates meet to destroy the world and each other in the egoistic sense, most of the people describe their relationships with feelings of pain, sadness, and deep hopelessness.

Twin spirits are the hottest, biggest loves in the world. Their unions are situations that come from eternity and go to eternity, that makes the unity of God. Therefore, they never come together in the world, like Romeo and Juliet, Ferhat and Sirin, or Leyla and Mecnun. Their realities before the world existed, and the point where they end up when the world ends with unity is one. Therefore, twin spirits are explained with the numbers 11:11 and 1:1.

The number 11:11 represents the periods in which the connections of the twin spirits with their spirits are not strong, the reality of spirit and body. When in the experience of 11, twin spirits see themselves a spirit and body; they look at the physical level and believe in the things they see with their physical eyes. Physical beauty; a beautiful body; and beautiful eyes, lips, clothes, and material things still seem appealing and tempting. At this level, 11:11 do not physically meet each other.

Then twin spirits go to the 1:1 level, the level that is with God. There may be a period between these two levels that lasts for a few days, a few months, or a few years during which they meet physically and live the highest dimensions of love, sex, and passion. Everything they live in this period, especially the egoistic situations that prevent their meeting, happens to carry them to the 1:1 level.

Since the twin spirits cannot carry the fire of love burning in their hearts to the world—in other words, since they cannot physically meet in this world, and this is especially prevented in the universe—they have to carry the deep situation to God's level.

There is only one way in this world for twin spirits who are lovers that cannot join: finding shelter in God.

The love in the hearts of twin spirits and the fire in their bodies carry them to unite with God since they cannot physically meet.

The number 1:1 represents the period in which they separately start their journeys to serve God. The only way of dealing with the deep emotions they live is to touch, reach out to, and embrace other people and to settle in the heart of humanity. Actually, on a level, they both become prophets. A deep perception, patience (the prophet's patience), understanding, and mercy settle in both of them because they have no other way. They are on the only path, the path of lovers, the path of God.

You enter the path of lovers when your heart starts to shred. At the moment when they really, in the earthly sense, are defeated to a love worse than death, the love the twin spirits have for each other, which is triggered through each other, is the love of the Creator. In their self and breath, they experience His self and His breath. This is huge. It turns hearts into pieces. You cry for days or months, but the pain of the first separation from your twin spirit—the first shattering—never ends. Twin fires remind us of the first shattering and therefore make us feel shattered. Twin fires can never stay together for a long time. They experience a longing for the truth and the pain of shattering of the twin spirits. This deep agony of first separation—yin and yang, female and male, Shiva and Shakti—ensures the formation of a deep understanding toward humanity within and ensures that the twin spirits stay at a level of the divine mission.

You can determine the people who have met their twin spirits—in other words, who have entered the path of lovers—by their eyes. They embrace humanity with a magnificent mercy, sincerity, and deepness at every moment and everywhere. The pain of longing and shuddering they feel inside is so deep and huge that the only chance for them to keep going is to reach out to and touch other people instead of their twin spirits they cannot embrace.

Our twin spirit is our other half that we never physically join with other than in our first- and last-world experiences, but we feel the presence all the time. Our twin spirit is not our equal. You can understand this as being siblings, but of course, not as siblings in the world. It is a relation of siblings such as yin and yang, black and white, light and darkness, night and day. One of the twin spirits is always white, and the other is always black. One lives with great devotion, and the other lives with great freedom. One needs freedom, and the other needs commitment. The most important thing is that it is impossible for them to be spouses in the world. Since they are their absolute opposite poles, they think they see themselves when they look at each other, but actually, the person across from them lives and contains the opposite possibility. It may take too long for them to understand this possibility. Generally, one of the twin spirits is one step ahead, guiding the other as in every life before, showing the path, being the light, and illuminating the path. Whichever this side is, it tries to show the other side its distinctions.

The biggest mistake the twin spirits can make is to confuse this experience with the experience of soul mates. Most of the time, we deeply meet and connect with our soul mates in the world. Therefore, most of the time, we experience that the person across from us in the spiritual depth is similar to or maybe the same as us. However, the case is the opposite with twin spirits. They are completely opposite each other. If one is bright, the other one is dark. One represents the afterlife, and the other represents the world. One is equipped with spiritual information, and the other is equipped with earthly experiences. One says, "God," and the other says, "Human." As long as they do not realize this, they may have big conflicts. When they look at each other, they see themselves at the spiritual level, but their characters they choose at the earthly level are their opposites. That is why this is called twin fire. It is almost impossible for them to understand and perceive each other completely, just as people are not able to see what is behind them. They represent their dark spots—everything they did not see, know, or experience in this life.

One of the twin spirits may be ahead of the other in terms of physical experiences, sex, touching, and physical love. The other may be experienced in universal love, divine love, and living at the consciousness level. They may unite incredibly, but they will not comprehend, because one cannot be in, beside, or around the other. One is always the opposite of the other. This opposition brings out a water-and-fire relationship that is hard to experience at the earthly level. One of the twins is fire, and the other is water. They are completely incompatible and opposite each other, but they are a whole when they are together.

This opposition and difference makes it impossible for them to stay together and walk hand in hand on the path of life. They are chosen to show each other what they are not. When they comprehend and understand this, their being together is the biggest lesson of the universe. When they accept that they are the opposite of each other and when they look at each other with this understanding, if they can get out of the illusion that they see themselves, they can understand that it is not only themselves they see in each other. When this is understood, the real lesson starts.

The real guidance starts when the twin spirits understand that they can see everything they themselves do not have in each other. They see the possibilities hidden within themselves and closed to themselves in each other, just like a person not being able to see what is behind him. They no longer need a teacher or guide apart from each other. Their differences and opposite sides can explain the whole world experience, including everything they cannot see and do not know—of course, if they can stand the existence of each other despite this difference and opposition.

Our twin spirit—in other words, our dark spot, or everything closed to our experience in the physical dimension—protected and looked over us in the lives in which we had a body, not as a body but as a spiritual being. He or she guided us by illuminating our path. The same applies to us: we may stay in the spiritual dimension with the mission of supporting our twin spirit in his or her life in which he or she has a body.

Twin spirits never split. They did not split before or after time existed, and they feel and know this in their next encounter. They have a deep sense of knowing toward each other because they stand at the furthest point in the universe, stating the things they do not know.

The best description explaining my twin spirit would be this: my other side whom I know was and will be by my side at every moment and for eternity, whom it is impossible for me to understand or see, and who teaches me every lesson. It is my dark side. The experience of humanity in which I do not even know the fact that I do not know.

The twin spirit is actually a symbol of the thought of human separate from God. Our twin spirit is the symbol of duality, just like the duality started with Adam and Eva at the beginning of the world experience, the symbol of separation. If the twin spirits can turn this deep feeling of longing within instead of living their lust to unite and join together, a desire that arises because of the intense feelings they feel for each other openly—in other words, instead of trying to reach each other or wait in an absurd cycle for a lifetime—they reach the point of inspiration where God exists. A great inspiration arises there.

Maybe what I say will not surprise you and make you run into a contradiction; however, our twin spirit is the only point that is impossible for us to experience in this experience of world. Our twin spirit is the only human who is impossible for us to understand and the only journey that is impossible for us to see, because whatever we are, the twin spirit is the opposite. Inspiration is hidden in this duality. Herein lies the mystery.

All poets write poems about the loves they cannot have, and all sculptors make sculptures of the ones they cannot have. This is the point where we can touch the imaginary world, cannot reach with the consciousness of world, and can touch the consciousness of God. It's the inspiration point. Since humans cannot reach God, the place where this experience is reflected is in our soul mate. When you turn the desire to reach within, when you let the burning fire touch your heart, then the purpose of existence arises. At that point, the Creator starts to use you and your burning heart. He is the fire you feel. The longing you feel is for Him. He is the one you cannot reach and cannot embrace with this existence. Somebody in this world should be the symbol of the longing you feel for Him so that you can be inspired.

The most loving and understanding people of this world are the ones whose hearts burn with love and are shattered with longing felt for the lovers they cannot reach. They understand the whole of humanity. They touch people.

They know.

This is the ultimate knowledge: divine love.

At this level, all needs for doing and being are deactivated. Seeing, fully understanding, and accepting that you cannot end up with the only person you want to reach in the world but cannot know your place is the biggest awakening you can have.

The presence of the Creator is one. If He is, then there is nothing else.

Within His truth, neither I nor my body exists. Therefore, the union will never happen, and the purpose is not uniting. Isn't it meaningless to go after something that will never and cannot happen? Therefore, I called our experience with our twin spirit absolutely meaningless. It is absolutely meaningless at the level of truth.

However, it is the most meaningful thing in the world, maybe even the only meaningful thing.

That is why twin spirits are confused with soul mates. Humans get lost if such a meaning is ascribed. This symbolizes the beginning of the journey of getting lost. In this case, humans are lost. Therefore, the biggest love you have in this world, the love between you and your twin spirit, means that you are getting lost.

What does this mean? If you are fooled (maybe the prophets always tried to tell us this!), if you confuse him with the love of God and confuse your longing for him with the longing you feel for the Creator, if you idolize him, you will waste so much energy to reach a person you cannot reach in order to be with him that you get wasted in the way. You will not even understand how time passes when you are together. You would do anything to be together. You would destroy the world, your world; give up on everything; and destroy your whole life, and you believe that this would be worth it. The more you cannot reach him; the more you are fooled; and the more you idolize him, make him a god, and cannot think of anything but him, you cannot do anything, and this means the end of you. Your life energy ends, and you start to feel exhausted, tired, and dead inside. Many young people are taken to the hospital or try to commit suicide when they cannot deal with this intense feeling of longing. Many people become addicted to alcohol and drugs.

The most important thing you must remember is that you cannot reach your twin spirit even if you are together. He is always a stranger to you in every aspect. Since he is a stranger, an incredible line of fire is formed in the world. This means physical attraction, sex, lust, and passion, but ultimately, you will get lost at the bottom of all these earthly feelings, and you will want to go back home from there, to turn within and be alone. As long as you cannot deal with your despair, as long as you cannot reach him, you will have two options: either you will live in this line of fire despite all conflicts by accepting that you can never understand each other, can never know each other, and are the complete opposites of each other, living every day with him with a physical mind-body, or you will leave him. Leaving him means being completely liberated from the physical world, the corporeal world.

If a person can let go of her twin spirit, the depth she lives with him, and the rush of emotions she loses herself in and can give up the chance of touching him and being with him, true liberation occurs because this is the hardest decision to make, the hardest thing to do in this world. It is a path chosen rarely.

If you have chosen this path, when you let go of the person you have understood you cannot reach and when you turn to God, you will realize that He has embraced you and has taken you to heaven.

The breaths you take will be heaven then. Your looks will turn into understanding, passion, and the messenger of the Creator. Your heart will burn with such huge love and longing that it will turn into an inspiration for the whole of humanity and make everyone you meet full of faith and love.

It gives you the power to change the world.

The kingdom of God becomes yours because you have not preferred just an earthly body, however appealing it may be and however big what you have lived and felt may be, over Him, the Creator. Now your way home is guaranteed.

At this point, you live in the world not because you want to express yourself, because you want to reach him, or because you have any other purposes but just because you will fulfill your mission. Your heart burns with the love of God, but you know that the only way of reaching Him is through taking all your brothers and sisters home with you.

The last person on the world will be your twin spirit—the last person who chose to go back home.

The last choice made will be his. At the moment when the whole world and your twin choose the truth, the holy plan is complete. You will know that there is no escape from this. This plan is made in this life.

As I have always said, you have misunderstood, and now is the time for correction. This is the twin spirit.

A soul mate is different. Since soul mates exist in the world, they come to every life together, and they go together. Therefore, they have a trust for each other at the highest level. If there is a person you are sure will hold you every time you are about to jump off a cliff, that person is your soul mate. We feel trust for our soul mates from the first moment we meet them. We get lost within them; we almost become one. We experience the infinity, holiness, and power of our spirit through them. When we look at our soul mates, we see ourselves. We find everything belonging to us in our soul mates. We experience spirituality through them.

Soul mates are excellent life partners because they know us well since we have been coming to and going from the world with them for centuries. They know what we will do and how we will proceed with our slightest movement. There are almost no uncertainties with our soul mates—there cannot be. At every moment, everything is definite and defined, like destiny. The uncertainty we live with our twin spirits does not exist with the soul mates.

Soul mates are our comfort zones in every aspect. We feel comfortable, safe, and unconditional when we are with them. We go beyond the physical reality, and we can experience the state of just being. Soul mates contain each other; they become interwoven. They can exit together, and they can

Awakening

walk hand in hand for long years. In my experience, if you are in your last life, wherein you also meet your soul mate, you will definitely need your soul mate at every level. Because the meeting of soul mates is so striking, unbearable, shaking, and incredible, we will need our soul mate to go through the love, truth, and awakening dimension. We need our soul mates in the dimension of knowing so as to proceed without panicking in the unknown dimension we experience when we meet our dark spot.

In summary, soul mates have marriages lasting for a lifetime. They have compatible relationships; they are couples who accept and love each other despite everything. Twin spirits are lovers who never understand each other, live in constant distrust and obscurity, and show and teach each other everything they do not know. These are the forbidden loves experienced in fires, the lovers who can never unite.

My soul mate is the person who understands me the best, the consciousness who represents me the best—everything I have seen, my whole self, my body, my mind, and my feelings.

My soul mate is my reflection.

We may have male soul mates, but we only come across one mate who truly represents us. He is our only mate in this world, the only mate of our spirit and body, and we came here together in all our lives. He is also the person who understands us best in this world. He feels who we are from a single look, from our posture. You will know this if you have found your true soul mate, your only mate in the world. Eyes reflect the soul. We enter the universe from his eyes, our hearts become one, the minds become one, the consciousness proceeds together, and he is the person with whom we will go hand in hand throughout the lifetime. He is our best friend.

The soul mate is the grand prize. He is the reflection of the decision of heaven. He is the symbol of unity consciousness.

The soul mate is also a symbol, just as the twin spirit is. While the twin spirit is the symbol of the consciousness of separation, our part that we see separate from us, the reflection of the decision of being a person separate from us, the soul mate is the reflection and symbol of union, of returning home. Therefore, we feel a huge peace, quietness, and safety with our soul mates. We want them to be with us for the rest of our lives.

Soul mates are inherently the ones who came to this world to be with us and accompany us in the journey of life. Soul mates accompany each other in the journey of liberation from the world. Therefore, I think you cannot meet your twin spirits before you meet your soul mates. It is not really possible to meet your reflection who reinforces you, ensures that you come in out of the rain, and reminds you of who you are and survive (I mean it!) this experience. You will need a person who holds your hand, who is by your side, and whom you know to be by your side at all times during the mind-blowing experience you have with your twin spirit, in which you lose yourself, or else it is almost impossible for you to have these experiences. The order is that you meet your soul mate or twin spirit when you become one with our spirit, when your spiritual side reinforces.

Soul mates resemble each other in every sense: shape, spirit, body, self, posture, look, and even walk. They perceive life the same. They see the same things in the places they look. This is the reason they click so well. They hardly have conflicts. Generally, they are really compatible, and they have deep admiration, love, and respect for each other. They do not have the experience of the line of fire, as the twin spirits do. Their relationships are not hard.

Everything is indisputable for soul mates. I think this is the best explanation, like a perfect plan for soul mates to find each other, just as it is a perfect plan for the human to turn to his core. When you turn to your core, you find your soul mate. The satisfaction from that experience naturally ensures that you meet your soul mate. This meeting brings about the breathing, a relaxation at the highest level, and a feeling of trust and togetherness at the highest level.

Our soul mate is the only person to whom we can say, "I was created for you." Yes, you may have many soul mates, but as you would guess, since you truly have one soul, you should have one soul mate. The others are your partners in periods in which you get closer to your soul, connect to your soul, and mingle with it.

Just like the ninety-nine names of God, or Allah, there are ninety-nine possibilities in soul mates. In other words, we meet ninety-nine soul mates during our life. They can be anyone—our relatives, teachers, colleagues, partners, and friends. Everyone you feel close to and about whom you can say, "It was as if I knew him before meeting him," is your soul mate. You have been together with the soul group in this dream since the beginning of the world. Therefore, you have a warm relationship with your soul mates at the first moment. They are your eternal friends, the people you have been living hand in hand and heart by heart with through the journey of life for centuries.

As you would guess, just as there is one of the ninety-nine names of God in the background of each human energy, form, and existence purpose, there is only one soul mate suitable for this existence. All people have one soul mate whose eyes they got lost in, with whom they intertwine and become one, whom they feel to be by their side at every second, and about whom they say, "Yes, he is me," with the breath of breath, the self of self, the posture, and the look.

Finding and meeting him is harder than anything for most people. It is a small possibility. Why? Because to meet your soul mate, who is the reflection of you in everything, you must be truly committed to yourself. You must never play roles and must always act as you are, or else you will meet that true reflection of yourself here and now, just like your other ninety-eight soul mates.

If you want to meet your true reflection, your one true partner in the world, you must first change everything you came to this world to change, liberate everything you came to this world to liberate, and, most importantly, be yourself at every moment. If you have nothing to hide from anyone, put yourself out there 100 percent, do not feel ashamed, and are not intimidated by anyone, then it means your soul is in the world. As a result, you can experience a 100 percent reflection of your soul in the world.

I feel lucky about this. Yes, I have come a hard way, as if I have been walking this way for centuries. I have always been on a journey of transformation, liberation, and healing since the beginning of my life. Some call this karma cleanse.

Let me get back to our subject. You should unburden yourself from every burden you have been carrying before you find your true partner. You need to live everything you came here to experience—love, relationships, jobs, success, failure, trust, fear, disease, health. When you live all these and when you are completely liberated from the meaning you have ascribed to this world, you deserve to meet that ideal partner, the only partner you choose with your experience of the world. Really!

My husband always says to me, "I would not have been able to find you if the past had not happened, if I had not lived what I lived." I agree. The ideal partner, the true reflection of our spirit, comes across us when we mature. Even if we meet our soul mate, when there is too much to live and to clean, when there are issues we've brought from the past, issues we ascribe meaning to, and issues we need to be liberated from, we become so busy with these meaningless issues that we might not realize him.

The most important thing I will say about our ideal partners, our soul mates, is that we meet them when we are ready. You cannot find your true partner if you are searching. My husband also frequently says, "I have been searching for you for the whole of my life." But unfortunately, you cannot find when you are searching. At some point, he stopped searching for his ideal partner, just as I did. At that moment, he met me, and the same goes for me. The moment I thought I would not be able to find the one true partner whom I would intertwine with, whom I would be one with on every level, and who would completely be the reflection of my soul on every level and stopped searching, I met him.

You cannot find him if you are searching, and he cannot find you when he is searching. Your soul mate, your ideal partner, is the chapter in which everything must be a whole—of course, with one condition: when you are you and he is he and when you and he live without any hesitation, insecurity, or dread in living as you are, then you will meet him.

If you tend to hide yourself for even a second, if you do anything other than you feel for even a second, you will not meet your soul mate. Not yet. The moment you start to live the way you feel like living without caring about anyone and when society, rules, and family stop being meaningful for you, then you meet him. That's the moment when everything changes.

3

Breath

The Journey

Are you ready for the journey?

Then let's start our exercise.

First, let me tell you where to start. Actually, this starts on the last day of my seminar called the miracles course. I will take up from where I left the group on that day, and now, together, we will reach the level of awareness.

The goal of our journey is this: ensuring you can differentiate between miracle consciousness and ego consciousness, between the truth and the world. I have only one purpose: to ensure that you can differentiate between the two and understand how the laws of the two work and what the two of them actually are.

Before starting, I would like you to determine a good intention.

What kind of a change would you like to happen when you finish reading this book?

What can you want?

Some examples might include divine love, wealth, happiness, health, completing the missing parts, being yourself, unity, love, power, peace, rising, awareness, and being in the moment.

Now I will tell you something that will surprise you. If you can understand what I am about to say at every level, there is no need for this exercise, because what I am about to say is already the expansion of your life.

All that we have mentioned our life.

Whatever your intentions are, you have them at this moment, this holy moment.

You awaken to this at the end of the miracles course. Now you need to open this so as to carry this awareness, this consciousness, to a higher level.

You might say, "I already have all these things. I already know there." Then why does not every day of your life reflect this? Knowing what you have is an experience. Feeling them deep down and using them is a totally different experience.

Yes, all these are my core. In my experience, you have someone who has committed to living with her own intentions, and she still intends for the truth every morning. If you understand this, there is no need for you to read any further. But people forget. The human system is the mechanism of forgetting oneself. The only things you do constantly are escape from yourself and forget who you are. The whole system of the world is founded upon this: schools, education, media, economy, and family.

Everything in the world is a reflection of the superior plan you make in order to forget yourself.

You might say, "I had forgotten, but now I remember. I am everything." You are right, but the real problem starts here.

People are awakening. In Turkey, every day thousands of people are participating in personal development training; meditating; working with their minds, thoughts, and breath; and awakening. However, nobody notices that this is a bigger problem than they think.

I wrote this book to awaken us to the truth. If you have come to this chapter, you should be aware of something now. Whether you believe what I have written or not and whether you agree with me or not, something should start to be clearer and more visible for you. Very nice! But remember this awakening may create huge problems for you if you do not read what I have written in this chapter or do the exercises I have recommended.

As you would guess, awakening to the fact that this world is not real but is a dream while still experiencing this world will not have a petty effect on your consciousness and life. On the contrary, it will naturally shake you at first. The things you have read in the first chapters of the book have affected and shaken you pretty much—am I right?

The problem starts at this point. Being asleep while not being aware that you are asleep is not hard. This is just like continuing to lie while not being aware that you are lying or realizing the effect you create when you lie or keeping up with your addictions when you do not know the damage they are causing.

If there is no awareness, there is no problem. All problems begin with awareness.

In my experience, I was aware of the fact since my birth. Even when I barely was in my right mind, I was able to see that everything is an illusion and is temporary when I looked around. Of course, I could not express this with words or tell anyone how I saw everything, but at least I was aware that people were exaggerating life in the world. For example, I remember asking my mother and father and my friends at school, "Why?" when considering the things they were sorry for, cared about, and pursued. I used to wonder why people cried over a dead person. Even today I remember saying when I was around thirteen or fourteen, "She did not go anywhere; it is just her body that died. Why do they think she is gone?"

I always knew that the people they called criminals, were angry at, and cursed did not actually exist, no matter what crime they seemed to have committed. I used to think, *Someone killed someone—so what? The person who died did not truly die; only his body left. Why are they so mad? The killer—poor man—thinks he has done something unreasonable, but actually, he did not do anything. He did twisted things. Poor man. Forgive him. Maybe he did it without knowing what he did.*

Do you know how big a problem this awareness is? How hard it is for a consciousness that thinks death, assault, and everything happening in the world is real; perceives everything as real; and takes everything seriously to be aware of the truth? I know this well.

Awareness—that is, remembering the truth—is a real problem for the world. Why would the world, a nonexistent place, be scared of something other than the truth? There is only one thing the world does not want us to do: awaken to the fact that it is real. An order is created to prevent this from happening. For example, consider the five senses. Colors, shapes, odors, tissues, tastes, and sounds surround us. Our brain can be manipulated so well that we can think that everything happening here is real. Therefore, we can get angry and mad. We experience question after question, madness after madness, and disease after disease.

Then someday someone comes to you and says, "No, none of these are actually happening. Why are you being mad?" The consciousness of the world—the consciousness that wants to keep the dream alive and wants you to believe a nonexistent place exists—gets angry when I say, "None of these are happening." I do not need to describe this; I am sure you have witnessed at least one occasion when you said, "Aren't you a bit exaggerating?" about a fact someone else believed in and you did not, and the other person got angry. Now imagine that you exaggerate in every area everywhere, and I say, "You exaggerate everything!"

Yes, you exaggerate everything, and you think everything in this world is real, but none of these things are happening.

The person you call a murderer and the person you think is bad don't actually exist. The assumptions we make that they do exist are not real. They never happened. They were never experienced. Now, get mad if you can—if you can be mad at anything.

The thing I am trying to tell you is this: the fact that I remember the truth does not do good in the world.

I will emphasize this again: the fact that I have awakened and am aware that this is a dream does not do any good. It will at least not change your life in the sense you understand.

Many people think that the fact that they are awake will change their whole life, as if when their awareness increases, they will be able to do anything they want, they will be successful and rich, and their lives will be on track, as if a magical wand touched them. There is no such thing. The awakening, or awareness, has nothing to do with the world. That you have awakened to the fact that the world is a dream does not change the reality of the world. Why would it? Also, if I am aware of the fact that the world is a dream, why would I want it to change? Why would something that never existed change? Everything can stay as it is.

You have ascribed so much meaning to the world that you want to change everything.

So it will not change. What then? What difference does it make? Anyway, the world was never real; it never existed. Nothing happened here. Why would you change anything?

If you understand what I have written, if you can feel this truth deep inside, you have awakened. But you are not awake yet.

Awakening to the truth and being awake are two different states.

Awakening

Awakening to truth—to the fact that the world and the universe are a dream—is the first step. This step is your second birth. When you take this step, your perspective of the world has completely and eternally changed.

However, do not think that everything has ended with this rebirth. Actually, it is all starting now. The journey of return has started.

Awareness starts the journey of return. The journey will end when you distribute this awareness to the world.

You have bought and read this book to wake up, remember the truth, and start your journey of returning home.

The journey is just beginning.

The same is happening for the ones participating in the miracles course. Most people come to the course because of obstructions in their breathing and thought system, not aware of the fact in the beginning. Then, as their breath opens, the miracle happens, and people remember. There is no need for me to tell you the truth anymore; your breath—your self—tells you and reminds you of everything.

Without this, before the awareness, you did not exist; you were not living. You had forgotten who you were. If you forget who you are, you are lost; you think the dream is reality. You are lost. You are sick. Being awakened to this is the first step, and you have taken that first step.

Remembering and knowing the truth is the smallest step you can take. Most people think even this is a big step. *Awakening. Enlightenment.* What big meanings we ascribe to these words. What big searches these worlds have in the background. However, awakening and enlightenment are really simple facts that happen when we can open our breath. People take courses for days and months for this. Both the time and the energy are wasted. When you connect with your breath, with your self, enlightenment automatically occurs; there is no need to exaggerate.

The real issue is not awakening; the real issue is deciding what to do with a consciousness that knows the truth.

People come to this world first to be born and then to die. Can you prove otherwise? This is the story. This is the fact. The cycle of the human, and the universe, is this. The earlier everyone wakes up to this fact, the easier it is—not because awakening is necessary. Do not get me wrong. Because it is inevitable.

All those courses you take to wake up, all those meditations, and all those books you have read do nothing but delay your awakening. If you let yourself be, awakening will inevitably happen. I cannot understand why people try so hard or delay their awakenings.

Now, this is the truth: "I remember! All these things are not happening." Okay, you have woken up. So? Now what?

Our exercise starts here. Everything I will give you is at this point, because my story starts here, not from the chapter of forgetting the truth. Such a thing never happened, at least in the period I know myself. Maybe I forgot myself when I was a baby, and then I had such a big trauma that I had to wake up at that moment. I do not know. I think the period between forgetting and waking up was probably too short for me. Personally, I cannot remember a period in which I forgot the truth.

My story starts with a connected but shallow breath and with remembering everything I have written here. The only reason I am writing this book now is that I was able to find the words to express the truth.

My story started when I was only four or five years old, when someone said, "You are not this; you are something other than this." I could not understand and believe, and I said, "No, I am complete and whole." I remember the first period I criticized. I thought, *What can I do if you cannot see my beauty, my perfection? May God help you.*

Until I was thirty, I lived remembering and knowing the truth, the fact that the world is a dream, but I could not tell anyone. Did the fact that I knew the truth do any good when I could not tell what I knew or share with the people around me? No, absolutely not.

The fact that I remembered the truth became the biggest problem in the world—for me, my family, and my beloved ones. When I was twenty-eight, I was literally mad. Everyone around me ascribed huge meanings to the world—as a price of my not telling what I knew and saw. They cared too much, and they claimed that the material world was valuable and that the things happening were real. I did not even understand what they were saying. I said to myself, "How do all these people look at the world to see what they are seeing?" I asked questions, such as "Why can't I look like they do? Why can't I see what they see? Why can't I value the world and the things in the world just like they do? Why don't all the earthly pleasures, properties, and experiences make me happy? Why am I more and sadder every day?" I wanted to come to a point where I really wanted to die, but I did not know how to do it. When all others had killed themselves and proven to themselves that they were dead, I, who wanted to do it but could not, started to feel like a stranger to the whole world.

I said, "God, please show me the path. What should I do?" My encounter with breathing was right after this prayer.

The answer came in my first breathing session. They presented with a to-do list, and I—who had said, "I do not know how to deal with this. I do not know what to do. I want to die"—thanked God for everything He has given, and I left that session knowing what to do with what I remembered, believing in my path. Since that day, I have been walking on my path. I share everything I know and everything I think with you with the courage given me by my breath.

With years of experience, I can finally say this: I think everyone diagnosed with a mental disease has awakened. They are so awake that not knowing what to do with this knowledge has driven them crazy. Every awakened consciousness has the consciousness to awaken in the world. Therefore, all of the people you call mentally ill are teachers. They all remember the truth, and they know the world is just an empty dream. Unfortunately, since they do not know what to do with this information, they cannot fulfill their duty of being a teacher, and they cannot wake up tens of sleeping people around them.

The biggest pain of an awakened consciousness is seeing the sleeping consciousness around and not being able to wake it up. This is how mental illnesses happen. All the people diagnosed as mentally ill know and remember the truth, but they cannot remind the people around them. They have come to train the people in their period, and as long as they cannot do this, the sleeping consciousness around them will not understand them and will consider them ill.

However, the "normal" ones are the patients.

Do not get me wrong: I have not been diagnosed with a mental disease, because I did not let that happen. I was lucky because my self-confidence never dropped below a certain level. I was aware of the truth I had within and the effects it created, but I learned the degrees of the effect of the truth with experience.

The state called mental illness is a lie. It is just a label made by the sleeping consciousness whose level of awareness is not enough to understand these people—and unfortunately, they are the majority.

Everyone diagnosed with a mental disease is actually a teacher. They only have one problem: not teaching, not telling what they know, or not being able to express it with the right words in the consciousness of the world, in a language that the sleeping will understand. As long as the teacher does not tell the students the truth, how will they know? They cannot know. They cannot understand because the things told by these people are above their capacity for understanding. As a result, the students label the teachers as mentally ill, and they go on.

Now the world is awakening. A hundred years from now, the people you call mentally ill will be your guides.

If you are diagnosed with depression, as it is called in the modern language, you are awake. You know, there is even a movie about the awakening: *Divergent*. Do you remember?

If one can see the truth and cannot ascribe a meaning to the world, if a person can see how meaningless everything in the world is, that person falls into depression. Awakened consciousness does not see the things seen by the others. He does not look at the world by perceiving it as real, ascribing meaning to the happenings, or understanding it. He is aware that he understands nothing. He is connected to nothing, and he cannot be. He lives as if he is in a constant void. Most importantly, awakened people cannot be mad at anyone but themselves. Actually, they cannot get mad at themselves either. They grunt, get bored, or get mad from time to time just because they cannot see the world as the ones with the world consciousness and the ones sleeping do. The awake people are actually a gift to the world. Every day more awake people are born, and the world changes thanks to these people. Most of them are not as lucky as I am in expressing the truth.

I came across the tool of breath at a time when I was really desperate. Breathing is such a powerful tool that I do not even need to tell people the truth. They can perceive everything I want to say by connecting with their breath, with their self.

Awakening

But not all awakened people are as lucky as I am. Since sleeping minds cannot understand them because the awake do not share the language of robots that the dream the world is used to, most of the awake are diagnosed with mental illnesses or depression. They cannot perform their spiritual teaching duty because they cannot realize that they have come to this world to teach the light and love they have. They cannot teach as they keep quiet, and as they are kept quiet, the world has turned into the place we experience.

Maybe this book and this chapter will be a pioneer to honor them and keep on with our lives. Who knows?

If you have someone close to you who's been diagnosed with a mental illness, please encourage him or her to do breathing sessions immediately. That person is just a teacher who cannot put what he or she knows into words, and it is our duty to clear his or her path.

That is why it seems as if everything turns into a nightmare when they complete the miracles course. You cannot wake up to the fact that the world is a dream and not say anything about it.

I have spent most of my life like this, and that is why I can really associate myself with you. I spent twenty-eight years of my life knowing all this but not knowing the fact that all the things I know are the truth, and therefore, I could not convey the knowledge to the people around me, and I felt like a stranger. At the point when I desired to die, I met breathing. Since I could not disconnect myself from the truth, since I could not fall asleep like the others, since I was aware, I wanted to die.

Being awake in this reality of the world and remembering the truth and not doing anything about it are huge problems. Not remembering is much better. Really. In my experience, since I did not know what to do with this information, I really wanted not to remember at all. I wanted to be like the majority, to think the body was real, because remembering the truth at a time when the consciousness that thinks the world is real is the majority and knowing that the world is a simple game is really hard.

In summary of your current state, maybe you have been living in a cave up until now, and this book broke you free. Or maybe you have gone out of the cave a few times before, but you could not stay there. Twenty-eight years of my life passed as I tried to fit a spirit too big to fit in a cave into a small cave. Do not get me wrong. I am saying that my spirit is bigger than any of yours, and that is why it could not fit in the cave. The spirit is already infinite and unlimited—whatever you do, you cannot fit it in a cave. However, most people live in the fantasy that they can fit it in a cave, in the illusion of the world.

I could not dream it. My journey passed by with my saying, "I do not understand how or why people fit themselves in caves, patterns, forms, and rules; I wish I could also do it and live happily in the cave with them." It turns out there is no life in the cave, and there is no cave at all. I could not see or perceive what they were doing in that cave.

As a result, I could not get into the cave. I thought the ones inside the cave could not see or hear me, but it turns out they wanted to come out and come to me. When my breath opened, it was as if I got my voice, and then I started shouting inside. At first, nobody heard me. Then thousands of people held the hand I was reaching out, and they came out and came to me. Those people are the tens of thousands of people coming to my seminars now. They are all dear friends of mine. I owe thanks to all of them, not because they held my hand when I reached out to them but because they fulfilled their commitments to themselves.

I am still shouting inside the cave from the outside—while knowing that there is no cave and seeing that the cave is not there but being aware that others have created such a place in their dream. I am not assuming a cave; I assume that you think there is one within. I call you, but you are not there, actually; you are here by my side. Wake up.

That is what I have done in this book. I got you out of an imaginary cave. Or rather, I woke you up to the fact that the cave does not exist. Now starts the real problem. You have woken up to the fact that the cave does not exist, but what will you do to the parts of your life that think they are still in a cave?

Maybe this problem will not be solved throughout your life, and you will continue to breathe with this in mind every day. That is what I am doing.

Now we will try to differentiate between the cave and true life, because if you cannot make this distinction—if you confuse the true world with an imaginary cave—you cannot wake up the ones in the dream of the cave.

Awakening

We all have a part in our consciousness that forgets and a part that remembers. Now I am representing the part that knows you and remembers the fact that the cave is not real. You are representing the part of me that forgets and perceives this world as real. This book is a reflection of us, our relationship with ourselves—the only relationship in the world.

The parts of us that remember and forget are different. I am sure you have understood this by now. In the reality of this world, both exist. In other words, nobody can forget completely, and nobody can remember completely. Forgetting and remembering are two facts that happen in this world. That is why they are the absolute opposites of each other. It does not actually happen, but it seems so for a while.

At this point within the point of truth, we can talk about true existence and, therefore, the one and only Creator; it is not possible to either forget or remember. In truth, you do not exist. Since you cannot forget, you cannot remember. But in here, we forget at every moment, and there is no problem with this. This is the nature of humans: forgetting and remembering. Of course, these have different levels. In other words, some may forget too much, and some may remember too much, but it makes no difference because in reality, we are all the reflection of one consciousness, and actually, we do not exist.

There is only God.

You need to forget the truth in the world. If you do not forget, you cannot perform your functions in the world. You need to remember because if you cannot remember, you cannot keep going in the world.

You can talk to God, you can tell about His love, you can feel it in your heart, you can take His light in your heart, and you can feel His joy, but are you aware that none of these have anything to do with God and the thought system of God?

Neither you nor your perception exists in the place where the Creator is, where singularity is, in truth. There is only Him—nothing else. Therefore, you can feel Him and understand Him, but you cannot be one with Him because you do not exist at that level.

Now let's start with duality.

Within the experience, within this dream, there is always a duality, and there will always be. Nothing happens by itself in the reality of the world. Okay, the world is not real; it is a dream. But even though this dream is not true, it has some features, a reality. For example, there is only God in truth, but in the world, there is everything but Him. It seems that there are plenty of different things.

As I have mentioned before, the world is just a thought in the presence of God.

But what is that thought?

What if there was anything else other than the truth? What would it look like? The answer is this: the way the world looks.

If there was a place outside the truth, a place that was not created by God, how would this happen or look?

We experience the state of the thought and the question "How would a place other than the truth, a place not created by God, look?" distributed within the cycle of time. Therefore, everything in this world is founded on the question "Why?" and there is no answer to this question. The question is based on the world. Can a question be the answer to a question? Can a question contain the answer of the truth? That is why God is not experienced in the world.

A place not created by the Creator cannot be created. But how would it be as an assumption? This idea could only be a concept, a design, and this is how it would be. Like this. The answer of God and the certainty of the day of reckoning lie here. The end of the dream is inevitable. The world can only be a dream because of the truth of the Creator, because of His features, and all dreams are bound to end. Therefore, death is inevitable. This is a dream; it will end at some point.

The idea of the world, in truth, is only an idea, and it blew when it came. The body can only be an idea, and it disappears the moment it comes. It is not possible for something nonexistent in truth to exist.

That is why the idea of being in the world, or the idea of getting lost in the dream, died at the moment it was born and even before it was born. Our way back was guaranteed at the moment when we started our journey of forgetting the truth. Because you cannot forget. You cannot forget completely. That is why you cannot just disappear here. Every disappearing should have its way back, and every forgetting should have a remembering. Each idea of being in the world brings about a spirit because the part that forgets the truth brought the part that remembers the truth along to the world. The medal of the world has two sides. Nothing here can be seen by itself. You cannot disappear forever because you have never disappeared. Since the happening you think to be disappearing never happened, your journey back is guaranteed—just like your cave dream. The cave was a dream. The world is this dream. It never existed. Therefore, you do not need to die to wake up. You are already dead.

If you want to see the dream of getting away from the truth, the return to the truth is also within that dream. In other words, the moment you start your journey to disappear, you also accepted your journey to return to the truth. Every path has a return.

That is why the body cannot exist by itself, and it comes along with the reality of spirit. Why? Because you cannot forget until forever. You cannot dream forever. You cannot just forget and just remember. Most people think the awake ones will never forget again, and the asleep ones will never remember. Neither is possible because one cannot exist without the other; it never did and never will. They both have different functions and benefits, and neither of them is real. The relationship of teacher and student continues at every level and continuously.

In my experience, one thing is really clear: my world is my reflection, and in my reality in the twenty-first century, both forgetting and remembering the truth happen. We get lost in the world; I can see this everywhere I look. And we can stay aware and awake with an open consciousness and remembering. I am both the one who forgets and the one who remembers. For the part of my consciousness that forgets, there is a part that remembers, and I can experience the relationship between these two. The point where I see, know, and allow this is the point where I am liberated, where I am free of the illusion.

The plan of returning home is also within the plan of getting lost. Therefore, there is nothing to worry about. There is just too much to live. That is it.

At the level of truth, there is neither forgetting nor remembering. There is only God. Both exist in the experience of the world, in the illusion of the world, and they are not separated. In case the balance is lost in one of them—in my experience, twisted breathing and thinking habits cause this, and this can be remedied—problems occur in the perception. As far as I can see, some people tend to more in the truth, and some more in the experience of the world. The tuning is off with most people. However, this tune can come back with the tuning of breathing and thoughts.

The ones in truth think, *Since the body is not real, we do not need to do anything.* However, even if it is not real, the system of the world has a state, the state of doing. This place is the world of action. There is constant action; it is a place where you are always on the move and get results after doing something. Yes, it is not real. But the fact that it is not real does not change the nature of the world. Since it is not real, nothing can happen in the world of doing without actually doing something. Here you need to do something even to remember the truth in the dream.

Some people say, "The reality of spirit may exist, but we live in the world," and they say we should consider the body instead of the spirit and the world instead of the afterlife or the core. In this case, since there is no spirit and no life in the body, diseases start at the physical level. Actually, both perspectives are true. But they both have different laws and rules. The real illusion starts here.

Now I will tell you where you are mistaken generally. But first, let's differentiate between the miracle and the ego consciousness in the duality. I will not mention mind and past-future cycle because I assume you have overcome it. I am talking about the consciousness here at the moment. This consciousness is divided in two: the part that forgets and the part that remembers. Both apply to the reality of the world. In truth, there is no ego consciousness and no miracle consciousness. Since there is no forgetting, there is remembering. Since the world that is forgotten is not real, the world remembered is not real either.

Neither the body nor the spirit is real. Both are states that occur in here, in the experience of the dream.

There is only God in truth—nothing else. There is no spirit separated from Him.

The miracle consciousness is more real than the ego consciousness because it is an agent of the truth. But what is important here is this: I can choose between the two. They both have certain laws, and these laws are completely opposite. My consciousness cannot choose two states at the same time.

For example, when I say, "I am whole and perfect," I remember the laws of the truth. In other words, I am in the miracle consciousness, and

I remember the truth. If you can understand this, you implement this in the world. Our natural state is whole and perfect. Okay, I am created to be whole and perfect, but when I say, "This body is whole and perfect," here starts the problem. When we remember our truth, wholeness, and perfection for twenty-four hours, we may start to see the body as whole and perfect, and that perfection can be reflected on the body. But if we say, "The body is whole and perfect," this will not be true, because it is not. I am not this body. I am the one who will make this body perfect by remembering the truth. I am the one who will take responsibility for this body and make it whole and perfect because it is obvious that the body cannot do this by itself.

The fact that I remember love is not enough for the world to be full of love. Because of the world, because of its idea, its formation is a mistake, an erroneous perspective. Love cannot exist here because of the nature of the world; I am the one who will bring it here. I can only do this when I know myself and remember who I am.

The world will be full of as much love as I can remember.

The world is just as how I know myself, because my consciousness is reflected in the world at every moment.

Here we get confused. "I am love. I am a foundation of love"—everyone says and reads this. Okay, fine, but do I mean Nevşah when I say this? If this is the case, there must be something wrong, because it would be wrong to expect Nevşah to be full of love at all times. Something with a name and shape cannot be the source of love.

Nevşah can be full of love as long as I can remember that I am not her, as long as I can remember my truth and the fact that I am infinite love. If I forget who I am, get accustomed to a limited body dream, and cannot remember that I am love, neither will Nevşah.

Here starts the real mission.

I have a mission here: remembering who I am and knowing myself.

Because who would if I cannot know myself?

If I cannot protect and defend my truth, then who will?

We cannot have something forever in the world of dreams. If you want to have truth, you have to protect it, and we can only protect something by sharing it.

Now I have a question for you: Can Nevşah, a mortal body, also be a foundation of infinite love? Are not there two completely separate facts?

If you thought I meant a mortal body when I said, "I am love," then you misunderstood me. How can Nevşah, a mortal body, something that dies, also be an infinite creation?

Neither your spirit nor you are infinite. Only God is infinite, and yes, you are a part of Him, but neither the part that knows itself nor the part that does not know has anything to do with a part of the consciousness and the Creator.

Know that neither your body nor your spirit is full of love. Only the Creator is full of love. Your spirit is the side of you that remembers Him and feels His love, but it is not the source either.

Remembering the truth—awakening—happens in the world. You do not try or do anything else for this. Remembering is the law of the illusion, just like forgetting.

Forgetting yourself is not a fault, just as knowing yourself is not a virtue.

Knowing yourself is not a virtue, and forgetting yourself is not a torture.

However, it is true that the ones who forget themselves live in darkness here and struggle more compared to the ones who know themselves. Forgetting yourself takes you closer to the fire of hell, and knowing yourself ensures you live in heaven. Still, both are an illusion.

What happens in the illusion of the world when you do not remember the truth? Hell. A total void. Unworthiness and nothingness. When you cannot express the truth here, when you cannot bring it here, the world looks at you as if it is without you, with a blank stare. Nothing you do or say will have any meaning. The world starts to seem like a tasteless, weird, sick place—and maybe dangerous, mad, old, and sad.

However, when you remember the truth and who you are, you get the chance to experience that identity here in the world. If you remember you are love, this place will be filled with love. When you remember you are light, this place will be illuminated. You are the one who will bring the trust, understanding, and peace here. These do not exist in the world. You will bring them here. This is your mission.

True life, the life explained as the afterlife, contains infinite love within the kingdom of God, yes, but infinite love is only possible by remembering Him in the illusion of the world, not by looking at the world.

Awakening

If you want, love, light, holiness, integrity, trust, happiness, and health in your life, you need to protect your relationship with your core, and you need to continue remembering the Creator and your true identity. Otherwise, this illusion can turn into a horrible place. You just need to turn to and look there to get love and light from your core, because that place, your core, is the place where you know yourself and the Creator, not the place you are searching for.

Our core is the place where we find ourselves. The world is the place where we lost ourselves.

The choice of miracle consciousness is somehow the journey back home. You have chosen this path now, because I am on this path, and you can find this book only on this path. Remembering the reflection of the Creator, the truth, is my plane to go back home. Looking at the world and perceiving it as real is the place where I enter the dream and plan the dream of the world.

One side of our consciousness is the place where the dream of the world is located. We see the dream of the world on one side of our consciousness. On the other side, the side where the world does not exist, we remember that this whole experience is a dream. One consciousness is not separated from the other in the experience of the world. They are just different. Why? Because I do not get completely caught up in the dream. Okay, I may be in a dream, and I may want to experience the possibility of a life outside the true life, but a dream cannot last forever; it is bound to end. Miracle consciousness came right after the birth of the idea of the dream of the world, with the mission of fixing the dream, and the idea of the world disappeared the moment it was born.

The choice of the ego consciousness never occurred. The truth never changed. We just had a dream for a little while, and this dream ended before it started.

Actually, all the experiences in the world are the reflection of this truth. Whatever you ascribe meaning to in the world, that thing will be taken from you because if you try to prove which dream is real by yourself, that dream ends faster—for example, the dream of love. As long as you tried to prove to yourself that earthly love was real, you saw that it was not, didn't you?

Therefore, the moment you intend to have this dream and step into the world, it is obvious that you take your step back. However much you wanted to get lost, that never happened. The step you think you took into the world, the disappearing, never happened. It may seem real in the world. People can get caught up in anything at any time; this is human nature. Your mission is to remind the human of the truth.

The journey of learning is actually the simplest, easiest journey. All you need to do is allow the true relationship. We all have a master and a child connected to the outside world. There is a perfect bond, a relationship between our spirit, our core, the guide within (of course, the word *within* is used metaphorically), our body, and our mind. One is our bright side, and the other is our dark side.

Let's dig deeper. The side that is human is our dark side. Why so? Because it knows nothing, cannot see ahead, and is lost in the world. Can our human side see its future? Can it see what will happen tomorrow? Can you say that it sees ahead in the world and takes all its steps with a magnificent confidence and wisdom? No, because it is in the dark. It cannot see ahead; it does not know where it is going. That is the thing. That is the reality of the human. Humanity is in the dark—and there is no problem with that. Why so? Because humanity is never alone. Humanity always exists in this world with its life, its spirit, its core, and its guide within its own system.

There is one problem: the true relationship is not established.

In other words, all solutions we look for exist in our own system; light and love exist in the spirit consciousness that is the opposite of human consciousness. We all have these two. All we need to do is accept both sides, see and understand that both have totally opposite features, and found their relationship on solid ground.

The result will be a healthy life in all aspects. I would like to explain this. How is a healthy life in all aspects possible? Does such a thing exist? Of course it does. Of course it can.

When you establish the relationship between the spirit and the body, the guide and the human, the master and the child, the core and its replica—and the shortest way to do this is through breathing—everything becomes simple.

Everything you do not know and everything you do not want to know as a human already exists in your spirit. All skills you can do spiritually exist in your human side. All your problems have already been solved. Your human side is in the dark, and it cannot see. But you also have a spirit. It sees everything and knows everything, so why don't you consult it instead of wasting your time on other things? It knows all the answers. Are you aware? There is a place within you that knows all the answers to all your questions. You just do not want to admit and listen.

This happened to many times in the past; the voice of my core never left me. I do not remember even a second when I did not have the guidance of my core. Sometimes I was able to lower the voice a little. I told it, "Shut up now. I do not want to listen to you," but it never shut up and never gave up in showing me the right path. You know well what I am talking about. You live the same thing constantly. However much you insist on not listening, you can never escape from yourself. As a product of your plan to escape from yourself, you can get sick or become an alcoholic, a drug addict, obese, depressed, or sick by not hearing and listening to that inner voice. But remember that voice never left you and it never will. Maybe it is time for you to escape from it.

There is nothing else you can do.

You cannot escape from yourself. You cannot be separated from your core. Your human side comes to this world with your spiritual side. The two cannot be separated. You are not independent of your inner guide. The human walks with its own master at all times. But then it starts to search for different masters. Despite having a giant guide, a divinity within, you try to idolize humans and materials. It is a pity!

You can stop doing that right now. You know that, right?

Then stop.

Thank you.

Remember the dream of the world never truly happened. Your idea of being a human never happened. Your spirit is the proof.

You never took the step to be lost in the world. The apple Adam had and the illusion he entered using his five senses never happened. Only in this dream can you perceive or experience yourself as separated from God. Only in a dream can you forget yourself or escape from yourself. Your idea of being separated from the truth and from heaven can only happen in a dream.

Since the dream is not real, you seem to forget and then remember in this dream. Whatever your experience of entering the dream is, that is your experience of getting out of it. Your entering the dream is the guarantee of your exit. If you had not entered the dream, you would not need to wake up. Here in this world, first, you need to sleep, but in truth, neither the sleep nor the waking up happened.

That is why awakening is inevitable, just as entering the dream is inevitable. Everyone asleep will definitely wake up. Every time you choose the ego consciousness, you also choose the miracle consciousness. Awakening is inevitable, but our free will decides when it will happen. But why not now? How long do you want to continue sleeping? How long do you want to continue to believe you live in a world that is not real?

The most important thing you should know before choosing between the ego consciousness and the miracle consciousness is that these two consciousnesses are completely different and opposite. You cannot believe in two worlds at the same time. You must make a choice in your consciousness. Either you will perceive this world, the dream, as real and continue to sleep in the dream, or you will accept the other world, the true world, as real. You cannot make both worlds your reality at the same time, because their features are totally different. You need to decide where you will be and where you are.

If you believe you are in the mortal world, you are a mortal. You will suffer and get sick. You will be sad and get hurt. Your power will have limits, you will sleep and wake up, you will feel hungry, and you will hurt. The moment you say, "I am someone who has a body and who dies," you will be that person, and you will die. The moment you say, "This world is real," and believe it, this place will be your reality. Do you really want the mortal world to be real? Do you choose to be a mortal body with your free will?

If you believe the mortal world is a dream and can see that this dream is temporary and that everything in this place is a mortal, temporal experience, you will exit the dream. This world will not affect you anymore as it used to do. If you can see that the world is a temporary experience, if this is your truth, the moment you believe in this, you will be immortal. The moment you say, "I am not a body that dies," and accept this truth, you are no longer a mortal body; you are immortal. You will not suffer. You will not get sick. You will not die. Whatever you believe, you will be that. Do you choose this with your free will?

The truth never changed. The truth that the world is mortal—a mortal dream—will never change, and you have free will to decide when you will wake up to this truth. You can delay awakening as long as you want, but you cannot prevent it.

I have seen consciousness that insists on not waking up. People can fool themselves for years or even centuries in believing the world is a fun, entertaining place. They think they can achieve happiness with earthly pleasures by eating, drinking, and having sex. I understand that is nice. Experience all the pleasures, and enjoy the world. But it will end at some point. Which pleasure you live and experience in the world is permanent? Which earthly passion stays with you forever? How long will you continue this game? When will you leave these toys?

If you say, "Not yet," continue. Continue wasting your time in the world of meaningless things; feeling remorse for doing things in vain; chasing momentary pleasures; and, when that pleasure ends, feeling guilty because you did not use your time right and did not chase after more permanent things.

I know certain people who, even though heaven comes to them, reject heaven, thinking they will be deprived of cheap pleasures. Why would heaven want to take away your cheap, temporary, momentary pleasures and desires from you?

Heaven promises you something bigger. A bigger life. A bigger existence. And you turn your back on it and say no so as not to leave the temporary, momentary, and guilty toys you have in your tiny life.

What a fool. But possible.

Sometimes I watch people get lost in the darkness after I tell them, "Come on. There is light here. Turn your face to heaven. Turn to your core. Leave those worthless toys." They do not want to give up. They do not want to give up their useless games, artificial loves, copy relationships, and nonsense trips. The funny part is that they cannot realize that there are people who can see that the things they think to be real are not real. They think they are fooling themselves. But they could never fool either themselves or us. Artificial loves, nonsense games, and copy relationships seem so clear that you will be surprised.

It is dependent on the rules of the spirit, the core. Our core continues to reflect its light to the world; therefore, everything is visible at all times. Hiding is not possible in the presence of spirit. It is such a huge light that if you cannot accept it, that is totally on you. But what if the others who can accept that light can see the places where you cannot accept it? What if everyone can see the places where you do not accept the guidance of your spirit? What if others can see your resistance, your problems, and the place where you got separated from your core and fell into the ego consciousness?

Well, precisely. Everyone sees everything. Everyone knows everything. I hope you start to be among the ones who can see and know at some point, or life will be hard.

Maybe I painted a sad picture, but this is the case. Thanks to the one true relationship, the truth always exists, and it always will. Thanks to this relationship and the spiritual guidance we all have, everyone sees and knows everything. The ones after the truth will always be seen someday, and the ones after things that are not real—copy toys, copy loves, copy relationships, temporary satisfactions—will be noticed. Our spirit is the awareness and light. Nothing stays hidden. Intention never stays hidden. Every step you take, all your behaviors show the intention, because our spirit continues to reflect its light to the world of bodies.

They say, "People only fool themselves." Only the human side can be fooled; your spirit or conscience never believed in the games you played and the nonsense you chased. You just never heard it; you never listened. This does not mean that I am not listening to it. Someone will listen. Someone will know.

The person choosing the miracle consciousness sees and knows everything thanks to the guidance of the spirit. You, the human, can fool yourself, but I, our true self, am never fooled.

The choice of the miracle consciousness is a total choice, all or nothing. You cannot choose half of the miracle consciousness or half of the truth. As I have said before, you cannot choose two worlds at once; this is not possible. If you have chosen the real world to be your truth, then you look at this one and see a huge void and a huge truth reflected on that nothingness. Everything turns into truth; everything is the creation of God. Only if you know and remember Him, accept His light as your own, and perceive Him with you will the world turn into heaven and become everything whole, perfect, and healthy. This wholeness ends the judgment, the worry, and the need to fix.

Only the people who have not fixed their own consciousness need to fix the things around them. Warning is the behavior of the ego consciousness. The spirit does not warn; it just declares. It says, "If you do this like that, it will be better for you, for your siblings, and for the universe. But if you do not, that is your call. If you want to delay your awakening, you can do it." Of course, you can get lost as much as you want to; you can sleep as much as you want to. Whatever you do to keep yourself in the sleep and whatever you ascribe meaning to, whether it is sexuality, food, drinks, fame, money, or property, just go on. Get lost in all you want; you have time. You will wake up at some point. Awakening is inevitable.

Spirit knows its path. It does not rush. You do not need to rush to fix the problem—because it never actually existed. Yes, the world is a mistake, but this mistake never happened. The mistakes that never happened do not need to be fixed. The same applies to the mistakes in the world. Mistakes may continue. People may break their promises, not do what they are supposed to do, not listen to their cores, get sick, or suffer. It is all okay. People can stay in the dark as much as they want. Until they become tired. Until they get fed up. Until they say, "That is enough!"

I wrote this book for the ones who say, "That is enough." If you have not said it yet—if your meaningless experiences in the dream have not bored you yet and you are not full—you may continue to deal with hunger, nothingness, and the void. Although you will get nothing and never be satisfied, you can keep on holding on to the world to chase after earthly facts. But awakening is inevitable.

This is what the spirit says. The truth is always there and always will be. The untrue never existed, it never will, and not knowing this did not change this even the slightest bit.

Choice of Miracle Consciousness

In my experience, with this choice, you start to be unable to see the world. Or rather, you cannot see it as a human, as other people do. When you look at the world, you see the things your spirit wants to see, not what humans see. This, of course, may shake people who are in the consciousness of the world. After all, the place you are looking at and the things you see are not what they are accustomed to. Wherever I look, I see a master, a divine guide, a teacher, and I experience everyone at the point of one true relationship between my spirit and body. I either learn or teach, and nothing else happens. This is hard for the ones with little true relationship experience. This might even be boring—or heavy or too big—for someone who is used to wasting his time in chasing after earthly things.

The light of the spirit can even hurt the ones who are not used to it. I had an experience of this. I had this experience with a friend of mine who wanted to stay in the dream—to drink and have sex all the time, eat and travel, and experience everything in the world. Probably she ignored the voice of the spirit for so long and dismissed the guidance of the core for so long that a state within the relation of spirit and body shocked her. First, she did not understand; then she tried to ascribe different meanings; and finally, she experienced getting detached before she got what she wanted. This was her choice. Everyone who chooses the world chooses the experience of not getting what he or she wants eventually.

People first claim they know what they want, and they chase after it. Then this chase ends with a huge disappointment. What could a person want? Humane things. Do you believe that humane things can satisfy you? How can humane, earthly things satisfy a creature whose core is the spirit? They may fool themselves for a while, but they eventually wake up.

What does a person chase? The experience of the five senses. Tastes, odors, colors, visions, and sounds. A touch, a view, a nice meal, or a good drink. Accomplishing something, producing, and performing. Which of these can satisfy you for eternity? Whatever accomplishment you achieve, it is temporary. However you enjoy something you have done, it will pass. Fall in love, but regardless of whomever or whatever you fall in love with, it will end. It is hilarious that you cannot see this!

Awakening

By the way, while writing about our human side, I say *you*, and while writing about the spirit side, I say *I*. You must have noticed this. This is a part of my exercise, an important part.

Now it is time for the experience of the miracle consciousness. Let me be clear: the laws, rules, must-bes, must-dos, and things to say in this situation or that situation were never my concern and never will be. I do not perceive or understand these. I might say this is my dark spot. If you are in miracle consciousness and your system operates with the laws of the truth, the laws of the world will not affect you. The laws of the truth operate with an accuracy and fairness superior to the laws of the world. In any way, the laws of the world arose from the laws of the truth. Do you have any guides other than your soul in the experience of the world that the laws of the world would not be written by the laws of the truth?

Do you know what the prettiest truth about the dream of the world is? Every problem has a solution. Since the world is the expanded form of a single erroneous thought in the cycle of time and since it was fixed before it was made, thanks to the laws of the truth, the world is where mistakes are fixed. We can call the world the place where the dream starts and ends or the place where the question is answered.

It is the place where nonexistent questions have their nonexistent answers.

This place is inherently a purposeless place, considering the purpose of the target, since it never existed. We always ask ourselves, "What is the point of being here?" You can never find an answer to that question. What if that question does not have an answer? What if that question is a question without an answer?

When you ask, "What is the point of being here?" you believe that there must be a point to being here. What if there is no point? What if the purpose is not here, and that is why you cannot find the answer? You must not think, *There must be a point to being here.* You must ask, "Does the world have a purpose? Does this world exist?" Then you will get your answer.

If you get the answer "The world does not exist," then ask, "Does a nonexistent place have a purpose?" It would be meaningless, wouldn't it?

I have met many people who ask this question, but I have never met one with the answer. I've met many who heard the answer, but that is not the case.

Maybe the answer is not within the question; it is outside.

The world is a dream that does not exist. Okay, we've got this. Because something that does not exist seems to exist, this world is an error, an erroneous thought, an illusion. Can anything not within the infinite truth, not within Him, exist? What a crazy question, isn't it? It is too crazy even to be a question. The question "Can nonexistent things exist?" is the erroneous thought.

The answer is right there. Why do you keep asking? This is the crazy one.

It could not, could it? This is the error. Is it clear for everyone?

This error is like a virus on a computer; maybe it has always been described as the devil. Entering into the dream, or your idea of being in the dream, is the devil. A claim that nonexistent things can exist and that a place not created by God can be experienced. Do you like to claim? Maybe the need to claim started here.

Because of the illusion of time, a dream that does not exist and cannot exist thanks to the truth of God is blowing up and growing like a balloon. In your example, it is your life of eighty years. It seems to exist for a while. It actually looks like a storybook, does it not? This is the secret. Your world, your role, and your identity are within a novel that was written long ago. You think the things happening here are new, but that is not the case.

Two neurologists discovered something called readiness potential in the brain in the 1960s. They hook you up to a device, and they can know what you will do eight seconds before you do it. In the other world, some part in your brain sends the message of what you will do. All people stay within their role in the scenario, story, or book they are playing. You think that your free will is waking up in the morning and choosing what you will eat. Humans are in such darkness. Humans are that shallow.

They need experiments, research, and proof to perceive the fact; otherwise, they cannot understand or perceive. Humans cannot invent by themselves. Out of nowhere, they cannot say, "I found it. I created it. It happened by itself," because that is not how the world works. Nothing happens automatically in the dream. Just like in stories, something happens first, and then something else happens. First you do something, and then you get your answer. Every step you take has an answer, a reaction, and every step you take has an effect. The story in the book constantly progresses; it never goes back. The past stays in the past. The past chapters stay as past chapters.

The fact that you think your future has not happened because you do not know what will happen in the future is really shallow. Did you know that? I am calling out to my human side and your human side: Does a new thing have to happen just because I cannot see and do not know? Hilarious! Maybe it already happened, but I do not know. Is it impossible? Oh, those maybes. The language of the spirit is always soft and well behaved. It never claims. It never pressures. That is why humans master suppressing that voice. Our spirit is so well behaved, honest, plain, naive, and connected to us that when you say, "Shut up," it shuts up. When you say, "Speak," it speaks. It never guides without permission, it is never rude, and it never claims.

Dream: it seems like this, and then one day you die. The story of the world ends with death always. How boring! Oh, this is a completely different issue. Aren't you fed up with dying? There is no point! Aren't you tired of thinking death has a meaning? How many times more do you need to die and resurrect to understand the meaninglessness of death? How many more loved ones do you need to lose to wake up to the fact that death is not real?

Since the life in the world does not exist, how long you dream and when you wake up do not really matter. You know the time. You determine the rate of the time. It is up to you how fast you will wake up.

Awakening happens in the moment. You can wake up now, or you can continue sleeping for a thousand years. As a consciousness getting spiritual guidance, technically, it is not possible for us to sleep any longer because the "I am here" truth happened.

A consciousness remembering the truth overthrows the dream.

Time seems long for humans since we believe that the world really exists because of the ego consciousness. Actually, time does not exist in the presence of God, and all these things never happened.

The miracle consciousness remembering the presence of God, your core, says, "Time is not real. The world is not real. Stop lingering. Stop chasing worthless things."

You come to the breathing training, to the miracles course, because you have chosen the path to wake up. The miracles course is the place where breathing is used right and where awakening can happen fastest. Why else would I have kept telling you, "Breath. Only breath," for all those years? I am calling out to the people with breathing exercises. Breathing commences the awakening; the miracles course confirms it. All methods I use therein are systems chosen specifically to ensure awakening with the guidance of the spirit. Since every step taken with the guidance of the spirit directly reaches the result and the success, we can obtain conclusive results, thank God.

Even one example tells a lot. It is impossible for the steps taken with the guidance of the spirit to fail. We fail because we listen to our human side. We cannot obtain what we want and cannot reach our goals because we listen to our human side. What can something in the dark tell you? How can it guide you? Our human side is in the dark, so stop consulting it. It knows what it wants and what it should do. The only thing it needs to do is to let the spirit take over and control it.

You will be at ease when you ensure this. Because the spirit is the light, the information, it shows the path. It illuminates, and it guides you. When you trust it, when you surrender yourself, you will be at ease. But there is one condition: you will do what it tells you to do. The world is a world of doing, a world of action. Remember what I said: you cannot get a result without doing anything in the world. Do not think that everything will happen by itself and that you can lie back and wait just because you have accepted the guidance of your spirit. For the things you want to happen, your human side must stay in action.

You are the one who chose to wake up.

You have chosen the way back home. That is why you are reading this book now. There is no other way because this book, this chapter you are reading, is the map to your way back home. A consciousness that wants to get lost would not read these words.

Follow the call to go back home; do not delay it. Do you know why I tell you not to delay? Not because you should not delay, not because it will be wrong, not because it is so important for your awakening, and not even because it is necessary. Just because it is time. I tell you this to remind you of yourself and of the point you are at. It is hard for a person whose time to awaken has come and whose cycle of time is prepared for the awakening to delay this. I know you are struggling, but now it is time for the easy path. Your time to go back home has come, and you already know that.

This is your last life. You know this too.

You are reading this book because it is time to meet this side of your consciousness, the side that remembers the truth. Maybe many people on the street are going back home. Maybe they know the miracle consciousness through different ways. It is time. Now this is the only truth.

People say, "Time heals all." Of course. Without time, there would be no awakening. Time is the most important part of the illusion. It starts with the illusion and ends with the illusion. And time itself is an illusion, along with everything else in it.

Since sleeping to the truth happens in truth, naturally, there was never awakening, but within the cycle of time, both seem to exist, and they actually complement each other.

The cycle of time allows being lost in the world and also returning home. The system uses both journeys, but still, it is the system of the world, the system of illusion, the system of the matrix.

The laws of the world and the laws of truth are complete opposites. There is an idea behind the system of the world. Just like every idea, this idea has two possibilities, like man and woman, day and night. Even the word *possibility* brings about a secondary. This secondary actually arises from the idea that a second person other than God can exist. Can it? If there is a true Creator, if He is the true and only, can a second existence exist?

If He is the one, if He is the only existence, if He is existence itself, how can you say another person exists? How can you not see that humans cannot be real?

Since most people have an incredible conflict within themselves, they cannot see the conflicting beliefs. They say, "God is one, and there is no other Creator," and they also say, "But He created other creatures." But if existence is one, then there must be just one existence. If the second existence, the human, was really created, then there is not only one God. There are God and human. They both exist. Then these two must be equals. Could I explain what assigning an equal to God in the religious books means?

Make a decision. Do humans exist? Does God exist? If both exist and both are part of creation, then the thing you call creation is split in two: one side is the human, and the other side is God. But you said God is one and only one. Isn't God the only existence in creation? Make a decision first. The rest is easy.

The laws of the illusion and the laws of the truth are complete opposites. Therefore, since these two are confused, most people cannot understand the truth.

You cannot understand the truth by interpreting it with the laws of the world. You cannot feel the truth in your heart when you are looking with the consciousness of the world.

The laws of truth are related to the true one. It does not change; it does not conflict. It is one; it tells singularity. It does not an opposite one. The laws of truth are the laws of existence. As befits the name "the truth," the truth is one. Or it would not be called the truth. The truth exists, and it always will. It does not change according to perception. The fact that you know about it does not matter. It exists whether you know it or not.

But the laws of the world are always conflicted because there is duality in the world. Everything has at least two states because it is not real. What is true cannot be two. If there is a truth, it is one. There is nothing in the world that can be perceived as one. The laws of the world are the laws of nothingness. They are just the effort of a nonexisting place to prove its existence. Therefore, if your system is managed with the laws of the world, you always try to prove yourself.

Humans need to prove themselves; their spirits do not. Humans need to express themselves and change the life they perceive; a consciousness remembering the truth does not have such a need because it knows in silence. It knows that the world is not real and that whatever there is, it is enough.

Since humans do not let their spirits, their cores, and since their breath and consciousness are not open, it is hard for them to perceive the truth. They try to do something. They think they can reach the truth and the Creator by working, getting educated, and reading for years. Humans cannot reach God. This never happened. There are hundreds of thousands of atheists in the world today. Why? Because they are in the consciousness of the human. Because they are not aware of their spirits, their cores.

Awakening

You cannot tell yourself the Creator, and you cannot prove His existence. Whatever you do to prove Him, all is for nothing. However much humans read or work, they cannot reach God. You can only remember Him with your spirit, your core, your conscience, and your side remembering the truth.

But of course, if there is no connection with your conscience and spirit, this does not happen.

In summary, it is not possible for one who is only on the side of human to reach God. But everyone whose breath and consciousness are open and who is connected to the spirit and core feels God in this breath and self at all times and can know God at all times. Breath is actually a mentioning.

We mention His name and presence with every breath we take.

First, we need to perceive that the human is not real, and I think this is the hardest part for most. In the tens of thousands of people I have worked with, I have seen that this cannot happen before the breath is completely open, before total devotion occurs. Even if you understand the truth, no matter how much you read, your mind will not understand Him. The human mind is not sufficient to understand the Creator. You can feel Him in your heart, soul, and core. You can have the guidance of your core, you can reach God in the path He let you in, and you can feel Him. But if you perceive yourself as a human and if you think you really exist, this is impossible. You can never know God because if you exist, if you perceive yourself as created, as an existence, there is no God. You must make a choice. Do you exist, or does He? Which of you is an existence? Is a dying body an existence, or is the infinite and only one an existence? It is obvious that you cannot call them both existences. If the mortal one exists, then the other does not. If the immortal one, the only one, exists, then the mortal one does not. How can both exist?

Can I say something? If Nevşah had tried to write this book, it would have been impossible. What can a person who knows nothing about the truth write? Nevşah is inside the illusion, and it is impossible for her to understand the truth. First, you must admit that. First, you must understand that you cannot reach God through Nevşah. First, you must come to the point of saying, "Nevşah does not exist; she is not real," and then you can connect with the true one.

If you call something unreal and untrue real, then you cannot comprehend true existence. If you call death real, how will you understand immortality? You cannot. Even if you enter that experience, that person will seem unreal to you.

Do you know what the human can comprehend—for example, what Nevşah can comprehend? The reflection, the truth. The things I am putting into words can only be an illusion because they are written using Nevşah's mind. Yes, I may share, write, and tell the information I obtained from the guidance of my spirit as Nevşah, but you are the one who will reach the truth and feel the Creator in your heart. There is nothing I can do about it. Why? Because Nevşah is just a limited body, just like your human side. She has her limits. The things she can tell and show are limited. Even if I use all the known and unknown words, even if I write millions of pages to show you the truth, there is nothing I can do unless you make the connection with your spirit and enter the true relationship.

Making a choice is up to you. Can you make this choice with your free will? Will you perceive yourself as a mortal body or as representative of the infinite life? Is this world real to you, or is the containing the message of the Creator real? You must decide.

Whichever you choose, the other will be invisible to you.

If you make the world your reality and perceive it as real, you can never reach the infinite love. Even if you do, you cannot know it, and even you can escape, fear from it. If you make the world your reality, then death becomes real, and it will be. When you die, everything will end. For most people, this is the case. Most people disappear; they become dust and leave this world. Do you want this?

Ego Consciousness

We have come to the most important part of our exercise.

You have misunderstood the ego consciousness.

You tell a person who uses all his potential, values himself, and is holy and connected to his self—and therefore is big and strong, or even a giant—"You have a huge ego." It is the ego that says, "You have a huge ego," to a person who expresses himself and his truth.

To see someone as being on a high horse, you must be really low. That person does not have a huge ego; he just did not make himself small, as you did. He did not humiliate himself, he values himself, and he cares about himself as much as God cares about him. And this is much for you. Then we must solve this problem because nobody can have a huge ego. Anyone can exceed his potential; may love himself too much; and may be aware of his power, his integrity, and who he is. This is not a problem but a virtue. If you see a virtue as a problem, I think you must change your perception.

Let's see what ego consciousness is. Ego consciousness is the consciousness that believes the reality of the world and the body. If you think the world and the body are real and you perceive yourself as having a dying, restricted, limited body, you will see a body that contains a consciousness that has accepted his truth as high and with a huge ego. Yes, it is. And this is not a problem; this is how it should be.

The person with the light of the truth knows who he is. He sees that God created him perfectly; he recognizes his purity and his beauty. Whatever happens in life, he knows his power, potential, and infinity. He neither fears nor limits himself. Therefore, he is unstoppable, free, determined, and clear. You cannot control him; he only submits to his spirit, his core. He listens to neither you nor anyone else. He yields to neither you nor anyone else. Neither the material nor the body can stop him. He is infinite, and he knows that he hosts an infinite power. He walks over whatever he wants, and he walks in his path with determined steps. You, who does not know about your infinity and thinks you are in a limited body, of course will see him as huge. He seems huge to you. However, it is just the highest possibility of humanity.

The world is the opposite of the truth. Whatever the true world is, the mortal world is not.

The expanded form of an erroneous, crazy question, such as "How would the world be if the world was outside the truth?" And this is the case. Everywhere. Look, and you will see. How would it be? Just like this. It would be mortal, finite, and limited; there would be no light or life. Love could have been reflected, but it would not be true. It would be just a dry earth without a sprout of love. This is what happened. It did not actually happen, but it seems so for a while.

We call this untrue world a dream, and we can also call it the mortal world or an illusion. It is the opposite of truth, and it has a system within.

If the world is the opposite of the truth, then everything here, including the whole system and all the rules, must be the opposite of the truth.

The body does not exist in the truth, but we perceive it as real in the dream, and the dream has its own balance. For example, this body gains weight if it consumes more than it burns. For example, if you do not take care of this body and mind, first the mind and then the body gets sick. For example, if you do not wash, this body starts to smell after a while. This body ages and dies. These are the realities of the dream, and they will never change. I hope you do not think your body will somehow be immortal just because you remember the truth.

This illusion has a system; it has formulas within. It is crazy to act as if they do not exist.

The two worlds have their special laws and systems. The material world and the spiritual world work with separate laws and systems.

What do I mean? I mean this: The fact that I feel great will not make me gain money. The fact that I feel extraordinarily beautiful will not make my body as fit as I want. At the level of the body, I need to do whatever is required to get what I want.

Did you ever meet someone who gained a muscular body just by dreaming of it and imagining it? If there is anyone who can see "I did it," I recommend you run. Nothing happens in the world contrary to its laws. Simple illusions are, of course, possible; a nonexistent thing can be shown as if it does exist. I am not talking about this. I will also mention this in magic.

How I feel about myself has nothing to do with obtaining the results I want in this world. Actually, sorry—yes, it does. How I feel about myself and my thoughts and feelings of course have an effect on the world. When I feel good, the world seems better, and everything is experienced with the highest possibility, but the fact that you need to do something to get results in the world never changes. If you do nothing and just sit, nothing will happen in this world. That is clear. The laws of the world are clear.

If you want to lose weight, you will eat less. Imagining yourself thinner may make you feel better, encourage you, or help make what you want to do easier, but if you consume more calories than you should, you can never lose weight. Actually, it is simple. The world is a simple place.

The opposite also applies. You may have reached all your targets and obtained all you want, but you may not be happy or feel good, because how you feel has nothing to do with the things happening in the world. The two are separate worlds. One is the material world, and the other is spiritual. Their systems are different. They are different from each other, and one does not affect the other.

The success you obtain throughout your life, including how much money you have, has nothing to do with how healthy, happy, and peaceful you are, does it? Why? Because you need to do other things to be happy, peaceful, and healthy, such as breathing, opening your breath, resting, meditating, and cleansing your soul.

The reality of the spirit and the world are two separate states. Neither is real; they both exist in this illusion. It is just a dream. They seem to exist, and they are both part of the duality. In other words, they are part of separation consciousness. Therefore, the two are separate. There is nothing in the world not separate from each other. Even I consist of two states: my body and my spirit.

Duality is everywhere in the world. You'd better get used to it.

Now we will see these two states separately.

Since there is not one self, it is obvious that there are two selves we must control. Since they both have different rules and systems, let's examine them both. Let's work on each of them separately.

Since the spirit is the part of us that remembers the truth, the part that is connected to God, it is easier for it to understand the truth. Even understanding does not happen in the sense we understand with the human consciousness because the spirit inherently knows. Maybe it does not know how much it knows or how infinite this information is, but it somehow knows. Knows what? Our true reality. For example, the fact that we all are love and light. We are all plentiful, full of life, and full of healing. Therefore, our spirit is the path to infinite love, light, infinite source, wealth, beauty, youth, happiness, and joy.

Thus, when we feel unhappy, we must know that our connection with our spirit is compromised, because if my connection with my spirit that knows what happiness is and connects me with happiness is compromised, I can only be happy again when I establish that connection. We can say the same for peace, trust, stillness, and inner peace. Stay in connection with your spirit, and be peaceful, quiet, joyful, safe, healthy, and young.

But how will we establish this connection? Or how will we maintain it? Right at this point, the importance of breathing comes into our lives. The only thing that reinforces our spiritual connection is our breath. If our breath is not open, this connection cannot be established. In other words, as long as you do not work with your breath, it is not possible to feel the beauties, peace, and happiness in your spirit 100 percent, and it is not possible for you to accept these universal presents. That is why our five-day breathing course is named the miracles course. It is really a miracle that we can get anything we want in our life—peace, happiness, joy, confidence, comfort, health—when our breath opens just like this. If your breath is open, you are connected to your spirit, the truth. If not, you are not. I think someone whose breath is not open will not come anywhere, even if he takes training on truth for hundreds of years, because he cannot understand what he is being told. He will need his spirit. He needs his self. He needs a spirit. He needs his core to understand the truth. Otherwise, it is impossible, for it is our breath that gives us this self and strengthens our relationship with our core.

Of course, I am talking about the proper use of the breath. Today most people can do something with breathing as soon as they know. There are a lot of breathing techniques. Unless you are directed to natural breath (the only breathing school that can do this in Turkey is NFS), the relationship with the core cannot be established. Our aim is to open this path for you, as we know the importance of this. I was more like advertising; now I will leave this area immediately.

Let's go back to discussion of the world. The material world, as you would guess, has rules completely different from those of the spiritual world. The formula in the spiritual world is look-see-embrace, and the formula in the material world is search-find-do-have the result.

One thing is clear: nothing you are searching for spiritually—love, happiness, peace, health, serenity, comfort—exists in the material world. It is simple. If you want these, then you will turn to your core, to your spirit. That is clear.

For the results you want to achieve in the world, you will turn to the body. If you want to get a result in the world, if you want to go somewhere, you will get on that vehicle (the body), you will hit the road, and you will advance. The world is the world of doing. Nothing will happen unless you do something. You need to do first, and then you will wait for the results. This is the system in the material world.

For example, the fact that I feel plentiful and safe does not ensure the increase of the money in my bank account. But it leads to a change: I can work more and in peace when I feel more plentiful and better. It is not that the spiritual world has no effect on the material world; it has no effect on getting results. I can feel plentiful independently from the material world, and that is my real need. Most people want the growth of their bank accounts so they can feel plentiful and safe, but they do not know that money is not enough to feel plentiful. Being plentiful is a spiritual state; it is an internal feeling. It cannot be obtained with the money in the physical world. We cannot increase our money and material things in the physical world by feeling good, meditating, and feeling plentiful and safe. Of course, we need to do something. This is the law of the world.

If I am connected to my spirit and am aware of the infinity of the spirit, I naturally feel plentiful. In fact, I am not only plentiful but also connected to an infinite power. Now, at this point, I can do anything. I've stepped into the unconditional probabilities level. Here "I can do anything" status is an energetic door, an opportunity in front of us. It is up to us whether to take this opportunity or not. I know plenty of people who feel plentiful even without a penny in their bank account, and it is already possible with breathing. If your breath is open, then your life is open; you will not lose anything. Life will support you somehow. Okay, is this all you want? Is that how much you will take this opportunity in front of you? That is the real question. You can live happily by feeling plentiful all your life. Is this what you want? Or do you want to be both happy and peaceful, to both stay at the highest level of the spiritual world and have plenty of money in the bank, and to advance in the material world by achieving earthly success? Why settle for one when you can have a combination of both? Here we, the NFS family, have miraculous results with the system we developed by considering the two separately in our seminars.

You have to consider these two worlds separately and work on each of them individually. There is no other way. Really. Let one of them be, and then see what happens. If you let the body be, it will not work and will not produce. If you do not do something, you will end up poor, overweight, and unable to express yourself. Maybe you will look miserable or ugly. If you do not care about your clothes, you may not get what you want; if you do not do what you need to do, you cannot advance in the material world.

If you let your spirit be, then you will be angry, combative, stressed, sick, disorganized, unbalanced, and cowardly. You need to take care of your spirit too.

Let's say you made a breathing session with the intention of feeling the energy of abundance and being plentiful. Most of you know now that when used properly, breathing is such an effective tool that whatever you want to spiritually connect with, you will be that. Okay, you left the session feeling plentiful, and all your insecurities are gone; now you are looking at life and the future with confidence. You do not care anymore how much money there is in the bank or how many properties you have, because you are free from the meaning you ascribe to the material. Super. But what is next? Now, here is the question: How will you pass this expansion to the material world? What kind of person are you when you are feeling plentiful, and what will you do next? Remember there is a real effect of feeling and being plentiful in our lives. When we feel safe, we became a whole other person, and even that feeling of safety makes everything go on track. What if I use my possibilities, my body, and my mind? Then I can really create miracles.

Even if a person works when he is feeling bad, he cannot do much. But someone feeling well can change the world with the slightest work.

It is all about combining the two selves you have and ensuring that they proceed together. In other words, we need to feel good; be positive; take care of our spirit, our breath, and our mind; and work and use the tool provided to us: our body. So that we have this possibility, we have working hands and feet. Then we can do things and be peaceful and happy.

I may see abundance everywhere, and I may be aware of the abundance I spiritually have, but unless I reflect this on the material world, unless I reflect this tool I have, the mind-body called Nevşah will be worthless. Good. I am plentiful, and I can feel it. So what? What will this serve? That is the question you must ask.

The flow of the energy of abundance is required. The tool you are using, Nevşah, must remember the abundance for twenty-four hours so she will continue her life remembering. You need to do something for this to happen. Maybe I will read a book, go to a course, or work more consciously, but of course, I need to do something. I need to carry my inner world to the outside world, or feeling plentiful will not mean anything.

The meaning is seen when we carry our inner world to the outside world. Not when we feel peaceful but when we carry the peace to our music. Not when we feel happy but when we paint the happiness. Not when we feel calm but when we reflect it to our living environment. Then all our spiritual features will have meaning. What is the point of being happy and peaceful if you cannot do this?

If you cannot share love, express love, hug, touch, or convey that love to art, life, your job, and your family, then what is the point of being full of love?

Our first step must be realizing, admitting, protecting, and increasing all the spiritual features we have. You are asking how to do it, I know. I am telling you: the miracles course. There is nothing else I can say because I have not seen anything better. The miracles course will furnish you with all the spiritual features you have: abundance, beauty, love, light, happiness, peace, and health. Breathing takes all these out; they will erupt so hard that you will not believe it.

Let's say you have one this. What now? Just like I say at the end of all courses, the real journey starts now.

What will you do with this infinitely beautiful, magical energy you have spiritually? How will you equip the body you have with the spiritual features you have? What will you do in the world with that body?

You should know that you need to employ Nevşah to carry your spiritual features to the world so that they mean something. You should first teach her abundance. The true relation between the body and the spirit must be established. Your spirit can constantly and regularly talk to your mind and tell it who you are and what it should do. Her spirit needs to remember this so that Nevşah can remember the abundance for twenty-four hours, and she should do something for this. You must understand that the human cannot remember his spiritual features without doing anything. The human is the one who forgets. You need to work, meditate, open your breath, and work with your mind regularly to remind it these features. Our participants in the miracles course know how to do all of these, because these are taught to you there. Once you have done these, you are regularly in the open breath and the open consciousness, and you continue to work on yourself. What now?

Now you need to work hard, because remembering and awakening to the core will absolutely direct your mind somewhere—and it should.

With the abundance consciousness, our human side naturally tries to adapt to this abundance and tries to make life abundant. This is the natural result of waking up: an increase. A consciousness that has woken up to the features of the spirit will increase in the remaining part of life—material and moral—because when infinity of the spirit descends to the world, it increases life.

But if you do not remind Nevşah about the features of the spirit, she will not remember. She cannot do anything about it. If I pray, saying, "I want abundance," will it come to me? No.

I am the one who will remind my mind that I am abundant. The mind is the one that will work the body to make life more abundant.

I am the one to remind my mind what health is, and the mind is the one that will direct the body to be more beautiful, feed it with proper food, make it do sports, and rest it.

If there is no relationship between my mind and my true self and if the mind has forgotten the truth, this is the first problem. When the mind cannot align the body with the truth even though it remembers the truth, this is the second problem.

We must spare some time to remember the truth and also some time to reflect the truth we remember on the world. There is no other way.

How does Nevşah express the information of truth in the world? By writing, talking, giving seminars, and supporting people to open their breath and reach the truth. How will you do it? That is your path. Nobody can know that path better than you.

Just know this: the world is reflected on the world by working the bodies and ensuring they produce. When you do nothing and remember nothing you know, no awakening you have will be useful. I even think that it does not count as an awakening. You will say, "It was an experience, and it passed."

If you want your awakening to continue, carry what you know, feel, and think into the world. Do not wait; do it right now.

Paint, write a novel, make sculptures, write poetry, produce new works, make designs or organizations—do whatever you want, but just do.

Work and do because in Nevşah's world, in the material world, there is a law of doing. The material world is the world of doing, the world of action. If you think that just imagining will get you anything, you are wrong.

The material world does not care about how you feel. What you do is what matters. How you feel, your inner world, is important to you—that is it. And remember you can do what you need to do, whether you feel good or bad. Always. What you do has nothing to do with how you feel. If you want to do something or accomplish something, all you need to do is do it. That is it. There is no need for anything else. You do not need to feel good to do something; you just need to do it. For example, you do not need to feel good to get up from the bed in the morning; you just need to get up. The feeling has no effect in the material world, in the activity world. Let's look at an example from sports. You can feel great, fit, and healthy and run for a hundred kilometers, or you may feel crappy, but you can still run for a hundred kilometers. How you feel will not affect what you do. Most people fool themselves by saying, "I feel bad. I will not be able to do this." What is the relevance? What does how you feel have to do with what you do? It has nothing to do with it as long as you do not think it does. Really. It is time to wake up.

You can feel plentiful, but you may not have a penny in your pocket, or when you feel the least plentiful, you may not have a penny in your pocket. Both are possible because there is not a relationship and interaction between the spiritual world and the material world in the sense you understand. They can happen independently.

The material world is the world of doing. You need to do. You cannot lose weight by sitting and doing nothing, you cannot make money without working, and you cannot be fit and healthy without caring about your diet. You may feel super and pretty, and that is great, but you need to work your body to take it where you want. That is your tool. How the goal is reflected on the world is what we see.

The spiritual world is the world of being; you just need to stay, to be, in order to accept the gifts you have. The more you try, the further they will be. You need to let. Your breath and consciousness must be open; you need to accept. You cannot get anywhere in this world by doing. You cannot do something to be awakened. On the contrary, you need to accept the light you have without doing anything. You cannot do anything to be filled with love; you just need to remember who you are. Of course, you need to do something for the human to be filled with love because of the laws of the action world, such as coming to a breathing course or meditating. Just as you keep your body clean or do sports to stay fit, you need to do something to keep your spirit clean—maybe participate in cleansing programs, do yoga, or open your breath.

As long as I am me, if I am here inherently, because of the highest reality I have, as long as I am in the dream of world. And as long as I am connected to myself, my core, and my breath, I will make the best use of the tool given to me to travel in this world, the opportunity I have: Nevşah. I will keep her at the highest levels both spiritually and bodily. I will do what it takes for this, and I have Nevşah to do what it takes.

That is called awareness. That is called knowing yourself. If you have understood this, then you have understood everything in life.

Our natural state passes from expressing yourself.

If you have woken up, you will know this, and if you are awake and can look at the world without the slightest judgment or perception, you will perceive the world as it is: a simple playground prepared for you to play. It is a wasted, tossed-away tool if you do not play. And remorse.

When you let the material world be, you have how crappy it gets; it decays and gets dirty, rusty, ugly, and old. If you let the world be, that happens when you are asleep, because you do not know what you are doing and what the consequences will be. This is your empire, your kingdom. How can you let it be?

If you let the world be and do nothing to change first yourself and your perspective and then the world, then your comprehension skill is not developed yet, just like that of a coward king who does not take responsibility. He has a huge kingdom, but he cannot take responsibility for it. He just watches. Then you do not see the world. You have eyes, but you are blind. The material world is the world of doing. If you let a field be here, that field will decay. Do you want that field to decay? Is this your reflection? Is this how you express yourself? Is this how the miracle consciousness reflects? Is your truth a decayed field?

If you are in the miracle consciousness, remember the truth, and know yourself, will the field decay? No, of course not. Would not a person who knows himself, his nature, who he is, and how great an existence and life he has resurrect that field? Would not he turn everything he touches into gold? Would not he make everywhere he steps on beautiful? If you do not do this, there is a serious problem. If you have let life be, then you are in deep sleep.

An awake person creates such a huge life for himself that his body works for maybe a week without eating, drinking, and sleeping. It always things makes better and more beautiful. A consciousness that is responsible for his kingdom never lets anything be.

That field will be magnificent. That is what the miracle consciousness, the awakened consciousness, is!

If I see even one piece of garbage in my presence at the point where I remember the truth, it will bother me. Why? Because I, the whole and perfect one, am the one experiencing this place. In my presence, everything must represent perfection. In my presence, there will be nothing missing, and I do everything for it. If needed, I will not let Nevşah sleep. If needed, I will work her at all times, but I will make my world the way I want it. That is how truth is reflected on the world. (By the way, the *I* used in my sentences is all of us. What I mean here is not Nevşah; it is a universal self—not the one in the dream but the one having the dream.)

Now I will tell you what you do most of your life. You ascribe meaning to the meaningless dream. Life eventually shows you that everything you are chasing—love, money, sex, alcohol, cigarettes, success, fame—is meaningless, and then you wake up. Then, if you are not liberated from the need to ascribe meaning to everything, namely the ego, you start to ascribe meaning to futility. You say, "Oh, so what? It is just a dream; I can let it be. I can do nothing. Anyway, it does not have any meaning." You ascribe meaning to the futility. It does not matter if the world is a temporary dream. It just is; it is neither good nor bad. Did this experience change just because you have woken up to the fact that this world is a dream? No, the world is as it is, and it stays there with all its rules and systems. You should do what you need to do, because this dream is your dream. The fact that it is a dream does not mean that it does not belong to you.

The fact that it is a dream is not a problem; in fact, you turn it into a problem. However, you could have understood the fact that the world is a dream is completely different. The fact that the dream has no meaning does not matter. That means you can do anything; you can play any game. There is no problem with that. You can choose not to do anything; you can leave the field to decay. Which game do you want to play? Decide this. Do you want to have an angry dream in which we kill each other with toys of war and make each other suffer, or do you want to have a dream of heaven with peace and love? Do you want to play in a field that is left alone full of rotten vegetables, stinking and filthy, or do you want to play in a clean and nice place? This is the choice. Whatever you choose will be the case. Which fits you better? The importance of knowing yourself arises right at this point, because if you know yourself, you know what kind of game you want to play and where—I do not need to tell you. This is awakening. Now you have woken up.

The Difference between Two Worlds

The fatigue you have felt in your body until today and the diseases you have had are all due to your resistance to doing and to your body. You do not want to accept its limitation, and that is the reason you get sick. You think the body is immortal. If you drink alcohol every day and consume fatty foods, your body gets too tired to get those things out and keep you healthy. What happens in the end? The motor of the vehicle bursts.

There is another issue: when the whole deal of the body is doing, you say, "I do not need to do. I want it to happen by itself. I am good as I am."

This body wants to do, move, produce, run a play, and work, and you say, "Stop. There is no need." You have one foot on the brake. There is nothing more tiring than trying to keep a body that needs to work and move still. That body is programmed to work. If you do not let it do anything all day, it will fail. It will end.

Did you know this? There is nothing more tiring on the body than being still. That is why you get sick. Resistance is the only reason for all diseases. The fact that you do not accept your body, including all its features and limits, and do not honor and care about those limits makes you sick. You do not act in harmony.

The tool you are using has a scenario. It has a name. It has a city it was born in and lives in, it has people around it, and there are things it needs to live. Every mind-body is included in a plan on the planet Earth. It has things to do and things to say. Yes, they all are in a dream. It has a scenario, and mind-bodies are not free of this scenario. Yes, whatever will happen in the scenario, our consciousness is under its effect, but this does not mean that the thing you understand—your experiences—will change. What do I mean? I mean this: You go to the school you are supposed to go to, you are born in the city you are supposed to be born in, and you marry the person you are supposed to marry, but the experiences you have with the person you marry, in the school you go to, or in the house you are born into are affected by your consciousness. With the reflection of consciousness, you may have peaceful, happy experiences or sad ones. Nothing happening in the world will make you feel anything. Your thoughts on what is going on are the only reason for your feelings.

Think about it: Do all the people living the same thing and even in the same place when it happened feel the same? No. All people feel the feelings that are a reflection of their thoughts on the event in their minds. That means your feelings have nothing to do with what you live, and feelings can change. You may live happily or unhappily in the same house in the same place with various feelings. Here is your effect.

Let me give an example from my experience. I am free of the dream. The true self is in the dream, but since there is a side remembering the truth, remembering that it is in a dream ensures its freedom from the dream. But Nevşah is not. She is a role, a character in the dream. She will do whatever she is supposed to. Nevşah is like a machine connected to the main computer; she always gets messages in her mind about the things to be done. You think you choose what to wear when you wake up in the morning, but that is not the case.

As I have mentioned before, two neurologists, Kornhuber and Deeck, discovered a reflex in the brain called readiness potential. This reflex is an electrical activity that happens eight seconds before we move. Neural activity happens eight seconds before a conscious activity. In a sense, our brain gets a message regarding what it should not, regarding our next step.

This is proven information; you can look it up on the internet.

We have solved a problem most people do not understand and get confused about. Yes, there is something called destiny. The tool we use in the world—the role that has a name, shape, body, and mind—has a destiny. True self is free in this destiny. Being free of the destiny does not mean that it can change it. But it means that destiny does not affect the true self.

The true self is free from this dream because the laws of the world cannot affect it. However, the mortal body, the player, is not free from this dream; on the contrary, it is a character in the dream that must be there. The dream is as it is thanks to it.

It lives what it is supposed to in the world. You married the person you were supposed to marry, broke up with the person you were supposed to break up with, and became friends with the person you were supposed to become friends with, and these were determined the moment the dream of the world started. They did not change, and they will not change. Self, core, and consciousness work at a level higher than this area; the system of the world does not affect or limit Him. He comes from and goes to infinity with the love and light it has inherently, and He knows the truth: the world and the mind-body are not real.

The experiences we have in the world do not have the slightest importance. Why would they change? Your true self does not want to change the world, so why would you be given this chance? You are the one experiencing the one, not the experience. You are not in this mortal body. You are not the role; you are the player. You are not the mortal body; you are life itself.

Then we can say that knowing yourself truly liberates you from the mortal world. First, we admit that the dream is a dream, we accept that everything in it automatically progresses, and we are set free because there is nothing else we can do then. That area does not exist, so how could you have something to do? When we comprehend this, we can start to deal with ourselves instead of dealing with the world and getting no outcomes. Therefore, since the world and my experiences will not change, I should enjoy it. I should be happy, peaceful, and full of love and light. Whatever I do and whatever happens in the world, I can accept it happily and lovingly and enjoy it.

This does not mean self-surrendering. This is the opposite: coming to your senses and taking responsibility for yourself. Up until today, you looked after the one thing you should not have: your body and the world. You struggled in an area you have no control over. You tried to change and stop the current and future happenings of the world. Now accept it as it is and allow it as it is. Set your brain-body and the other brain-bodies free, and let them do whatever they do. You care about the truth, not how you feel, what you think, or how you look.

The mortal body with a name and a shape is not free. You pretend that it is, but it is not. It has things to do and things to say. You need to follow the rules. There is no other way.

I am the reflection of eternity. It is different but still in the dream.

True self is still in the dream. Outside the dream, it does not exist, the mind does not exist, and the self does not exist. There is only God. There is nothing other than Him.

One part of our mind is the ego consciousness, the human consciousness that thinks the world is real. It operates the functions of our human side. The readiness potential in the brain is connected to this part. What you are supposed to do in the world, the role you are supposed to play, your destiny, is recorded here.

The other part of our mind is the miracle consciousness—the side that remembers the truth and knows that the world is a dream. This place sometimes says to the lost side of the mind, "All these things are not real. Actually, they are all just a dream," and it connects to the area where you remember the truth, which is defined as a dream you have when you fall asleep at night. There, in truth, everything is possible. That area is the area of infinite possibilities, the place where we connect to our Creator, our core, love, light, and truth.

The ego consciousness is the place where we perceive ourselves as earthlings and believe in the world—and this is necessary. One side of our mind needs to perceive the world as real when we look at it; otherwise, it cannot proceed in the world and do what it is supposed to do. But the other side needs to remember the truth—that all these things are just a dream—so that I can remember myself. In short, you cannot get lost in the dream forever. Every dream is bound to end one day.

When the dream ends, will you be enlightened? If you are enlightened in the dream, then yes, and if not, then no. If you die while you are lost in the dream, you will continue to come and go until you find the way back home, however long it takes. Experience as many billions of options, ways, and vehicles as you want—they are all possible. Of course, they are limited, but they are possible.

It means that one part of our mind is lost, just as one part of your humanity is lost, and you are the reflection of all. You are responsible for making it turn back, for waking it up.

Awakening is inevitable, but you have to decide when to wake up.

You are responsible for deciding when the ego consciousness will return home to the truth and to its natural state independent from the scenario. If you have entered the illusion that you can change the scenario you play instead of going home; if you are still dealing with the mortal world and have ideas about how the world is supposed to be; and if changing the world is important to you, you are delaying your awakening.

You are not doing what you are supposed to do regarding the earthly issues. You ascribe too much meaning to the things you do, the things you say, and the things that happen. You waste hours thinking about these, and you delay your awakening, saying, "Could it have been different?"

If you have a body in the world, you have a body in the world; you cannot escape from this. How stupid it is to think you can be free from this experience by stopping the experience of the world or cutting your relationship with the world. It will not work. If you are in the world, you are in the world. Period. You cannot pretend as if you are not. Your body in the world has things to do, and none of them are even real, so why would you limit yourself? Conscious of knowing and remembering that it is in a dream would be about how it behaves or what kind of a place the world is.

There is nothing to do in the world to wake up. When you stop ascribing meaning to the world and pondering earthly issues and saying, "What can I do differently?" and when you stop caring about what is going on, you will wake up. Or the opposite: you will stop all these when you wake up. This does not mean doing anything and watching your life from far away. On the contrary, it means being deep inside the mortal world and doing everything that is supposed to be done. If you cannot, then you care too much about the world and your character in the world. You are still asleep.

If reputation is important to you, if you are political instead of being yourself, or if you live according to the world and not how you would like to, then you are asleep. You think the dream is real. That is why you care about what is going on here.

The assumption that awakening starts not when you start the world, is not real; but when you see that you cannot change the scenario in the sense you understand.

What does it mean to say that the scenario does not change in the sense you understand? It means that what needs to be done will be done, and what is supposed to happen will happen. Yes, our consciousness and what we choose in our consciousness affect life constantly but not in the sense we understand. It does not change the course of things but just how they happen. It does not change what has happened but the way it happens. What does this mean? You will do what you are supposed to do, you will go where you are supposed to go, and you will marry whom you are supposed to marry.

You do not get to choose what to live in the journey of life, but you get to choose when to live what and how to live.

The life in the world is independent of what we live. This is about how fast you learn and whether you are a murderer or a saint. The ones who insist on not learning their lesson, take the dream too seriously, criticize, analyze, discuss, try to understand everything, and try to do everything right and by the book will waste time. As long as you are not yourself and do not live as you want and do what you are supposed to do, you delay your test. The only way is to live whatever you came here to live and do whatever you came here to do. If you are free of this world and aware that you are in a dream, you do this. You live at full speed without caring about who says what, paying no attention to the meanings ascribed to the steps you take. You learn all the lessons you are supposed to learn, and you end the game and go. Only when you do this does everyone around you learn. When you are loyal to your core and closed to the outside world, progress under your own guidance, and have the courage of your convictions, then everyone who knows you is your student. You live; they watch. You do; they talk. You end the game; they discuss, and they follow in your footsteps.

Awakening illuminates everyone around it. Every step taken is a lesson. Every decision you make embraces, affects, and changes thousands of people. A mind that represents the infinite light has the power to change the world. Only a single look of His is enough to end or give breaths. He is aware of this power, because when there is no awareness, there is no true power. Awakened consciousness is free of all kinds of fears and shame. It does not fear from anyone, does not yield to anyone, and does not listen to anyone but itself. It is unstoppable. If you stay in the way, you will be crushed; if you stay behind it, you will be illuminated. Because of the consciousness chosen, the human has no chance but to let Him. The human either lets Him or gets crushed under the power.

How does this crush happen? Naturally. The true power does not want to crush, but that is why it has already crushed the ones who do not respect that power. People are afraid of standing up, preventing a consciousness that is the representation of the power. They cannot look into the eyes because they know that when they try, they will not be able to do so; their masks will fall off, and they will not be able to hide anything from Him. An awakened consciousness illuminates everything and sees everything.

An awakened consciousness does not care about what is happening. He knows that what happens will happen and that he will not get anywhere by dealing with it, thinking about it, or analyzing it. Therefore, he only cares about himself, his consciousness, his core, and guidance. He knows that if there is anything he does not like about what he lives, the one thing that he needs to change is his consciousness. He does not waste time. He gets better, healed, and more beautiful every moment. He gets stronger every moment. He gets closer to the truth every moment. He does what he wants to do; he is independent of the outside world. He knows that this is what is supposed to be.

You are running late for the lessons you have to learn. You are wasting time. You think getting angry at Him and resenting His works. But it does not work.

Analyzing what happens is delaying your way back home.

If all had dealt with their own issues and stopped caring about others (for this, all need to be aware of their own power), they would easily learn their lesson and wake up.

You only deal with the people stronger than you; you criticize another because you know that you cannot change him and because you know his power. Criticizing is lame. Lame people criticize the ones stronger than they are. Write this down.

The world is a trap. It is a trap that will make you take it seriously; perceive it with your five senses; and think that the events, feelings, emotions, earthly perceptions and values, thought systems, and judgments are real. The only purpose of the world is to take you away from your core and keep you there. If you get fooled by this, your awakening may be delayed for thousands of years. Yes, everybody will wake up, but everyone will decide when to. As the awakening gets late, the agony will increase. Humans are so keen to get caught up in the world that as far as I have seen, they are ready to use every experience to fool themselves. They ascribe meaning to the things happening, and they get angry and pissed off and curse. They cannot see that they are the ones doing these things to themselves. On the other side, they are afraid that if they follow the wishes of their core, humanity will judge them, so they cannot be themselves. As if the judgment had any effect!

Wake up! Both judging someone else and avoiding judgment are equally a waste of time, and they both delay your awakening.

I do not get why people keep talking for hours about things that are impossible to change, about the past, while there is too much to do in the world. I write a mail, and people can talk about it for months, saying, "Would it have been better if you had not written this like this but like that? If you had not done this but that?" Why do they not want to understand? I would do it differently if I could. Why would you keep talking about something that already happened? You are wasting time. I am moving forward. I got a thousand years ahead of you while you were talking and judging me, and you did nothing but discuss me and talk about me. You ran around in circles.

You should avoid criticizing not because you cannot criticize but because it is nonsense, and it does not work. You should not do it because it wastes your time, delays your awakening, and, more importantly, does not have the slightest impact on the person you are criticizing.

Personally, I laugh at the minds criticizing me. Why so?

1. I am not affected. I do not even understand what they are trying to do.
2. When they criticize, they are negative, their vibrations drop, they become stressed and nervous, and they get sick. I cannot stop asking why people would do this to themselves.
3. It delays the awakening, and it wastes time.

It brings no outcome. What did you do? "I criticized." What good did it do? "None." So why did you do it then? "I do not know; I cannot help it."

Lack of awareness and blocked breath and mind are like that. People with open minds, with bright minds, do not criticize people; they turn everything into creation, an action. They do not talk; they do. They do not react; they answer. They do not defend; they prove.

A person who thinks the dream of the world is real tries to change it and deals with the things people do and say. A person who is conscious of the fact that the world is a dream, an awakened consciousness, says, "Let them do whatever they want," and he does whatever he wants. If he has an answer to anyone, he does not ponder it; he just gives the answer. If he has anything to do, he directly does what he is supposed to do. If he has a letter to write, he writes and uses the system of the world. If he has anything to say, he says it. Maybe he curses, and maybe he punches someone if necessary. He does whatever necessary because of the unconditionality.

As you can see, people mostly misunderstand the truth. An awakened consciousness is love itself; he loves the world. He loves all the pleasures in the world. He knows that none of them are real. He never gets addicted to any of them, but he is connected to them and loves them thanks to his devotion to himself.

The awakened minds are not well behaved; they do not just sit around silently as you think. Why do you think Jesus Christ was crucified? Because he was so well behaved, followed all the rules, was political, and gained everyone's love?

You have misunderstood the message.

The ego always misunderstands.

The truth is, do whatever you want, learn your lesson, and go.

Awakening

Live the way you feel like living. Do not follow the rules or the system, and get eternal freedom.

As I have mentioned before, awakening does not happen by praying to the skies, being a divine person, or experiencing supernatural powers. It happens when you go down to humanity and make all your wishes and desires true. This scenario will not end unless it is lived.

You need to live everything in your scenario in the dream of the world; otherwise, it is not possible to free yourself from the world. How will you learn your lesson unless you finish the thing you are supposed to live?

Sometimes I find myself in acts whose endings I already know. For example, I do or say something that I know I will be criticized, lashed, and judged for, but I say or do it anyway.

I do what I am supposed to do because I woke up. I woke up to the fact that there is no other way.

Here is a lesson for you if you want the dream of life to end forever and want to learn every lesson you want to learn: the world itself. Live everything you are supposed to live, no matter how stupid, dangerous, or risky it may seem. Do whatever you are supposed to do, say whatever you are supposed to say, rise to the clouds, become free from this place forever, fly, and go.

Remember well-behaved children are the ones who take the world too seriously, the ones who are still asleep.

As long as you deal with the scenario—with what you do, what you say, and what others do and do not do—you will not work in the place you are supposed to work. Be sure of this. You will miss life and the lessons you need to learn, and you will come back here. Criticism and analysis only make you waste time. Aren't you sick of it yet? Live however you are supposed to, finish it, and leave!

As I have mentioned, I do certain things while being well aware that they will bother someone or make someone angry, because I know that I learn the lessons all of us should when I do them. If I do not, one lesson will be missing. I know that too.

As long as you continue to deal with what is happening in the world, you are not working in the place you are supposed to. There is no good or bad scenario. There is no point. Something that does not exist can be neither good nor bad. Dreams, storybooks, and the things happening in the world are neither good nor bad. They just happen, and there is no point in this. The fact that the world is meaningless is neither good nor bad. It is just meaningless. The dream is meaningless. The fact that the dream has no meaning is also meaningless. Most people think that the dream, a nonexistent place, must have a meaning, a reason, and they say, "What do you mean it is meaningless? This is horrible." I say to them, "No, a dream is a dream, and it is meaningless, but the fact that it is meaningless is also meaningless. Something meaningless and nonexistent that is not even true is neither good nor bad."

In summary, (whatever your name is) is a machine. The name of the machine I am using in this dream is Nevşah. She is connected to a computer, a collective consciousness. She does whatever she is supposed to do because she knows in her consciousness what she is supposed to do at all times. The vibration of the consciousness may change, and it may be positive or negative, but the scenario does not change. It just becomes harder or easier according to the vibration.

Nevşah has no impact on her scenario. Imagine you are in the play *Romeo and Juliet*. Romeo is just a character; he is not real. Romeo has no impact on what he says. Does he? In your real role of Romeo in the storybook, for example, there is not a chapter in which Romeo says, "I love you." Romeo does not revive and say, "I actually did not mean to say I love you." And you—the machine—do not revive. You are bound to sleep in the universal cycle. Whatever is supposed to happen in the scenario happens, and you are not the writer; you are just a character. You cannot affect the scenario. Stop struggling.

The machine, the mortal body and a part of the dream, Nevşah, is not authorized to change what happens. Just like that. This is what destiny means. You do not have a free will about the things happening in the world. Free will is a different thing. Here is something else you have misunderstood.

We said, "There is only one relationship in the universe, in the dream, and that is the relationship of the spirit and the soul, the relationship between your core and the human side." In a sense, I wrote this book for myself; this book is a love letter written by my core to my human side.

In summary, the protagonists are not authorized to change the story.

What is the relevance? Imagine Don Quixote revives and comes out of the book to comment on the things written in the book. This is exactly what you do when you criticize the things happening in the world, and it seems as funny as this example.

You are not even the writer of the story; you are just a simple character, and you make judgments.

Romeo will say whatever he is determined to say. Nevşah will do whatever she is supposed to do, like it or not. If you do not like the things Nevşah is doing or saying or do not like the things happening in the dream, that is your problem. Fix it as soon as possible; otherwise, you will not remember. This is the only place where you can work; you can control your inner world, the character itself, not the role.

Where does the ego consciousness get activated? The ego is activated when I started to think I am Nevşah. Because then I start to care about Nevşah, and what Nevşah will live becomes more important than what the life will live. Or the opposite. I lose my connection with integrity and unity, and because I lose my connection, I start to think everyone else is like me.

People who say to me, "I think you are not in the miracle consciousness," or "You are contradicting yourself," actually see themselves. You should know this by now.

We are only responsible for our consciousness, our perception. We cannot change the things happening in the dream of the world, but we can change how we perceive it.

But why is this change important? Because perception prevents me from seeing the truth. Would the consciousness you see me with change my consciousness? Would the fact that you think I am contradicting myself or think I am stressed affect me? No. I am what I am. I am happy if I am happy. I am peaceful if I am peaceful, or the opposite. You see me however you want to see me.

If you are curious about your level of consciousness, look at me. Whatever you see in me is you.

I know this is harsh.

When you choose the ego consciousness, you lose your connection to the truth and identify yourself with the thing with a name, with your simple role in the scenario. Therefore, you perceive yourself as something mortal and helpless—something that can make mistakes; has limited power; and gets hungry, tired, and sick. Isn't it natural that you fear and become stressed and nervous? I would also fear if I believed I was something mortal. What would I fear? Death.

If you want to act as if the body will never die and be free from death and the fear of death, you cannot fool yourself like this. You need to free yourself from your body, from this mortal thing.

All those who perceive themselves as a body have fear because that body will die. If you do not want to fear, you must stop perceiving yourself as a human.

I know it is not that easy, but it is possible. It is possible with a good breathing specialist and a well-designed breathing seminar. It is a matter of time.

What happens when you choose the ego? A tiny character in a huge storybook becomes more important than the others. You ascribe meaning to it. You care about the mortal name, and you deal only with it and enter the nonsense as if you can change anything. You are wasting time.

The dream of the world is a mortal story. It eventually comes to an end. This storybook was read and finished the moment it was designed; it never changed, and it never will. Can you change the astrological course in the universe? Where do you get the idea that you can change your course? Which twisted perception does this come from? You are knocking your head against a brick wall. You are wasting time; you are getting lost in the cycle of time in trying to change the story. I, the core, am telling all these things to you nonstop because I am determined to get you back. You cannot come back like this.

You need to work in your consciousness and mind for your journey back. This place, your consciousness, is the only place you can control, where you have your free will. At this point, you need to work on remembering.

Always remember: "I am whole and perfect." Constantly.

Do what you are supposed to do in the world. Stop dealing with that area; stop pondering everything. Do not get hung up on that area. There is no other way.

Do whatever you want to do, because only then will all our siblings finish all their lessons, experience everything they came to the world to experience, and become free forever.

When you do not say what you want to say or do what you want to do, everybody is affected. Neither you nor your siblings learn the lessons, and you cannot see the things you need to see. Something stays missing, and then you have to come back again and again to live what you are supposed to live.

Instead of interpreting the world, you need to ask yourself, "What should I do?" Herein lies your destiny.

Everything—the whole dream of the world—is in the past.

Actually, neither the past nor the future exists. Time is an illusion. Future has already happened; it has ended. The story has already been written; it has ended. The idea of the world ended the moment it was born. The cycle is determined. The things to be lived are determined. The things to happen are determined.

The ones who deal with astrology know that every fifty to sixty years, the same type of people and the same thoughts come to the world on the same latitudes and longitudes. You cannot change the things you are supposed to live and do in the world.

Knowing the truth and remembering it every day, every moment, are different.

Many people know that the world is an illusion and is not real, but too few of them can remember and really play in the world at all times.

Even if they do remember the truth, most people do not work in the area in which they are supposed to work; they do not work with their consciousness. They hold the things happening and others accountable for what they feel and what they think. However, the things happening will not change. They will continue to happen, but you can control what you feel about them. If you do not want to look at the world and ascribe meaning, comprehend what is happening wryly, and see attacks, mistakes, and problems, then you need to work with yourself and your consciousness.

I will tell you something really radical: you may not see an attack even in a situation wherein somebody kills somebody. You can live completely free from the things happening, and you can accept what is happening as it is, without any judgment. Like others, you can only do what you are supposed to do, and you can see the truth.

The point when you reach the peak of your potential is the point when you confront the thing that scares you the most. Be sure: the thing you are scared of will not happen. Even if you are a mortal body, you can be here within a program, and nothing you did not choose to live or are not equipped to face will happen. Why would you be afraid?

You are ready and equipped for everything you came here to live. All you need to do is go ahead—without thinking for a second and without ascribing any meaning to anything.

This is true freedom. Too few people can get to this level, because this level is the one most prone to criticism. Nobody but you can understand you. The mortal body does what it is supposed to do and the things it can do, and this point is the point where we are gifted to the universe, where every creator bows before us. But the people perceive this as fear. Since this is a power and self-confidence they never have met before and since some people fear the people at this level, they step aside. These people are generally the ones with little awareness. The fear is not related to what is happening; it is related to the person. Whatever happens in the world, you may not fear. You may not see any trace of fear within anything, any behavior, or any step. Or you may. It depends on what you choose in your consciousness. Nobody can be scared of anyone. People choose fear in their consciousness, and fear is not real. It is just the place you want to look and see. This is the only truth.

If someone says to you, "You scare me," or, "You are trying to scare me," this actually means "I choose fear in my consciousness now," because nothing that happens scares you.

Whatever you do, nothing will affect me, and I will not see fear if I do not choose fear in my consciousness.

The consciousness that reaches the true power, the ones without even a trace of fear in their system, may scare the ones who continue to choose fear. The point of nullity is a giant mirror showing people themselves.

A brave person makes you face your fears; a loving person makes you face your lack of love.

Fear is not a feeling you have for something that will or will not happen; it is your choice. It is not something someone makes you feel. It is something you choose to see.

Remember you do not see fear anywhere you look; there is a level at which nobody is trying to scare you: the level of true power.

The doors of the universe are wide open for the people in front of whom the whole world bows down and steps aside—people whose greatness is seen by the awakened minds and whom all the asleep ones fear. They are given infinite power because they use their powers to help people learn their lesson and get free, not because they use their powers for evil. They know this. They do not get affected thanks to that infinite power. No criticism, comment, separation, tiredness, hunger, indecisiveness, speech, judgment, or fall at the level of the world, at the level of humanity, will affect them anymore. These people dive into life with their whole heart. They live as they want to, and they always grow and progress before the surprised looks of the criticizing minds that think they are doing wrong.

A person at the true power level grows with criticism contrary to common belief. That person gets even stronger with each criticism and each judgment. He turns into a total monster in the perception of many. He is the body representing the divine right. His one look will burn; his posture causes the birth of innovations. He is the one that starts and finishes the change. Most people feel that he came to teach. Every speech given by him, his every behavior, is a lesson for the humans.

Humanity meets the true lessons with screams first, and they strongly oppose the true discipline. Then, eventually, they surrender one day.

Since they see that there is nothing they can do, there comes a moment when they listen to the things being said and told and see the power of the true power—in prostration. Until that moment, everyone keeps ranting, criticizing, and making many comments about the world and the things happening in the world, right or wrong, at the same level. In a moment, the divine power enters the heart through the body accepting that power. When it enters, the ego shuts up, and the world stops spinning.

What is the difference between the people living with the divine power and the other ones?

The most important difference is that they do not care about the things happening. This does not mean they do nothing, stay ineffective, or are unresponsive. This means they do what needs to be done without hesitation; they perform what needs to be performed without thinking. A person at the point of true power does not stop, think, or care about other people, and that person uses the system in the world, the order, the rules, astrology, and the whole universe in the best way to serve the highest possibilities. When a consciousness that is one with the divine right is reflected on the world, it adapts to the system of the world. The system of the law, morality, the body, the immune system, the rate of metabolism, the webs of the mind, telepathic powers, and the whole universe come under his control. There is only one reason for this: the intention of one person, God's will. He has longing and love for the Creator and his home. He wants to get back home fast. He knows he does not have time, so he does not waste time. He uses each moment for the expression of truth. He does not wander idly, he teaches constantly, and he aches for his siblings to go back home. Some people do not want to learn their lesson. They try to delay, they spend time, and they deny living at the true morality, the true right level. They care about the aims of the world, such as buying a house, buying a car, and spending time with their families. The representative of the divine right finds them, and he sacrifices himself so that they can learn their lessons as soon as possible. He sees the lessons humanity can learn from his steps and the hardness of the path for each of the parties. They will be criticized and even cursed.

But this is the goal: for the truth to be visible and to release the curses, evil, judgment, and anger inside people. The representative does this.

The divine right representative steps forward. He does or says something to people that they will definitely judge and curse.

He does this to make people face the criticism, mess, complications, contradictions, fear, and judgments in their own systems, not because he thinks he will not be criticized or because he is unable to see the consequences of his actions. This happens. Many people want to run away because they are secretly aware of what is being shown to them. The fear, curses, and evil inside them surface. They look at the divine right representative, and they see attacks, bad intentions, and mistakes in him. They see their own consciousness. They are afraid of this, and they do not want to stay there in his presence. It may be hard to face their destiny; they try to run away. They do not know that the divine right representative will follow them even in their dreams. The true power controls the whole universe, but they cannot see this.

But why can so few people get to this level?

Because most people are lost in the world. They cannot see what is in front of them because they are too busy dealing with the world, judging the steps taken and the behaviors, and making the distinction between good and bad, beautiful and ugly.

Most of the time, people do not even recognize the true teacher.

Do you know who your true teacher is? The person you are afraid of. The person you chose to break up with. The person you ran away from. The person you think is doing wrong. The person you think is not sincere. The person you think is trying to attack or hurt you. That person is your true teacher. Everyone you have chosen to be together with is, in one way or another, in the same consciousness with you. They think like you and see life as you do. You get along well, you agree, and they listen to you and say, "You are right. You are right to break up with him. Yes, he totally attacked you! Yes, he is trying to protect you. That is why he is doing all these things. He does not love; he is mean."

Your ego feeds.

However, your ego cannot expand in the new horizons ahead of you. While learning what you do not know, when you look at the person who does everything you have criticized in your life and forgive him, when you stand by that person even though he does the thing you do not want, your ego gets shocked.

Try sticking by the person to whom you said, "Oh, that is enough. That is too much!" Think about how hard it will be for you but how great a lesson it will be to stick by him and face your criticisms, judgments, fears, and lovelessness—to face how you punish yourself.

You could pile up all the people in the world, and it would not even compare to the lesson you will learn when you can hug that person and choose to stay by his side.

There are many examples of this, all experienced by me. People break up with each other, saying, "I choose love, which is why I do not choose you anymore." They cannot see the state that they cannot choose love in that person's presence because of all the criticisms they make. While they think they choose love, actually, they just delay their lesson.

All breakups are people's escapes from themselves.

You only want to break up with someone because you fear confrontation and your features that you cannot tolerate. His presence makes you face the judgments about him. As you look at him, you face your fears and lovelessness, which you try to blame him for, but actually, they have nothing to do with him. The mistakes, evil, and attacks you see when you look at the person across from you are all made up by you. You try to break up because you do not what them to be revealed because you do not want to face your mistakes. Facing your past mistakes is hard for you.

The learning period for most people is slow, of course, in my opinion. Why? Because they do not do what they are supposed to do. Even you do not.

1. You always blame others for how the things happening in the world make you feel. You tell others, "You threaten me, you attack me, you tire me, you make me mad, you messed me up, and you put me in a dilemma." You do these to yourself; others do not do them to you. You are the one who generates fear, is in threads, gets angry, criticizes, and contradicts. If that were not the case, you would not see these things where you look. You only see yourself where you look.
2. You do not take responsibility for your criticisms and judgments. You are the one who calls something good or bad, right or wrong, lovely or loveless, thread or not. All these do not exist in the world. No matter if the majority agrees with you, there is no behavior to which I can say, "This behavior is an attack." No matter what anyone does, even if someone says to you, "I will kill you," you cannot say, "This is threatening." Because everything is relative in the world. Whatever you believe, you see what you want where you look. You do not realize this.
3. Until you make peace with everything in the world, until everything is okay for you, you cannot see that everything you see outside is related to your inner world; that freedom is doing what you are supposed to do—even if this means punching someone—unconditionally and unlimitedly; and that these are universal lessons.
4. An infinite being takes this as a mortal body and tries to follow the rules of the world. You try to be a person who fits the criteria of the world, and you think this is important. But being good by

the standards of the world just feeds your ego and prevents you from learning your lesson. That is it. If you can, do something everyone will criticize. You cannot, can you? Your ego will not let you. You are selling your soul not to lose face, to be someone who fits the standards of the world.
5. Realizing your core, the truth, is one thing, but living under the guidance of your true self is huge. You need to be big and brave.

You need to be the messenger of the divine right. That is why everyone cannot be the divine right representative. Most people have such a huge ego that they do not want to let it go. What if you are not loved anymore? What if you no longer have anyone by your side? What if nobody approves of you and everyone criticizes you? You do not want that, right? Your ego will be hurt a lot.

Your real purpose, your real lesson, is to destroy your ego, and you cannot see this.

You are scared to death when you see a consciousness at the point of true power, living without any boundaries and conditions and caring so little about its reputation that it can kill someone if needed. Of course.

Freedom scares the minds that have chosen captivity.

You have two things to do.

One is to surrender to the scenario. It is obvious you will not be freed before you live everything in your scenario, and obviously, you will be given chances to be humiliated, criticized, and judged and to destroy and crush your ego and take the lesson you came here to take, like everybody else. That is the point. Because you cannot be free from your ego without letting this. That is why the religious books say, "Everybody will be judged." This will happen in the world. Because without this, you cannot face yourself, your ego, and you cannot wake up.

The second point is what you need to do for this. As I have mentioned before, do whatever you are afraid to do. Just do what you feel like doing in the system of the world, and you will definitely come to that point one day. If your breath is open, this happens automatically. You are given chances to disgrace yourself and be criticized and judged every day.

In summary, if you want to be enlightened, do whatever your inner voice tells you to do. Do this nonstop without thinking. If you are supposed to think, you will think; if you are supposed to get up, you will get up; and if someone is supposed to tread on you, it will happen. You may curse or be broke, but you will be enlightened at that moment.

What I have written is the opposite of what you were thinking, right? Because your ego made you believe the opposite. Don't you believe what I am saying? Then think: Why did I write this book, and you did not? Why can't you have such awakenings in your mind regarding the truth? Anyone who is ready and awake can experience and write this book. Why didn't you? Can it be because you have chosen your ego? (This comes from the core to you, to me, and to everyone.)

When you let everything that is supposed to happen in life happen, the guidance you get becomes stronger. When you allow this at the level where your breath is opened in the best way, at the highest devotion, what do you surrender to? To the scenario. To yourself. To your core. Your core already knows what you are supposed to do, what you are supposed to live. Therefore, the people with a strong connection to their core are also the ones who have surrendered to their destiny. They do nothing to change the world and the events in the world, and they do nothing to change themselves either. Their only purpose is to live their scenario because the only purpose is to do whatever you are supposed to do and be whoever you are supposed to be.

But naturally, it is not easy for the ones who have preferred their ego instead of their core.

Even today, in the age of enlightenment, concepts such as doing the right thing according to the system of the world, going by the book, acting according to the rights of other people, lingering, and being liked are important for most people. That is why most people have a hard time understanding the consciousness, which does not start with this wrong motivation and which lives only with the infinite representation of the core.

But how can you live free from the world and people, the human side, and the ego consciousness?

1. You never care about or listen to the desires, wills, ideas, thoughts, and comments of your human side, your ego self. Therefore, you

do not care about the desires, wills, ideas, thoughts, and comments of others, because you are related to the core, not the human, and that core is someplace within every person, a place only that person can reach. Nobody has reached his core through another person. Your core self is a place only you should reach and only you should open.

2. If you are free from your human side, the ego self, then you totally liberated your human side. As I mentioned earlier, you never care about what your human side does, says, or eats or where it goes. You do not think about these even for a second. The person who has chosen the miracle consciousness does not care about the ego self, and he does not care about what the people do with their human sides. He lets his human side free. That means if the human side wants to sue someone because of the scenario, it does. If it wants to go to war, it does. If it wants to eat, it does. If you do not meddle with the human—your human side and the other people—everyone freely does what he wants to do, the lessons will be learned, and the progress will happen. Everybody will be content. People actually become unhappy because they care too much about what others do and don't do, the paths of others, the human, and the ego self. If they could let it be and if the human side and all humans could do what they are supposed to do in the scenario, a magnificent balance, order, and divine right would work in the world. You cannot act against the scenario; it is not allowed. If you intend to punch someone, it is only possible if it is within the scenario; otherwise, your hand will not work, or you will not meet that person. If you need to talk to someone, you will talk to that person if that is in the scenario. If not, you will never meet that person. There is a perfect order in the world, and nothing happens against that order. No matter how much you judge, you will only end up wasting your time. If I am doing what I am supposed to do, this is because it is in the scenario.

3. If you do not choose the ego consciousness and you do not care, gaining a reputation will not matter. In other words, you do exactly what you want to do; you live as you wish. You live the way you feel like living, not for reputation or honor. It is obvious

that your ego will be hurt when you do this because all have their own rights and a path to walk, and only they can know what they are doing and why they are doing it. Therefore, the paths of all, the paths they walk representing their core, are open to criticism by the other people. The more a person is criticized, the more that person lives his core. That is that. The representation of the core makes everyone do different things. If you live representing your core and always do only the things you can do in the world, you only represent yourself, your core. You have a way of living your life, and this is not the same with anyone else. Thus, the people living by representing their core at all times are open to criticism.

Since a person who has chosen his core and abandoned the identities in the world lives under the guidance of his core, you will never know why he is doing what he is doing. All you can do is let him. He does whatever he wants, and how he does it, how he decides, and the steps he takes might not resemble yours—and they do not need to. A person living with the representation of the core is unique. He does not follow the standards, the general rights. The things to be done and to be said according to other people, according to the perception of others, do not interest him, and they do not affect him either. He does what he wants as he wants. Therefore, he is the inspiration for the whole universe. He is the star of the universe. The ones who choose the perception and rights of humans, the ones who do the right thing, will be like sheep within a flock and will not be noticed, and the ones doing things with the representation of the core will shine. The person who is himself will be different from the others because only then can he do things that nobody else can do. He leaves works of art in the world. He may get judged and criticized a lot. Remember you will never understand a free spirit living with the representation of the core with the human perception. You will always judge him and criticize him, you will not understand his steps, and you will not be able to fit him anywhere. He will always seem unbalanced and weird—because he is. Of course he is! Otherwise, we would not say, "He is always representing his core." We would say, "He is like everyone who lives up to the rights of the system of the world." A person who represents his core will never be standard like the others; he will be unique.

When you look at that person with your human side, you will not understand him because you search for an explanation, for a formula for what he does. The formula is him, and the formula only exists in him. Therefore, only he can do what he came here to do, and only you can do what you came here to do.

That is why the ones living with the representation of the core are great people. When you see someone who is who he is, goes on his own path, and listens to nobody, remember—know that he is a gift to humanity. Nobody else can do what he does, and he knows that. Nobody else can do what you are supposed to do, but first, you must have the courage to do this. He is the one who has this courage. Even though he knows that he will be criticized and judged and that many people will not like him, he does not care and continues on his path because he does not care about the ego. He does not care about the human, his human side. He has chosen his spirit, his core.

The people who have chosen the miracle consciousness do not care about other people. That is clear. They care about their spirits. They do not care about the world; they care about their cores. They know that all people have variable thoughts and perceptions, and they do not value people because they do not choose their egos, the human. Therefore, the consciousness who has chosen the human side will feel worthless and unimportant, like a piece of meat, in their presence. Of course. A consciousness that has chosen the spirit treats the human as a piece of meat. They always say, "Who the hell are you?" and they keep this position.

The consciousness who has chosen the human may feel like garbage, a lie, or a mess. They may feel worthless and purposeless in the presence of the people who have chosen their spirit, their core. Of course. Would a person who does not care about his human side, his ego, and who crushed his human side care about your humanity? Would he listen to your ideas, comments, and critiques? That would be funny.

If you still care about your human side, including the comments, ideas, and judgments, and still ask yourself, "What are those people trying to show me?" then you are doomed. Let me tell you something: those people cannot show you anything. They do not have such a capacity. Everything you want to see and know is in the path you need to take by yourself, in your core. What can a mortal person and his absurd comments, criticism, and point of view show you? Nothing. A human can only show nothing, just like himself.

Personally, I think my ears are shut to the people who make comments, criticisms, ideas, and human speeches, such as "I think this is the right thing." I shut myself to my human side. I do not care about my humanity, and I let neither my human side nor the other humans affect me. I do not listen to that nonsense. When the ones who care about their humanity, ego, personal ideas, and points of view read these lines, they get mad. I am sure they are saying, "So you are saying my ideas are worthless?" Yes, they are, honey—sorry. In saying this, I have just crushed your ego, haven't I? I know how you feel. How can I not? I do this to myself every day.

It helps people to live their core, be themselves, and step into the singularity. You enter the consciousness of singularity. What does this mean? Whoever you are you are. Only you can do whatever you are supposed to do however you're supposed to do it. You are single; you live in singularity. You are the single copy of the Creator. You walk in your path alone. The result is that nobody but you can understand you. They cannot understand what you do and why you do it. Only you can walk in your path alone; you cannot let anyone else in. Since you cannot, there is only you on the path of the core. Nobody else knows that path. Only you can experience it. Everyone has his own path. Therefore, when people try to understand the path of others, they get confused. They can never understand. Only if they walk in their own path, have no other shape than the representation of the core, and make unique decisions, even when they are criticized and not understood, will they understand you.

You need to be freed from the world; you need to let your humanity go and choose your core. Let it be. Let (whatever name you are given) do whatever he/she wants. You only live your destiny. Do not meddle—not because you are not supposed to but because it is meaningless. Personally, I know that I cannot change Nevşah. She is who she is. She will live whatever she came here to live; she will do whatever she came here to do. I know that when I let her be, the other people will not understand her, but this is how it is supposed to be. When I let Nevşah be, sometimes she will not live up to the general rights of the world, but I let her because the reputation, name, and dignity of Nevşah do not interest me even a little bit. I do not care about Nevşah or the other names in the dream with a

Awakening

name and body. I do not mean I do not care in the sense you understand; it is just that she is not worth dealing with and thinking over. She will stay as she is, so why would I waste my energy? Oh yes, if a mortal thing, your identity with a name, your ego self, is so important to you and if her walking on the path according to the rights of the world and being loved, liked, and understood by others is more important to you than your core, then you should care about her. You should control her; you should not let her be. If who Nevşah is was important to me, it would be important to me to control her, educate her, and show her how she would be liked—if I cared about the ego self and the reputation of Nevşah.

But I do not, and because of the representation of my core, I do things that seem crazy and incomprehensible to you. Here is the secret of life. Nevşah just represents her core, her single side—that is it. But you live your life like every other human. You try to be like everybody else; you try to blend in. And I am sure you have blended into society and have a great reputation. Congratulations. Still, you are the one who is reading this book, not the one who has written it. Could I make myself clearer?

I am sure there are things you came here to write or tell, things only you can write or tell. Remember the whole universe is waiting for you to do this, and as long as you do not do it, all doors will be closed to your face again and again. As long as you care about the ego self, as long as it is important to you to be loved, liked, and understood, you will always be a student; you will only read the things written by others. But it could have been me reading the things written by you. What a big loss for the whole universe. That is the reason for all the losses you've had in your life—because you delay the thing you came here to do.

It is time. Today is the day.

Whatever is supposed to happen in the world, it should happen. It will be better if you surrender to life. You do not have the power. The system is stronger than you. The story has already been written; it has ended. Nevşah has nothing to do with it. Looking at the point of self in truth, I do not care about Nevşah. Let her live whatever she lives. The scenario will not change, so why would I bother with her? I should deal with the place that will change, with my choice, because this choice is a choice to make through her. This choice is made while all these happen. They do not actually happen; that's quite another story. This choice is made while the whole scenario continues. It is made only when you surrender. When you look at the miracle consciousness, at the point of the choice of truth, you will not care about the scenario. You will not fight with the scenario.

If you fight with your scenario, the role you play, and the things you should do, you will see wars everywhere. You perceive the slightest movement as war and attack. You see attack everywhere because you attack yourself. You think someone, the system of the world, the laws, or whatever else are limiting you because you do not let yourself be free. You are the one limiting yourself. You are the one who does not love yourself. Since you do not love yourself, it is hard to see love in the world. You experience lovelessness when you look at some people and some behaviors.

Neither love nor lovelessness exists in the world; the world is the place you see yourself.

If you want to be free from the world and stay in light and love, you accept the scenario as it is, and you go along with it. It's that simple. If Nevşah is supposed to eat salad, she will eat salad. If she needs to do sports, she will do sports. If she is supposed to sue someone at work, she will. She will do whatever she is supposed to do because there is no other way.

I hope the message was clear.

Being in the miracle consciousness is not seeing that the attack is real and not doing what you are supposed to do in the world. There is only what is happening in the world—no attack. This is what you need to see. Even if someone punches you or beats you up, there is no attack. Neither is a war an attack, the law system a thread, or the death of a body an end. It is you who ascribes meaning to the things happening; it is you who sees an attack, thread, or evil where you look. You are the one who calls wars bad. But a war is neither bad nor good; it is not real, just like everything else in the world, just like you. That is it. If you have woken up to the dream, you can live as you want; you can do whatever you want. This is life!

If am aware that I am not Nevşah, I should stay where I am supposed to and do what I am supposed to. I should work there while this world of doing continues, while everything is continuing to happen. We can stay in truth by doing what we are supposed to do, living what we are supposed to live, and being free from all those. If you do not let the world, yourself, the role you play, and the other roles free to be as they are, you cannot return to truth.

Do not get caught on this.

Do not try to stop or prevent anything. When you want to stop or prevent anything, admit your wish to stop or prevent.

Accept everything as it is.

Remember everything is possible in the dream.

If you are still dealing with the world of doing, if you think something will change when your consciousness changes or when you wake up, you are wrong. This will not happen. The fact that you remember the truth will not change your role in the world and the things you are supposed to do.

Therefore, it is stupid to judge people by what they do. Even a killer may be ahead of you and more awake. You cannot know.

The truth is independent of the dream of the world. The truth cannot be affected by the things happening in the world; it does not change. The things happening in the world do not change when you remember the truth. The scenario is what it is. When you remember the truth, everything is a game. When you do not remember the truth, the world is heavy; it is full of fear, threads, and mistakes. Everyone is asleep, just as you are, and nobody knows what they are doing. This is how the world works. Nobody actually knows what they are doing in the world. Can't you see that? If you rely on the perception and judgment of your human side, it is really bad for you. That is hell because in that perception, wars, crimes, and punishments are real. However, in the perception of truth, these are the meanings you can ascribe to things happening in the world, but even if you are in jail, this is only in the movie.

The Place Where We Really Are

Here is another problem of humanity. Are you ready?

You think you are in your body, but you are not.

I can almost see the surprised look on your face. I told you: the truth will surprise you.

Lift your head and look around. What do you see? Look carefully and slowly. Focus on everything. Determine everything you can see, and memorize it. Save some time for this.

Now look at what you cannot see. Determine what you cannot see.

For example, if you are in the living room, you cannot see the kitchen, the bedroom, or the bathroom, unless, of course, you have a kitchen in the living room. Look closely, and determine what you cannot see. For example, if you are in your office, you cannot see your house, right?

You can only see the things located where you are, right?

If you are in your office, you can see your office; if you are in your bedroom, you can see your bedroom; and if you are in the airport or on a plane, you can see the airport or the plane.

Okay, if you can only see the things located where you are, then where are you now?

Are you inside or outside your body?

Are you in the place you can see or in the place you cannot see?

You are in the place you see.

Now, here look around at everywhere you can see.

You thought you were inside this body for years. This is just hilarious!

If you were inside your body, you would be able to see your stomach and your kidneys. Right? Do you see your stomach now or the couch across from you?

Then are you here in the place where you are, or are you inside your body?

Is the place where you are the place you can see or the place you cannot see—your body?

Where are you?

Who are you? Which one are you? This body or what you can see?

When I said, "The world is a giant mirror in which you see yourself," I was not bullshitting.

You are in the place you see. You are everything you see.

You see the place where you are. Then are you inside this body or this room?

Now can you see how silly it is to deal with the body you think you are in?

Your focus is either the dream of the world, the scenario, or the truth. You cannot have two focuses at the same time. Therefore, which one is your truth? You need to make this choice.

If you are dealing with your core—I will speak for myself—you cannot deal with Nevşah. You will not care what Nevşah did, if what she did was true or wrong, or if she had any effect on the world or not. If you care about this, if you care about the world, then your focus is the world and the truth with a body.

The saying "We are all one" does not mean the world; it means the lives of all of us are one. Bodies are not one, and they never will be. Even the union in sexual intercourse is not a total union.

The separation from truth, or separation from God, never happened. Because He is whole. Therefore, the world is not real. There is no duality at the level of truth. There is duality in the perception of the world. Therefore, this perception and this world are not real.

When we entered the illusion of separation—in other words, when we got lost—we thought we were separated from the truth. But this never happened.

This dream of leaving home naturally gave birth to the dream of returning home. I am saying it created; I am saying it gave birth. Neither leaving home nor returning home is a creation; it is a birth—birth to the dream. This has no difference from death. They are both in the illusion.

The consciousness we have in the dream is divided in two. One half of the consciousness is the ego consciousness—the human that thinks the dream is real, believes the things the eyes of the body see, and lives with the five senses and its perception. The other half of the consciousness is the miracle consciousness, core self or spirit, or life and even the breath.

One half of the consciousness has forgotten, and the other half remembers. You need to sleep in order to dream.

One half of the consciousness perceives the experiences, passions, pleasures, and pains of the body, and the other half knows that all those are not real. It seems that God has put the remembering side there, but of course, this is not the case. The plan of awakening is part of the plan of sleep, and it would be weird to associate both with God. Only truth stays intact. A nonexisting thing, such as a dream or duality, cannot be in Him. Truth cannot be two; it can only be one.

Just like two halves of an apple between the two halves in the consciousness—a round trip on the same path. There is no difference between them. They seem different because everything seems different in the world. One is the dream of getting lost in the world, and the other is the dream of remembering the truth in the world. I think people understand what this path is when they meet their twin spirit. Our twin spirit, the other half of our spirit, chooses the other consciousness. It's like a chase.

When I look at the truth, he looks at the illusion. When I believe in the truth, he believes in the illusion. When I get to the side of the illusion, he stays on the side of the truth. We can never look in the same direction. Whatever I choose, my twin spirit chooses the opposite. We can never look at each other; it is hard for us to see and understand each other. One day, when total balance and serenity are ensured, when both sides get what they will from the world and the truth, they will take a deep breath and stop. The door to the union will be opened. That day is already determined.

You need to choose now. Until you do not, you need to make the choice: the ego consciousness or the miracle consciousness. One is not better or worse than the other. One is the path to the world, and the other is the path to the truth. One is the path seen with the eyes in the world, the path on which you experience the world. The other is the path you see with the eyes of the truth. This is what we need to understand.

Personally, my story begins with being surrendered to the miracle consciousness. I remembered the truth from birth. Since the day I was born, I've said to myself, "All these things are not real." I have been living an experience within the true relationship.

Since in my experience of the world, the miracle consciousness is the consciousness that reflects God's answer and carries God's message, the only need for the consciousness forgets and gets lost here. However lost a consciousness is, this consciousness is like water to it because getting lost and returning home are definite, but the reality of getting lost brings a feeling that you will never go back. Therefore, when you see a consciousness that is on the way back, that reflects the truth, the ego consciousness has only one answer to it: being mad. For this state, everything this place looks for depends on the shape. But this does not change the fact that the two are the same paths. Yes, also the ego thinks that. The ego consciousness thinks that the miracle consciousness is superior, because the ego is the one that does not know, and the core self is the one that knows. The ego is the mistake, and the core self is the answer. The ego, or human, is the product of erroneous thought; the true self is the correction. Therefore, when it sees the miracle consciousness, it wants to be like the miracle consciousness and gets mad because it can never be. The path of the ego consciousness will never lead to the truth. The ego consciousness will not reach to the miracle consciousness; it will never reach its features.

Therefore, the people who have chosen the ego consciousness are bothered by the freedom, comfort, carefreeness, and apathy of the people who have chosen the miracle consciousness. They want to be like that, but they cannot because of the consciousness they have chosen. Instead of changing the choice, they waste time trying to change themselves, and they get even angrier.

As a child who was born as someone who already had chosen the miracle consciousness and remembered the truth, I can say that I was open to the attacks of the ego consciousness, and I learned much about humanity from those attacks. The human, or ego—whether you have realized this or not—stands at an aggressive state. It always attacks; it is always attacking with criticism and judgments in the mind, with the body—with everything. Thank God it is a human, or ego; therefore, its attacks are not real. Let me detail my sentence: the attack is not real. I do not mean that the other things in the world are real, but the attack is not. Since the thing that is always attacking, the ego, or human, is not real, the attack is not real either. But the human and ego are aggressive; it is in their nature. Of course, people who do not accept their nature will argue otherwise.

At the level of truth, it does not matter if you choose the ego consciousness or the miracle consciousness; neither exists in the truth. But one is the way to the dream, and the other is the way back. If you are reading this book, it is time for you to choose the miracle consciousness, but this is the truth.

The miracle consciousness is the place the ego consciousness wants to reach. The ego, or the human, tries to have the features of its true identity. It always thinks it will be whole and perfect one day. Pity. It does not know the fact that the human will never be the true identity because it is in sleep; it chases after targets that cannot be reached. It gets jealous of the person who has chosen the true identity and lives freely, carelessly, and listlessly the way he wants to, the person it cannot limit. It wants to be like him, but it cannot. The more it tries, the worse it gets, and eventually, it turns green with envy. That is the moment it wakes up. I wish God would grant everyone such envy. I want to say, "Work, and you will get there," but unfortunately, you cannot choose this identity by working.

The ego consciousness sees the miracle consciousness as a place to reach. When it meets a free spirit that has chosen the truth, it looks at the place where the free spirit stands, sees the spirit's place as a place to reach, and then struggles to reach that place. However, you cannot reach the truth with the ego consciousness. As it cannot reach and cannot be free and be a free spirit, it gets angry, panics, and runs away. It cannot stand seeing the person in the miracle consciousness, the person it thinks is superior, so it runs away. It runs to find its mistakes and make it like itself in its own dreams. However, true identity will stay intact no matter what the ego consciousness thinks about it. It stays with the same truth, power, love, and light; it continues to grow, progress, and create.

Whatever the ego consciousness does, it cannot stop or prevent someone in the miracle consciousness. For a person who has accepted his true identity, all doors will be open, even in the world. All his works will run in course; there will be no obstacles because he has taken down the one obstacle. This makes the ego consciousness, the person who runs into and struggles with limits and obstacles, even madder.

However, truth is not a place to reach. Our true identity is the identity in which we have the truth. It stays there without any changes and just waits for us to choose it. But this choice is risky because when you make this choice, when you let your human side free, the ego will not know what that side will do, and it fears. A free person can do anything. This makes the ego and the world scared.

Would you understand me if I said most people are afraid of their true selves? The power, infinity, and unconditionality of the person who unites with the free spirit can scare the whole world. And it should! Because the world has no power to stop such a person. When the consciousness remembering the truth is chosen, this happens, and this is permanent. It stops when it wants to, and it progresses when it wants to; the ego cannot control the free spirit. Therefore, the free spirit is dangerous for the ego. It does not fit the etiquette, the box of "good person," the descriptions, or the rules.

No matter if you are in the ego consciousness or in the miracle consciousness, you are on the same path. One is the departure, and the other is the return. Which side of the road are you on? This is the question you need to answer.

If you are reading this book today, it is because your return has begun. It does not matter where you are in this journey. The reflection of a consciousness that has returned home and the reflection of a consciousness that is lost are the same. Only the choices are different. One has chosen to be lost, and the other has chosen to return home.

Choose your direction. Now. Right now.

Will you dive into the world? Will you go back home?

You can go back home on both paths. These two points are the point of twin spirits. A consciousness that remembers the truth and a consciousness that is lost are the destroyers of each other. The side that remembers destroys the side that forgets. The side that remembers is always a thread for the side that forgets.

In a seminar on relationships, in which I detailed soul mates and twin spirits and in which we performed exercises on this subject, one of the participants said, "I believe these two should unite." Maybe the fact that is in a separation is the hardest point to admit for the ego. The human and the spirit are part of the plan of the world, part of the separation. At the level of the world and the consciousness, at the level of spirits, the union is not possible. True union is only possible in singularity. What is single is one. What is two cannot be one, and it cannot unite. There is only one, and it is God. Therefore, the union of twin spirits is just a fantasy. They may come together, they may meet, they may come across, and they may be friends or lovers, but as long as one looks in one direction and the other looks in the other direction, they can never understand each other. They are like two people with their backs facing. They are programmed to look at different directions. However, they can create miracles when they are one in the single purpose point, work together, and act together for the truth to be remembered. Since they are like the halves of an apple, they can see the places the other cannot see. They can watch the world 360 degrees together. Therefore, everything they create together lays the whole idea of the world in front of them. This is an important step for the awakening of the world, and they both know this. This means the union, cooperation, and cocreation of the twin spirits. When they work together, the world starts spinning. The channel of light is opened.

Another participant commented, "When I speak and act as Yonca, as the reflection of God, there is no duality. Spirit, body, etc. These two should unite."

There is duality because when I start, the idea of God and *I* is born, and this duality is impossible. There is only God in truth. He is the one; therefore, the reflection of God is not real.

The truth is one. At that level, there is no ego consciousness or miracle consciousness. There is no consciousness. There is no distinction, separation, or duality.

If you say, "God and …" you need to stop there. There is no *and* with God.

He is one and the only truth. There is no *and*. He does not have a continuation, front, or behind.

In truth, there is no ego consciousness and no miracle consciousness; there is only God. There is only one truth, and when I say *God*, everything ends.

If the truth is one, the one that never existed and never will at this level is either double or plural. Nothing that is not one—nothing that is plural—can exist in the singularity and union of the Creator. Here is the truth.

Can plurality exist within infinite singularity?

Can hatred exist within infinite love?

If there's infinite light, is there darkness anywhere?

When you call the truth one, is it possible for the singularity to exist in a place that is not real?

When I said these things in the miracles course seminar, another participant said, "Singularity must exist in the world for God to descend to the world." In my opinion, this is one of the thousands of explanations the ego makes for the truth. The ego always argues that it knows the truth—this is incredible. On top of all, it does this nonstop breathlessly.

I answered, "God will not descend to the world. The one that is infinite, the one that is single, does not enter the world of duality. The world is not even real, so how would you expect the truth here? This will not happen. When I said *God*—when this word is formed in my mouth—*God* loses its meaning. When the mouth of this mortal body says *God*, that word is far away from describing God. Therefore, maybe writing is the best way so that a mortal mouth will not say it. When I utter the word *God*, it loses its meaning. In His presence, there is neither ego consciousness nor miracle consciousness. There is no consciousness; there is only Him. Nothing else."

Is the light of the miracle consciousness the true light? No! Is the miracle consciousness or the prophet consciousness the consciousness of God? No! He is not something this world can comprehend. You cannot comprehend the Creator in the world. You do not exist in His presence. How can you comprehend Him? But you can feel Him. When? When you are nothing.

Because you are nothing in the presence of God.

God cannot exist in the world.

Existence cannot be inside nonexistence.

Does existence have nonexistence?

The dream of the world is a place that never existed. It was never created. It is just an idea, a motion. It is nonexistence itself. How would existence be in nonexistence? It cannot; this is not possible. You are having a dream, and you see that you are having a dream. There are two consciousnesses in the dream. One is the world consciousness, which is caught up in the world, and the other is the consciousness that remembers the truth. That is it. Only these two and the relation between these two exist in this dream.

For example, when you dream at night, you get caught up in the dream, but part of you knows that you are dreaming. That part is the miracle consciousness, and the part that is caught up in the dream is the ego consciousness. When you look at God, God is not in the dream; He is awake. He is the light. He does not know what you are dreaming about. He does not even know that you are dreaming—not because He cannot but because you do not exist.

Do you choose the miracle consciousness or the ego consciousness? What do you see? What are you doing? That is the question.

Existence cannot exist within something nonexistent, and something nonexistent wants the existence to see and accept it. In other words, the story of the devil being kicked out of heaven is the creation of the devil.

Can the light itself know darkness?

For example, think of a dark room. When I turn on the lights, is there a dark room anymore? Can the infinite light know darkness? What happens to the devil within infinite beauty and infinite goodness? It does not exist. But it wants to exist, it wants God to accept its existence, and also it wants God to kick it out of His heaven. Do you know what oppresses the ego consciousness? The fact that God does not see and accept its existence.

When I say, "You are nothing," to a person, he becomes furious. The dream ...

The ego consciousness gets mad when it is not seen.

Every person has an angel and a devil side. This duality is the confirmation that it is not real. The two sides of the medal are the proof that the human and the world are a dream. The truth cannot be two, because it is one.

The human is the person who experiences the idea of "If there was a place outside the truth, a place that was not created by God, how would it look?" The person who will be able to see the world with the eyes of the world is the protagonist in the dream. I need to experience being a protagonist to be able to answer the question "How would it feel to be inside a storybook?" Right? How would it feel to be in the world? How would an experience outside the only truth of God be? Just like this: the world of duality.

The Dream World

Most people want to believe that when a person dies, his spirit will rest easy and go to the side of God. I understand you; I am sure this belief comforts you, but unless the consciousness does not choose to wake up and return home, the death of the body is just a rebirth. Remember the experience of seeing the light in near-death experiences—a tunnel with a light at the end. That tunnel is just the womb of another mother. Unless you live everything you came to this world to live and do everything you came to this world to do, no matter what role you play, unless you complete the requirements of that role, you will not get far. You will still ascribe meaning to the world; care about your reputation, the human, and the world; not live your true self, your truth; and not play your role.

Unless you play every line of your role, you will not be freed from the world.

None of the roles in the world are good or bad. None of the experiences are good or bad. Being poor is no different from being rich, and being disabled is no different from being a famous athlete. Of course, these experiences are different at the level of the world, but in truth, they are all the same illusion, the same dream. Would it matter if you are poor or rich in a dream? They are just different experiences. The experiences in the world can be neither good nor bad. They are not real. They are equally not real.

Some have families; some do not. Some live great loves; some never know what love is. Some work a lot; some do not. It does not matter. It is what it is. None of these experiences have any meaning.

Neither good nor bad exists in the world. There is no world. There is no such thing. Because of God's truth, there is no world in truth, nor is there a human. There is no world, and this truth is under the protection of God. Since the absence of the world is guaranteed by the Creator, this world is the world of body and spirit—duality.

Only knowing the distinction in your consciousness is important in the world.

As I said, your consciousness is split in half. One half of your consciousness serves the ego consciousness, the dream-world consciousness, and the other half serves the miracle consciousness, the truth. The side of our consciousness serving the world is asleep, and the side serving the truth is awake. The sleeping side will never wake up, and the awake side will never fall asleep. When you are able to make this distinction, all your problems will end because you will give up on trying to wake up your ego and turn to your awake side when you no longer want to be asleep, and when your things do not go right in the world and when you want to accomplish something in the world, you turn to your ego. That is it.

Your ego knows what to do in the world. Ask your ego, your inner voice, and it will tell you what to do. But listen to it. If you fight it, it will not be simple, and you will never win this war. Stop challenging the scenario, and play your part. Since you are not the one who wrote the scenario, you are not the one who will change it. Don't bother trying. Do whatever you are told, listen to your inner voice, and be at ease.

Make the distinction. The place where the ego is located is the world of doing. If you want to advance in the world, you have to do something. However, the true world is not like this. Your awake side remembers the truth, the world of being, the place where you remember existence. You do not need to do anything in this area. You are supposed to stay, doing nothing. That is why people meditate. When you stop, your true identity gets activated. Everything you need spiritually is in that area. You do not need to do anything to feel good, peaceful, calm, and happy; all you need to do is stop and accept your true identity.

You cannot understand the truth by trying to understand, and you cannot know by trying to know. You will get further away from your true identity as you struggle. All you can do is let it. It all starts there. There flows the truth. When I accept that I am me, the time flows. When you try to remember, you cannot. You will remember when you acknowledge your side remembering and when you accept it.

You cannot wake up if you try to wake up, because your human side that is trying to wake up, your ego, will never wake up. Why would you try to wake up something that will never wake up? Is not this wasting your energy? Instead, isn't it better to turn to your awake side? Your true identity is light; it is always awake. Why are you trying to wake up the other one?

Remember the side of you looking at the world thinks the world is real. Everything you see with the eyes of the body seems real to your ego, and you cannot change this. You can only understand that the eyes of the body cannot see the truth. Okay, let them see what they see, and let there be a part of you that thinks these things are real; it is okay. But also remember that they are not real. Then all your problems will be magically solved. And this happens before none of your problems are solved. If you remember that none of your problems are real, there will be no need to solve them; you will just laugh at them.

When you actually look at the world, it is the world of dreams. Adam chooses that dream, the world of dreams, and goes to experience the world, and Eva goes after him to turn him back. This is the scenario.

I can say this especially about the female energy: Adam knows why he came here and what his life means. Eva does not even know why she came here. Probably she came after something, and she is searching for it. The man does not have such a mission.

The only problem of Eva is Adam.

There are not many men waiting for the women of their lives, but there are many women waiting for the men of their lives. This is the thing of the woman because she has this mission. The woman comes to this world to turn the lost man back. But many women forget this. They are waiting for me to remind them. The man is busy with other things; he does not even care about going back home. If someone asked me which I would like to be, a man or a woman, I would say, "Both," because they are both great experiences. I think I became a woman because I wanted to guarantee my return home in this life experience. I probably did not want to risk it.

Yes, the man is on the journey to the world, but there is no difference between departure and return. They are both inside the dream. I think the journey back is a little boring. You always remember the truth, but people do not remember as you do. You wait for everyone to turn to his true identity, see as you do, and know what you know. This may be boring sometimes—and sometimes very funny! I cannot stop laughing at the things that make people mad and the things that make them motivated. Especially, I really laugh at my human side. She acts like a little child most of the time. *Like* is an overstatement. She is a little child—like the whole of humanity!

Really, the journey of getting lost is more fun. You know nothing, and you do not know that you do not know. Enjoy it!

Look at little boys—cars, activities, and sports from young ages. They are in a different event. Then look at little girls, whining, whining, and whining. I am sure you get it.

There is no way out of the world, the world with bodies, other than seeing that it is not real.

A participant of the miracles course said once, "So there is nothing to do. We are stuck here." You know, yes. As long as you have a mind, there is no way out of the world. You need to go beyond the mind. This can only be done through breathing. In my opinion, the only way out is through breathing. You always try to prove something to yourself in the world with bodies. Actually, there is nothing to prove, but when you think, you are a prisoner of your mind, your ego, and the collective consciousness, and not thinking is not possible. Thinking is necessary in the world. In the world, you need to act after thinking; otherwise, you will never get to where you want.

The consciousness remembering the truth is at the level where the mind is disabled when your breath is completely open and connected. Humanity tried everything to reach this total consciousness state for centuries: meditation, yoga, prayers, intentions, and breath. In addition to all these, being free from your mind and reaching the consciousness remembering the truth is only possible with connected breath.

If you cannot understand what this means, let's try now. Close your eyes, sit comfortably, and start taking deep and connected breaths from your mouth. Wait before inhaling and exhaling. Take connected breaths continuously one after another.

Do this for one to two minutes.

Could you think while doing this, while taking connected breaths?

No.

If the breath is connected, you can be free from the cycle of time, the ego, and the illusion of time. Maybe the illusion is not going anywhere—the body is there when we open our eyes—but when the breath stays connected, we can always stay at this level. When you exercise enough, this breathing can turn into habit.

Now you have stepped into the area where this book is written. This book is written thanks to my open and connected breaths. After my exercises of long years, I am maybe one of the people whose breaths are at the most open state, and this state allowed this book, because if the breath is open, we can stay at the level of truth all the time; we can always remember the truth and the fact that the world is not real. Whatever happens in our life, we can continue by remembering the love, light, and pureness within confidence.

Remembering the truth does not cause any changes in the experience of the mind-body. The course of events—what happens, what the ego self does—never changes. But I can easily see and accept that I am not that person because if my breath is connected and open, I am free from the world and the illusion of time. I am free from my ego self and my human side.

Some of you may ask, "How can I open my breath at the highest level?" I will answer you with all my heart sincerely: there are many studies in Turkey and in the world on this subject, and there are various breathing systems and seminars, but as you can understand from the information in this book, if you really want to go to a further level with breath, jump to another dimension, and be free from your identity in the world, the only place you can do this is the miracles course because this course is

Awakening

prepared for this purpose. The plan of the miracles course contains your total freedom from your body and mind experience, your awakening to the truth, awakening to the dream, and your freedom from everything happening in the world—all negativities, all diseases, and the erroneous world. You can have special sessions to open your breath, and you can go to various courses, but if you want the highest level, as I have mentioned, if you aim for the highest point, you can only reach it in the miracles course.

Maybe you can understand the information told in this book on an intellectual level. Of course, there will be parts that seem reasonable. But as long as your breath is not totally open and connected, as long as you do not have natural breathing at every level, with your human perception, you will twist even the information written here.

I have worked with thousands of people in the last twelve years, I have trained almost a thousand breathing coaches, and still, I see how the truth can be twisted. I am still working to free you from human perception in every training and in every staff meeting. In my opinion, this is an endless road. Whatever the reason is, this was granted to me, and for some reason, I accepted this before coming to this world. I accept my mission, and I correct nonstop. The perception is trying to twist the truth. If someone claims that certain things in the world are real and others are not, I correct and say, "Sisters and brothers, none of them are real."

There is nothing in the world.

Neither the concrete world nor the abstract world is real. Neither the body nor the spirit is real.

There is nothing.

The world is the product of the mind. It is just a thought in the mind, and it is a dream, along with everything in it. It is the extended version of the thought *If there was a place outside the truth, how would it look?* The ego consciousness is the place where the dream of the world starts and the path of the world. The answer to this is the miracle consciousness, the place where the truth is remembered, the way back home. In truth, neither of them exists.

There is no way in truth.

Therefore, talking about what happens in the path is not necessary.

The ego, having the dream of the world, perceives what it sees with the eyes of the human body—death, attacks, wars, physical damages, bloodshed, diseases, sex, hugging, laughter, frowning, and other earthly experiences—as real. It takes orders from the main command center, the collective consciousness, and it does what it is supposed to do.

The spirit of self-remembering sees with the eyes of the heart. It remembers the truth: the world is a dream, and everything happening in this experience is an illusion. It only sees itself wherever it looks. At the level of "Here is the world, and I am watching," it just stays where it is without interfering with the experience of itself and other people or ascribing any meaning to any experience. It lets it all be, free from all of it.

Let's go back to twin spirits. The big bang and the moment of deterioration—the moment when the dream of the world started and the moment when the dream of the world ended—are actually the same moment, because the dream of the world ended when it started. Maybe there are millions of years and billions of different experiences, but actually, all these were experienced by the split consciousness. The spirit was first split in half, then into four, and then into millions. Then it will return to duality. This return will be a completion.

When the spirit is split into two, one half goes right, and the other goes left. The experience starts with split consciousness. One side, the man, enters the experience of getting lost in the world and goes deep in the world. He chooses to experience earthly pleasures, fantasies, wishes, and feelings. It goes to the right side.

The other consciousness, the woman, starts the journey of remembering and reminding of the truth. She wakes thousands and millions of consciousnesses to truth. Actually, there is only one consciousness she came here to wake up: her twin. But they both need to come to the end of the world and the journey of truth to stay at the point of balance. The woman knows this; she waits for the man to wake up. The man waits for the woman to come to him. This waiting provides the balance.

Since the twin spirits go to opposite sides, they cannot see what happens on the side of the other. They cannot see their own back, as if they're standing with their backs facing and looking in opposite directions. Therefore, conflict is the natural state of the twin spirits. One cannot see what the other one sees, and the same goes for the other one. In this case, the union will release a tremendous creative energy, they can look at the world in 360 degrees, and they can correct all mistakes. They act like a channel, just like Mevlana and Shams. Healing, power, creativity, and great inspiration are released with the union.

It is hard for the twin spirits to stay together. They always want to go in different directions, to proceed in different directions. But if they find a balance, they will be unstoppable together. There will be a power and noise as if God has descended to the world. They do great things for humanity.

If you are wondering, your twin spirit is your back. He is behind you, at the point where you cannot see yourself, Therefore, unless a person makes peace with his shadow side and accepts and embraces his good side and dark sides, including his anger, ambitions, agonies, and the deep longing he feels, he cannot proceed with his twin spirit in a balance. You take a journey beyond your expectations with your twin spirit. Therefore, your twin spirit does not need to be your spouse, lover, or life partner. This is a small chance because fellow travelers go in the same direction; however, twin spirits do not go in the same direction. They are like the two halves of an apple, going in opposite directions. When they are together, a great inspiration is released, and then they are separated, and their guidance is released. They guide and lead hundreds or even thousands of people in their own directions. They only unite—which happens after long intervals—to experience the union, experience the point of view of 360 degrees, and channel the information. They do not have purposes, such as sharing life, walking hand in hand, or being spouses or friends.

When the twin spirits unite, there is only one purpose: reflection of the Creator in the world.

If you feel the things written here not intellectually but deep in your soul, then you are spending time with your twin spirit, channeling together, and descending divine creativity to the world. The meeting of twin spirits has no other mission.

The twin spirits need to be in balance to spend time together. This does not mean having a relationship, because it is almost impossible and unnecessary because of their differences. They must have a balance inside them and in their lives to have a peaceful, happy, and calm experience together. Twin spirits cannot be together when they are struggling, materially or morally, because the times of struggle are the times when people are deep in their journey and when the twin spirits go in opposite directions. In such times, twin spirits only torture each other. It is like wanting to hold someone's hand, wanting to be together, but then life throws you to the opposite side.

Twin spirits know or feel that they need to step in harmony, like dancing, in common time and the environment. One takes a step forward, and the other takes a step back. One goes forward, and the other watches. Then it is the turn of the other. They do not go forward at the same time; they do not attack at the same time. When one attacks, the other needs to wait, and this balance should be well established.

Therefore it is said, "When one twin spirit is in the world, the other twin spirit guides the other." Generally, when one is in a body, the other is not, because if you want to go ahead in your path without interruption, you do not want your twin spirit in the world with you. You want to go ahead in your path, and you do not want that power that will turn you from your path. But one day you wake up, and the time to return comes closer. In that life, you will eventually meet your twin spirit. In all other lives, your twin spirit needs to illuminate your back because you cannot see. In the life in which you are enlightened, you want to see your dark side, and then you meet your twin spirit.

Twin spirits and soul mates are different.

If you have met your soul mate, nobody else will have his depth, nobody will understand you as he does, and nobody will see your truth as he does because he is the one who knows himself and you—the reflection the soul. There is a great harmony at the level of true soul mates. Many people say that people can have many soul mates. Yes, we may meet ones who seem to match our soul, have the same values, and have the truth on the spiritual level, but we all have only one soul mate, the reflection of one side of the one spirit. That is our only mate in this world—the person you cannot leave, the reflection of your soul. Since you cannot leave your spirit, you cannot leave him.

If you are a whole with your spirit, when you know yourself, you come across someone who knows himself. Therefore, he knows you because he knows himself. The shortest description regarding the twin spirit is this: the one who knows me better than I know myself, or the one who knows and understands me as much as I do.

Many people get divorced or cannot make relationships last because they cannot find the person they belong to spiritually. Of course, people need to establish 100 percent connection with their spirit and live with the truth of the spirit to meet their soul mates, just as with the twin spirits. Otherwise, it is impossible to form relationships that last for a lifetime without any effort, which continue because of the spiritual truth.

The training on soul mates and twin spirits lasts for three days. If you are interested in the subject, I recommend you participate in my soul mate and twin spirit training.

Let's go back to twin spirits. Twin spirits are separated from each other in the first world experience. During the experience in which they will live everything they came to the world to live and finish the dream, they meet again and come together. Their meeting is mostly confused with sexual experiences and unions or spousal relationships. However, as I have mentioned before, the union of the twin spirits has a greater mission. They come together to see that the universe does not exist and to prove this to themselves. What does this mean? It means the last step of the journey of truth. If they can take this last step, which will bring about huge courage, confidence, and unconditionality, the twin spirits have the power to wake up the whole of humanity. The only condition is working together unconditionally and fulfilling their mission they came here for. Because of the extra attraction between the twin spirits—the whole universe waits for this union—their first meeting may be confused with sexual attraction or some physical feelings. However, as their relationship matures, they will wake up to the fact that this is beyond a physical attraction and that they came together for a greater mission. They both accept this mission before coming to this world. First, they will be lost in the world; then they will find each other, go home, and get destroyed. They must do this willingly; they must let it happen.

Twin spirits meet in their last lives, and then the cycle is complete when they go back. Sorry—instead of meeting, I must say they come into bodies at the same time, because what happens with twins spirits is not meeting; it is a union.

When that moment comes, when they are both ready, the union happens at the most unexpected moment. The experience is the experience of finding each other; they both know and feel this. When this happens, the first sign will be this: there is nothing for either of them to learn when the process is completed. They already know everything they experienced alone in life. They neither accept nor get any guidance from anyone. This may seem like a problem, but it is actually a deep state of knowing oneself.

A person who knows himself will not accept guidance from anyone or listen to anyone. He only does what he is supposed to do. He is his own guide; he is the light and the information. He sees ahead and only does what he wants.

Everybody cherishes his own way of doing things.

The reason a person who met the twin spirit knows himself is that the side that guides him in the life in which they met is also in the world. The twin that guides him from another dimension in the previous lies is now in the same life, in the three-dimensional world, and she has come to take him home now. They know they will complete their mission and go back home.

The only place the twin spirits can get guidance when they meet is their own spirit because you have woken up to the fact that there is no place you can get guidance from.

The most important part is that the twin spirit is not what you think; it is your dark side. Your twin spirit is everything you did not make peace with, everything you got mad at, and everything you wanted not to be and not to be done in your humanity. Your twin spirit does them all. However good you are, your twin spirit is that bad, and however bad you are, your twin spirit is that good. Therefore, you meet your twin spirit in the life in which you make your peace with humanity at every level.

These two opposite poles are drawn to each other because they came to finish, to complete the mission. They cannot help it. But their experience is a little weird compared to earthly experiences. For example, you are both a whole and separated. Whatever you are, your twin spirit is not. Whichever direction you have gone until now, your twin spirit has gone in the other direction. Here is an example: If money is a problem in your life, it is not a problem for your twin spirit. If relationships are a problem in your life, they are not for your twin spirit. In the world, you went in one direction, and your twin spirit went to the other side. Your twin spirit brings you a reality of humanity that you never saw, knew, or experienced. In a moment, your twin spirit displays your whole dark side. He is everything to which you say, "I am not this."

Awakening

Splitting of Soul, and Duality and Inception of the World Experience

Since this separation started with pain, terror, and everything that was earthly, the worst part of this experience is your being put into a body and coming here. The world is the pit of hell. You are doomed if you get carried away.

Humans in the world have a deep longing in their hearts, a longing for the truth they will never reach. With the longing comes pain, fear, illness, and death in the world. You are burning and boiling in that dream called the world—again and again—and finally, you wake up.

All those things are too terrible to be true.

Yes, thankfully, you woke up! The world is a place too terrible to be real because it is the place where there is no truth.

Then what happens? You leave the world and come back to the truth. How does this happen? When you burn and broil in the world and cannot stand anymore, you say, "God!" You scream, "God, save me!" There you go; you are in the truth.

You wake up when pain, limits of the body, aches, soreness, and separation reach an unbearable degree, because you jump up to the truth at the moment when you just cannot bear any more. You don't want to spend time anymore in a world that burns you, and more importantly, you have no choice.

You fall back on God.

The base of this experience is the one you lived with your soul mate. Separation—ideas, ways, directions, humanly desires, and all—hurts you so much that you fall back on God just to stand.

The experiences you went through with your soul mate are much softer and more comfortable.

How do you know it when you've met your soul mate? You know it by the endless composure and tranquility. With your soul mate, your need of proving, explaining, and sharing yourself ends. You can sit quietly for hours with your true soul mate. You can sit next to a window, staring at the same point, for years with him, for you are already looking at the outside from the same spot, the same window. He is the reflection of your soul. You are at the same place, same spot, and same house with him. You experience your memories of a home with him, and you experience heaven.

You can meet both your soul mate and twin soul when you are ready, when you forgive and accept the world and the human race just as they are.

Your relationship with your soul mate embodies the world's biggest happiness, composure, and trust. It is amazing. You can be with him until the end of your life, and you wouldn't want to die; you experience heaven on earth. My spouse always says to me, "Experiencing even a few years with you is enough for me for a lifetime." This is what a soul mate is.

The twin soul is a phenomenon that brings all the pain and fear in the world that you avoid but experience anyway. That makes you face your dark side. When you look at your twin soul, you feel a melancholy, sadness, and homesickness because he is the symbol of division. The pain and longing brought by being in a bodily experience, by not being one, get so deep that you face yourself, you face your biggest weakness, and you decide not to get into this dream ever again. You say, "This will be the last time." The only thing you can do is fall back on God. That's why twin souls are called 11:11. The number 1:1 is the reflection of duality here.

But this is not the case for soul mates. A soul mate is the truth you can't get enough of: your soul. You probably have been coming with him since the beginning of time, and your deal is not being able to get enough of him already. The case with the twin soul is this: "He shall be the furthest possible from me." But you cannot be that far because you are involuntarily drawn into him. This gravitation is like some sort of call for duty. Of course, there is a dilemma if you see from the worldly point of view.

Twin souls die at the same time. They probably kill each other.

What do you do to be outside your body? What can you do? This is the question.

To lose yourself, what can you do?

You know, we do this with breath sessions. We go to a platform when the breath is clear, and there is no you, no body, and no mind in that platform. You are out of it. But of course, it can be a different way too—for example, getting lost in doing a job you love, cutting loose, doing whatever you do by going into a trance, getting lost in the act. This will make you leave your egocentric point of view. You'll leave egomania and work for a bigger cause.

Ultimately, you arrive at a beautiful point where you get out of yourself, and this is the exact formula.

Personally, I can look at Nevşah from the outside because every moment, I live in the act. I don't let myself go. As Mevlana said, I know that if I ever let myself go even for a moment, if I ever stopped acting and progressing even for a moment, I would fall into the mind, body, exegesis, and criticism and become egocentric. I never let myself go; I always continue to walk, move, work, and produce, because I know the moment I let myself go, oh, poor me! I burn in hell. I don't do that. I don't let myself go. I always walk and move. I always keep myself in me. I always keep myself in the life, in the act, instead of in my ego.

This is where life happens: outside. The place we perceive as outside is actually inside.

You are here outside at where you look at. You are not where you think you are; you are not in your body.

Think. If you were in your body, wouldn't you see your organs instead of this page? You see where you are and what you are in. Look around. Can you see anything other than the room you are in? Can the eyes of your body see anything except the place they are in? No. Thus, you are wherever you are. You are in that space, not in your body.

Actually, we are all here in the life. But you see an illusion inside another when you think you are in your body, and you become egocentric.

One only sees where he is. Therefore, you are inside where you are. The room, the park—whatever it is, you are in it, all over it.

This is a trick of your ego. It tricked you into believing the existence of the body, so now you cannot see yourself. You perceive yourself in this thing that actually doesn't exist, in your body. However, you are here. You are here and everywhere. Everywhere you look and everywhere you see you are.

Why does the ego want you to perceive yourself as a body and in a body? Because you depart from the truth and your true self while you are busy with your body, your ego self. This is the aim.

You miss your true identity while you strive with what you call the inner world.

The thing I am about to say will hit you like a joke: the abstract world, the thing you describe as your inner world, the mind, emotions, and feelings are all empty. Rubbish! These are not in the world and not even in life itself. They are illusions within the illusion. You see, the ego has exaggerated creating illusions. The world is already an illusion. Even in this illusion, there is another world that is also an illusion: the world of thoughts and feelings. Geez!

Your thoughts and feelings are lies even in the dream called the world. Aren't you aware of this yet? So then why are you trying to be free from them? You should try to be free from them because these lies prevent you from realizing that you are asleep. You are asleep, but you cannot see, and your illusions within the illusion—your thoughts and feelings—are the reason for this. When you start to work on your thoughts and free yourself from the feelings they create, you will be able to look at this world. You will be able to see the truth of the world and human. So what is this truth? The truth that you are constantly burning in flames in the world.

Let's sum up the knowledge of the truth.

The world is an illusion, and every birth leads to death. Youth leads to aging. Everything you perceive as life in the world leads to reproduction and death. The result is death. Therefore, there is no life in the world. That's why life after death, heaven, and hell are spoken about. The world is where you are dead. That's why heaven and hell are here. Heaven is your spirit, your essence. Heaven is where you remember the truth. Hell is the world. Hell is where you sink into the world.

Think of the world as a tree. Think of true life, the energy of life squirted out of the Creator, life, and liveliness as an apple. But the world is a pear tree. It never gives you an apple.

The world is not where you are given life; it is where you give your life.

The world is a cloud of dust. It has no base—nothing, emptiness. It is an empty screen. Nothingness. And my reflection. What is reflected on the empty screen? My choices are. If I perceive myself as a body, it is reflected. One's concerns, fears, and criticisms are reflected everywhere. However, if I know my true identity and myself, then this identity is robbed of me.

In the world, I can know myself; I can remember myself within the twenty-four-hour cycle of the world and each second, even though a part of me is dreaming. That's how I always face the truth beyond the images of the world. I face the war, and I see love. I face the body, and I see life. I face death, and I see the truth. I face human, and I see God. This is possible, and just so you know, the world doesn't have to change to make this happen. When this happens, when I know myself, the world and my humanity do not change. I am the same person; I do and say the same things. But my truth changes. Instead of my human part, I look at my true identity, and I only see that from then.

This hand of the body—is it the Divinity's hand? No, of course not. But if I remember my true identity, it can change into the Divinity's hand. Even the body's hand can remind me of the deity's. If I choose my spirit and remember, everything reminds me of Him. But if I choose the human, then I feel lonely, exhausted, and hopeless.

So if I see from the opposite view, can a cloud of dust summon the Divinity? No. Can it make you experience the Divinity? No. Is the Divinity in the world? No.

But I remember Him as long as I remember my true identity and bring Him, the Divinity, to the world. The Divinity Himself cannot come to the world. The unrestricted cannot enter within the borders of the restricted. The immortal can't step into the land where mortality is present. The one who is not born, cannot die, and has no steps cannot take a step into where steps are taken. He, the true, cannot be among the untrue. The world does not exist, but God is existence itself. He is not absence but existence. He is not mortal; He is eternal. That's why we can neither see nor experience Him in the world.

The only thing we can do to reach God in the world is to listen to our heartbeats bearing His memory. We cannot and will not reach Him because there is no ego or self where He is. Ego and self are nothing and will remain what they are.

When we remember our true identities, we remember the divinity in the world too. Here too we can breathe with His memory. Maybe we cannot reach Him, but we can live while we remember Him. That's how I can turn the world into heaven, where true life is remembered. The world can never be the place I share with the Divinity because there is nothing but the Divinity in that place. But at least we can remember His existence.

We have that power. Then everyone gets his memory. Everywhere becomes the echo of truth. Even a wall, a hand, a foot, or a table can represent the Divinity's memory—not because they are His memories but because I choose to see that way. Yes, this wall is a cloud of dust and not true. This body isn't true either. Nothing in the world is true. Without the life in me, I am like a piece of meat, a dress. I, lively when there is life in it. I, because I am here.

I am responsible if I am the one here. But I am responsible for accepting every existing thing, forgiving, and giving space to love and light. I am not responsible for the things in the dream. I can experience my eternity within the time. I can remember the truth while dreaming. Instead of getting attached to the body and the world and paying attention to the things done by the world and my human side, I can let it happen. I can stay within the truth.

I am life itself, and I can remember that. Here can you see what remembering the truth does? I am life itself. Therefore, this body is life itself within my existence. Can this body without the life in it give birth to a child? No. But I am here. I, the true identity, can make the body do it. I keep this body healthy. Life squirts out of this body as long as I am here. As long as I know myself, this body can stay within the truth, with the protection of the truth.

The Divinity can never be a mortal character in the dream. He cannot be in the dream, the illusion. But I can remember Him every moment, even in the dream. I can feel His protection and existence beyond everything there is. Whatever happens to me in the dream called the world, whatever my human side goes through or does, I can remember that none of these things existed, and I can be free. Even though I am a mortal character in the dream called the world, I can remember the Divinity with the help of the spirit, my essence, and by remembering the Divinity, I can keep His memory alive. I can turn the dream into the dream of heaven. This does not mean changing the world. This means that there is no death, attack, or war and that I can see that all of those things are a childish play.

The world will never be a life I share with the Divinity, but it can be a place where He is remembered, we speak of Him, and we return to Him.

I know that the world seems to you almost real. The ego self will always be there. It believes in the world and thinks the world is true. You cannot change that. Leave the human, the ego self, alone. Let it do what it needs to do. Set it free so that you will not be seeking freedom.

You are the one who is free, not the human.

You are love, not a mortal, ego, me, or human.

You will leave your ego alone when you quit trying to turn that human into something it can never be: truth, love, and light.

Since the dream called the world is almost real to the eyes of the body and the five senses and is real to the perception of the body, I can use it for my own truth. I can keep the Creator's memory, love, and unconditionality alive. I can embrace both my humanity and all the humans, even though they are killers. I can remember that I am not the one who judges and criticizes, but a mortal mind is. I can set it free to let it criticize, but also, I can remember who I am and embrace what happens with love. I can embrace my human side and other humans with my existence. This is not my human side embracing everyone. This is my existence, my essence, embracing everyone. This is embracing one and everyone when my human side does not. This is embracing my human side when it does not embrace someone—embracing my human side's inability to embrace first and then embracing the other person, the unloved one.

Most people recognize unconditional love, light, abundance, health, and healing as human because they confuse spiritual truth with the truth of body. It can be confused if your point of view includes your ego. But it is not like that.

Unconditional love is there even when bodies attack one another. It is there when a body dies and when a body suffers. Unconditional love is in the background of people who make each other suffer. Don't seek it in the world. It is a feature of your spirit. Don't seek it in the human. The human cannot forgive and embrace everyone. If you want your human side to forgive everybody, you throw yourself into a bottomless pit.

The human cannot love unconditionally. It has a conditional mind, a limited perception. How can it love unconditionally? How can it embrace everyone? You can embrace everyone with your energy, existence, breath, and true identity, with your spirit. But physically, you cannot do that. Don't bother. If you try this, it is certain you will fail, and this will only bring you anger. Don't do this to yourself. Accept your human side with its limits. Stop asking it for the things it cannot do. It's a shame, a pity.

Your spirit, heart, and bodily appetites are the individuals who say, "I can love everyone and everything." The human, or ego self, who is on a physical level where love and lovelessness are, cannot love everyone. Give up on that. You are delaying your awakening.

Everything will look different when you accept your true identity.

At the point where I know myself, even a dead hand is true. That hand is heaven. Every smell I obtain from every flower or human I touch is the smell or touch of heaven. Why? Because I am here, and I remember heaven. Of course it will be like that. Nothing can be outside of heaven when I am here. Even war is a part of the forgiveness plan. Every attack and desire for revenge in the world melts in love and disappears. Their nonexistence and meaninglessness become visible. This does not mean the end of wars, disappearance of death, or cease of bloodshed. This means that even the bloodshed and the desire for revenge are now replaced with the divine reason.

If I live my every moment with divine reason, the world disappears under my feet. Every step taken by my human side becomes a true step, a divine lesson, when I remember the truth. This is the true remembering.

Here is another important topic: I can remember the Divinity. I can remember that I am one with His features and even Himself. As a consciousness who remembers that, I can see a mortal thing with His memory and His truth; I can sanctify that thing, but I cannot deny that thing. I cannot turn the human into the Divinity or His holy features. A human cannot love like the Divinity. Spirit can remember and make all humanity remember the truth, the love of the Creator, His light, and eternity, but it cannot turn the world into the Divinity's creation. You can project Him and the truth onto the world. You can see the Divinity right now, even if you are dreaming. You can see His memory, light, and love everywhere you look. You can turn the world into a tool to remember the Creator. But you cannot turn the world into the true life.

I can only sanctify the world with the memory and truth of the Divinity. The sentence "I am the Divinity" cannot come out of a mortal thing's mouth.

Yes, I am the one who will remember and bring the Creator, His love, His eternity, and His uniqueness. But He cannot come here. The immortal cannot be in a world with mortality. Waking up—that is it.

Waking up to the dream called the world is waking up to what is and is not possible in the world. It is waking up to the fact that the world and the human will not change. It is to stop trying to make the human Divinity-like and remembering that the human side is nothing and will be nothing.

The human is part of the dream called the world, so it will remain in the illusion. It and ego are with the illusion; they cannot be separated. Your identity in the dream is a mortal body with a mind, a body, an ego, feelings, and thoughts. It is part of the illusion and is asleep. It is certain that if you try to wake it up, you will fail.

The world is a world of acts. You must go forward, express yourself, create, and reproduce without stopping. Otherwise, you get rusty, soft, and rotten.

You must go forward in the world. You will walk. Whatever happens, you have to look forward and walk forward without looking back and getting hooked on the past. Otherwise, you burn. The fire burning at the root of the world catches you and burns you.

You must accept your true identity instead of trying to develop a humane love, because your true identity is love itself. If you are connected with your spirit and essence, if you see and know His love, your unloving identity in the world doesn't bother you.

If you don't accept your true identity, it is important for you that your human side love everyone and everything. Unfortunately, you are working for the things you will not acquire, and it is guaranteed that you will fail and become angry.

We are surrounded by people who wanted to hit the road to home but misunderstood the message. They still care about their human side and try to make it full of love, truth, and light, whereas a person who has accepted his true identity does not try to make his human side loving. He says, "I am love." The person who lives the truth within himself can remember that he is full of love.

If you can accept and know your spirit and essence and can say, "I am the light and aware of it," you have already seen that there is not a human who can never love.

A human cannot always love and always be enlightened. The human is in the duality. There is always a dark side. If you try to make it enlightened all the time and don't accept its nature, the darkness in you keeps growing just because you don't see or accept it.

You cannot make the human pure light. Give up on this meaningless endeavor. It bears the light and the spirit, but it is not the light and the spirit.

If you choose your true identity, you love. You love even when your human side does not.

You are light. You are light even when your human part is in the dark. You are composure. Even when your human side has no composure, you are composure.

You are in peace. Even when your human side is in the reality of assault, separation, and war of the world, you are in peace.

Know that the rules and the system of this world are under the collective conscience's direction, not yours. This will never change. When you choose the truth, you will look different and perceive differently, but they will not change.

When you choose your true identity, you will see love even in the lack of love in the world. You will be able to remember that humanity, your humanity, and other people's unloving behavior are all love themselves. Then people won't even have to be loved. Your search for love in the world will end. If you find the true love, you don't seek love in the world, and you don't try to be loved. Do you seek food when you are full? Does the person who knows there is love, who has chosen his true identity, seek love in the world? Does he try to make every behavior of his human side loving? What does it matter if I am the one who knows himself? Does it matter what my human side does? Does it matter if my human side is loves or not? Consciences that are hungry for love seek love in the world. The one who is full does not seek love. He just loves. The human loves when he doesn't. He is love when there is no love in the world.

You cannot love a person by hugging him or always supporting him. The true love is beyond what is visible in the world. It is in both war and death and even in unloving behavior. Anyway, the human doesn't know about love. The love your ego describes is being nice to people and embracing everyone. These things just keep you away from your nature, your humanity.

The human distinguishes, judges, and criticizes. You cannot change this fact, so make peace with yourself.

This is the true love: accepting a person as he is with his perception, judgment, criticism, and anger. If you want your human side to be loved by everyone, you burden it with a great, unnecessary weariness. Let it be; it cannot love when it cannot. You are love itself; let it go, and get ahold of yourself.

The human is just a simple actor in the world scene. Don't expect anything from it but to play its role. Don't expect it to love, accept, forgive, or embrace everything. It cannot do that. He will slap if his role suggests so. You cannot stop that. He will act as his script says. Remember that there is no good or bad role; there is just the world scene. Spirit and true self are beyond this scene. They are not plain roles; they are the actors. Whatever will be will be. There will be moments of love equal to the moments of anger, because the human cannot only love; he gets scared as much as he loves. That is why his love is not real; it is just part of the act. Humans love because the act suggests so. One loves the person he loves; he doesn't love whom he doesn't. But the spirit is different. It loves because it is true. It loves everyone and everything.

The spirit is not in the play, not in the world. It is the abstract world within the world. Love of the spirit reflects upon the world as acceptance, forgiveness, giving space, and freedom. Good behavior, hugs, and acts that are part of the play cannot represent the spirit.

Your true identity is beyond the world scene. You cannot see it in the acts, words, steps, and experiences in the scene. It is behind all the experiences. It is in the role of an assassin, an attack, a war, lovemaking, food, drinks, and sleep. It is everywhere. The spirit is everywhere. Love is endless and everywhere; it is not possible for it to be in some parts of the dream called the world and not in others. There is unloving human, but there is not unloving spirit. That is why if you stay within your true identity, you can see love even in unloving humans. If you cannot, if some people, situations, and behaviors seem to you unloving, know that you have forgotten yourself. You could reflect your love even if they were unloving. You could see them as your loved ones even in their unlovingness, ambitions, and anger.

Every human has a role in the world.

Every character of the story, every human in the world, has things to do and say, and most importantly, it is all written. It is certain. Your role is your role in the world. There is no problem here. The problem starts when you try to lead your role out of the script by saying, "I mustn't have said this. I must have said that," or "It is better if I do this like that." Every human can be whatever his character traits, role, destiny, and way of life are. Thinking you can change your way of life or direct your role and destiny in the world is the biggest mistake you can make. There is no free will on the level of your role. Free will is something else.

With your free will, you can only choose with which consciousness you will look at the world; you cannot choose or change what you will live. Whatever will happen will happen. Whatever will be will be.

You can change neither the time nor the course of the things you will live through. The world spins, life goes on as it must, and you have no impact or control over that. If you think you do, you are wrong, and also, you are delaying your awakening by chasing the impossible.

The human must be considered as a simple machine. Every human has his abilities. Another person cannot manage to do things you are here to do. Another person cannot live the things you are to live. Every human has his own path, just as every machine has its things to do. Whoever you are, be sure that you are doing what you are here to do. You cannot change that. A washing machine washes clothes, not dishes. If you want it to do so, you break it. Humans are just like that; they break, and they get sick. You are trying to be someone else instead of being who you must be and doing what you must do. You are no different from a washing machine that wants to be a dishwasher.

That's how humans get sick. Instead of living according to their limits and making the best of what they have, they try to change things. They try to be someone else. When they try to be different from the person they already are, they get sick. Because the thought that you can be different from who you are is the disease itself. You cannot be different from who you are. You must surrender to existence. Your part is your part. You must stop messing with the character traits that you show by heart; otherwise, you get sick.

In the twenty-first century, most machines are broken. How do I know that? Because of the pharmaceutical industry. Humans are living in such a twisted manner today that they take a fistful of pills a day and still think they are healthy.

Know that your role—your character traits, or your ego, which is a blessing over you—is messed up just because you don't like it and do everything to change it. It is not possible to experience the role you are destined to experience happily and peacefully when the machine is broken. Here you are a nervous, sad, anxious person.

Your human side is perfect with its imperfections, perception, judgments, feelings, and thoughts. Your human side has no problem. You, not accepting it as it is but trying to change it relentlessly, are the problem.

I have been teaching courses to people who see themselves as problematic with their human side, character traits, thoughts, and feelings for years. I help them take better breaths, and they stop perceiving themselves as problematic. Do you know what I saw in those courses? Those who are ready to accept themselves with all their flaws, perceptions, thoughts, feelings, experiences, and humanity learn how to breathe better on the first day of the course. I learned how to breathe better and more clearly with only one session. But there are people who have the habit of messing with their roles in the world, their humanity, and other humans.

With a breathing coach, a life coach, an NLP trainer, or even a miracles course leader, nobody can help them accept themselves as they are. They keep trying and trying. They want everything and everybody to change. They think the day will come when they will turn into metahumans. People will change too—nobody will criticize each other, everybody will be a better person, wars will end, differences will disappear, everybody will love each other, and so on. That's what they think. I cannot understand how deep their sleep can be.

None of that will happen.

You will wake up to the dream when you accept humanity and the world as they are, with their rights and wrongs, illnesses, arguments, deaths, and inabilities. You will see that we are one, and you will wake up to a dream.

You will see how perfect the dream is.

This dream is perfect as it is already, with night, day, war, peace, fights, birth, death, love, and fear.

It is whole and perfect. The problem itself is perceiving some parts of the dream as bad or ugly and perceiving some parts as better than others.

Separation in the world does not exist as you perceive it. There is a perfect wholeness behind all the dualities.

What should we do to perceive the dream called the world and humans as they are and as a whole? What should we do to wake up?

First of all, we must stop fighting with our role and attacking our humanity and the humans in the world. I am not talking about a physical fight. If I talked about stopping a physical fight, I would be attacking the world, the roles, and humanity. I am talking about leaving the world as it is, not fighting a fight, fighting a war, or fighting the fear but leaving everything as it is, not messing with the physical world, letting the physical world be as it is, leaving the ego, leaving it as it is, not trying to make it something else, and accepting it as it is.

Do people want to attack each other? Let them do it. It is not even real, so why would you stop that? Do people want to make love? Let them do it. Do people want to make war? Let them do it. You cannot change the world, and it is none of your business. The world is none of your business. Why do you care about what happens in the world? You are living a destined life, so why are you denying or fighting it? It is okay if you are trying to make yourself sick. Everybody is free to be as sick as he wants.

Why am I writing this? Because every person knows what he does and does not want on the inside.

Every person's destiny is within his mind that directs him, within his ego.

Nobody can go against his destiny, because people cannot go against their desires and wills.

Whatever you want will be because those desires of yours are your ego, your role. Of course they will be. All you have to do is let it be and leave your human side alone. It already knows what to do.

I must fix the machine at the beginning of the road so I can continue to love and embrace myself. It looks bad when the machine is broken. First, there must be fixing. Breath and conscience must be fixed. Where you fix it is the miracles course.

The person who is trying to do things against his character and destiny is sleeping in an unreal mind cycle and in unreal feelings. First, you must leave that artificial mind cycle and transfer to the true mind cycle of your destiny, ego, and desires. First, your life must be on track. You will know when it happens. Everything is okay and going well. Things happen as they should, in an order, gradually. The scenes in the script are being played out one by one. Because you have let them happen. True healing—true health—is this.

We are all humans first and then spirits or spirits first and then humans—whichever you choose—but these two phenomena will coexist always.

Waking up in the world means remembering you are asleep here, remembering the world is not real, and letting the human and the world be as they are.

If you remember being asleep, you are not asleep. You must seem to be asleep. But you are not totally awake either because you know that the human cannot wake up. The level at which you know the human cannot wake up is the level at which you wake up. All those are possible at that moment. They are possible if you stay in the moment with a clear breath and conscience. The world gives you thousands of ways to open and clear your breath and conscience. There are hundreds of breathing coaches and lots of courses that will help you work your mind and be enlightened, even in Turkey. I think you must ask this to yourself before you go to these courses: Can a person who has not woken up to his humanity wake me up?

If a person promises you enlightenment, it means he is still asleep.

An awake person never promises enlightenment, because he has woken up to the fact that he is asleep and will never wake up.

I can promise you clearer, better breaths. I can help you wake up to the truth and clear your conscience. But I cannot wake you up. I can wake you up to the fact that you are dreaming.

Awakening is possible on the level of conscience, not another. For example, it is impossible to wake up on the physical level. A person who has woken up to the truth continues to make mistakes, blaspheme, get angry, and do whatever his human side does, but he doesn't care about those things, unlike the ones who haven't woken up to the truth. He just laughs at the mistakes and inabilities of his human mistakes. He remembers every moment that all of these things are just a dream.

Asleep consciousnesses work for the world. They try to change the world and humans. They confuse the dream with reality. The person who thinks the dream is real tries to change the world. A consciousness that has awakened to the truth accepts the world and the human as they are.

Awakening is possible when you don't take humans and the world seriously; you let your feelings, thoughts, and perception slide; you do not care; and you can accept everything that is happening in this world. You cannot wake up from the dream. You can wake up to the dream. This is only possible when you free yourself from the mental cycle that is a reflection of the world. Also, in my own experience, it is possible when you have the best and clearest breathing. Your intellectual understanding of the truth does not wake you up to the dream. I think this is the most important thing you must understand.

Worldly experiences wake you up, not your intellect, the books you read, or the information you obtain.

You wake up to the dream when you quit perceiving yourself as Nevşah—or Ali, or Ayşe—and see that the divine identity is here. If you are in touch with your true self, you have another existential experience to compare with your humanity. If you don't have a second and truer self, you cannot see what your human side is and its perceptions, limitations, judgments, or dark and light sides. The true self makes us see our flaws and human side.

You woke up to the dream when you saw the world as it was with its good and its bad, when you saw it with its burning flames and accepted it.

Body and spirit are part of a dream. The spirit has the dream; the body is in the dream. There is no dream, nobody who has the dream, and nobody who is in the dream in the truth.

The only thing that can make a difference to the dream is my choice.

Do you want to stay with the side that has the dream? Or do you want to remember that you are in a dream and live life without assigning meaning to it? Do you want to live life as if you are flying, let things happen, and accept everything in the dream called the world? Do you want to experience all of it? Or do you choose to stay in the dream? Do you want to get lost in the dream and believe in your five senses while believing that everything in the world is real?

Do you choose to look at the world and burn in flames? Or do you choose to look at the truth and sleep in peace?

Miracles Course

A summary of the whole book is as follows.

The world is a war zone. This is not the place where you are; this is the place where you make war and struggle. You *be* when you go to the world of spirits. You have to move, try, and go forward here, because that is why you are here. Thank God the human in the dream of the world, the body, and the soul are not real, just as the experiences in this world, the war or sex, are not real.

The human is a whole with its ego, and they cannot be separated. You have to accept this. The human lives a certain perception because of his ego; he interprets and criticizes with his own perception. The place where the ego is connected to its destiny is this perception, however you perceive it.

You cannot escape from the truth. The human is as happy as he is unhappy, as joyful as he is sad, and as good as he is bad, and he is everything he sees in the dream. If you ascribe meaning to certain emotions and escape from them, you limit your life, and you get sick. You need to respect the fire burning inside you. God put it there so you can see the truth. Do not run away from it; let it burn you. That fire keeps you in the world; your normal is feeling good or bad, balanced or unbalanced, happy or unhappy. Stop running away from yourself. When you run away from yourself and from feeling certain emotions, your blood values drop. You will get a fever and get sick if you resist that fire, so do not fight that fire; walk through it.

Your war is in the world, not inside you.

The fire burning inside you and all those feelings you run away from are the energy keeping you in the world. That energy is keeping you breathing, keeping your ego and humanity alive, and ensuring that your scenario happens. Instead of suppressing it, you need to fight with the planned world. As long as that energy is suppressed there, it turns into a bomb, and when it blows up, you may want to kill someone or tear someone apart. There is no need to limit yourself to that level. The pure anger of a child never kills someone; the anger of a person bottled up for years and blown up in a moment can kill someone.

Live. Stop suppressing the things making you live, your feelings. The fire burning inside the human connects him to the world. If you run away from that energy, you will die. If you stay in that energy and burn, you will be free.

That energy is what keeps you in the world. The place where you connect to the energy of the world, the magma, is the place where your diaphragm is—your breath, yourself, the place where the world starts. When you become a whole with this energy, you can take giant steps. You can experience the peak of your power. That area is the place where you are effective in the world, the place where the human is the most effective and experiences the power. It's the place where Hercules gets his power. Hera is the place where we connect to the human emotions we thought to be dark, the place where the human body becomes like a god. Yes, a human cannot be God, but he can unite with His burning fire. Then he becomes unstoppable. All doors of the universe open to that person just because he was brave enough to touch the fire. All those feelings you do not want to feel—ambition, anger, desires, wishes, dark and deep energies—come from the place that is the potential of the human body. Your muscles, your brain, and all those moving emotions work with that fire, the energy of life. Your cells regenerate with the desires in that area, and the hunger for the life you feel there and all your animal instincts make you survive and stay healthy, strong, and dynamic.

We never saw a well-behaved and polite person change the world. The ones who change the world and wake people up are always the ones who accept their humanity and change the deep feelings inside humanity into creation.

The feeling you perceive as ambition is not even ambition. It is just a moving energy, emotion—living energy, live energy. It's the energy that regenerates your cells, the burning fire. You may call it ambition, wish, desire, or whatever.

This energy has nothing to do with competition, being ahead of others, or being different. You can see it in a small child; he expresses himself as he is because he is alive and connected to the fire burning inside humanity, to life. He is what he is.

But if you are connected to this energy of life, the truth deep inside humanity; are living your life touching people; and are living inside you and your nature, this will be reflected even in the looks. Maybe the eyes looking at your body will not see it, but the ones looking at your eyes and your heart will feel the deep magnetic energy, the depths of the life in you.

The one who can touch his own humanity can touch the whole of humanity.

If you are connected to that depth, to your humanity, even once, you start to connect with the depth inside all people. The whole world sees this.

If you touch the right person, the deepest point inside a person, you connect to the truth of the person. You know we are all in the same hole, and we are one. We are different, and we all have different characters and different perceptions, but at the level of experience, we are one. We are all humans.

Therefore, awakening starts when you accept your humanity. It starts with being a human.

When people try to be more than human, they become separated from the one.

We are all humans; we are in the same feelings and states, and at the point of the truth, we are one.

Therefore, when we are just human, when we try to connect to nothing but our humanity, to the things we know and do not know, the things we understand and do not understand, we experience being one. When you connect to the humanity, you are connected to humanity—to all those deep emotions—and the whole of humanity. You can feel the fire burning deep inside all the people in the world, their heartbeats, and blood clots. You become the whole experience. If you have touched that depth and if you know about the deepest emotions of humanity, you have touched the humanity, and there is no greater satisfaction.

This is true happiness: touching the human—every person you meet, first your humanity and then the whole world—and being immortal, unlimited, and everything.

The people who have touched their humanity leave a deep trace in everyone they meet. They can go deep inside everyone, and they can touch the places where the human does not want to be touched. They affect and touch because they are the ones who dared to go deep into their own humanity.

Those people understand the human—all the humans—and humanity knows this. They can see the truth in their eyes.

Feeling the human, the humanity, is huge and deep. It brings a great understanding to humanity and also a great depth and great maturity. If you can go deep in the experience of humanity; face yourself without running away; and come down to the agonies, ambitions, and wishes of the human, you wake up right there.

I am sure now you better understand the moment when I woke up to the dream, as I told in the beginning of the book.

One morning, I got up and faced the world and my humanity, and then I started crying. All I could do was cry for months. I cried for moths. One morning, I got up and fell inside the reality of the world. I could not get out of that depth for months. I thought I was going crazy. I just did not run away. I did not try to run away. What a depth, an endless well, it is! I had an incredible experience. I felt the agony of the whole of humanity deep in my heart at one moment, and it destroyed me. It was unbearable—an incredible depth, human, a deep despair, loneliness. At first, I thought I was crying for myself, but as I let it, my heart burned so much that I understood that this is the truth of the whole of humanity. I saw. I heard. I learned.

I accepted that I am nothing.

Then love happened.

I understood. I understood that I am just a human, and I accepted the only name given to me.

That name became this book.

All I know is that I have understood the whole of humanity since the day I came to the world. I really understood. I felt it in my heart. At first, I tried to hide the love I felt in my heart. Then, one morning, I could not do that anymore, and that love woke me up.

I never got angry at anyone all my life. I cannot. Because I know. I know what humanity is in. Awakening is not what you think it is. You do not need to wake up to the truth; you already know your true identity. I need to remind you of that and what true awakening to the human and to the world is.

When you wake up to what the world and the human are, you truly wake up.

The point is not remembering the truth; it is seeing the human.

The point is not touching the truth or telling the truth; it is touching the humanity.

Now you also are awake. You have woken up to your humanity. You do not need to run away from yourself anymore.

You are the same as everyone reading this book, me, and all other people. We all have the same problems and emotions. You do not need to hide this or hide yourself or your humanity.

The path to awakening goes through your humanity.

All those deep emotions stay deep inside all people, in the core of their core; they are bloodred, burning. Running away does not work. We are at the end of the book; I am sure you are going through awakening with the summary of all I have told. You are accepting, forgiving, and understanding yourself and your humanity.

There is nothing you need to run away from or hide. False pretending is not working; your self knows the truth. Do not try; stop faking being happy. It does not work.

First, be a human. First, be a true human. The rest is easy.

The ego makes you think you will die if you connect to these feelings—I know. You will not die. Your true self will not die, but your ego will. That is right. You will not die. I stayed in that place, looking at human beings, for months. I could not get out of there, the humanity. I am still there; nothing is happening. Yes, I live the world deeper than everybody else, I have an incredible understanding and love toward the human, and my heart burns every minute, but I did not die.

Sometimes I am so busy with daily works that I do not even show it. But I am still there, and I know what it is. I cried for months. What happened? Nothing. I did not leave my bed for months; I was at the deepest point of the well. I did not use any drug, and I did not do anything else. If such a thing happens, people go to the doctor immediately. Then they get many psychiatric drugs. That moment is actually the moment of awakening. If you let it be, if you stay there, you will have a great awakening. If people cannot stay there, since nobody can help there, the doctors push drugs. I used myself as a test piece, and I did not go to the doctor; I did not use any drugs. I stayed there. A truly splendid thing happened.

Remember—you get out of the miracles course, and you run away, saying, "But I feel bad." That is the point. The miracles course brings you here. Of course you will not feel good; awakening is not feeling good. You will go deep down in humanity first, and the miracles course gives you this. You can dare to do this. You can handle those feelings. Now you have incredibly strong breath. You can go to this depth, and you can continue to be a human in this depth, in this wisdom. When you stay at that point, you can understand everyone. I know you all have chosen this.

Breathing Sessions

As I said before, when you go deep in pain, you see that you are nothing.

I think the most important thing is the following. For example, fictionally, it goes like this also: look at Nevşah in the beginning of the training and Nevşah at this depth right now, and look at what you are feeling now.

When you see that you are nothing and if you go deeper in that emotion, you start to laugh. You start to laugh because everything seems funny—it's a funny scenario.

Do you want to know what happens when you start laughing? Your mind takes over and creates a fiction so that you will not go any deeper. Laughing is the stupidest thing humanity has done since the beginning of the world and the most artificial. To quote Nietzsche: "It is man alone who laughs; he alone suffers so deeply that he had to invent laughter." It is a fiction to keep you away from your suffering. The feeling of joy has nothing to do with laugher. That is why it seems funny. It takes you from there and brings you here. I am telling you this because I know what it is; you will go a little deeper. Here we have not gone up to higher energies; that is why I am telling you something seems funny. This is in the mind; it shows that energy is here. This energy is such a deep well. There is no comedy here. There is bloodshed. There is physical pain. If you are here, this place is not funny. This is the least funny place on the earth. If you are in this endless well, nothing is funny. Everything is just as it is. There is not even the slightest comedy. It is really hell. That is okay. It is not a torment. Ego is the one who calls it a torment, or hell. That is the place where you are enlightened. Ego tells you this to delay your enlightenment. It says,

"Do not go there. That is hell. You will suffer; you will be destroyed." As a person who has gone there, can hang out there, and lives there, I am guiding you and saying, "No, this has nothing to do with torment." It has nothing to do with hell. You just need to ache for it. When you ache for it, a magnificent mercy comes out of it, because when you go deeper here, when your process ends, your energy jumps to the heart.

You have experienced it before. I kept all of you here first, and then, when I told you, "Open your eyes; open your heart," your heart opened differently because when you deepen here, there is such a confrontation regarding the human that a great mercy is felt. Let me put it this way: if the whole world could stay here, touching humanity, it would be impossible for someone to hurt another. If you could know what the other person is in, what emotions and despair that person feels, and what he runs away from, you would not be able to do anything that would hurt him. You would just want to lend a helping hand and hug him. This happened in your experience a little while ago. When you feel that point, you cannot do anything to the person across from you. He is in all those deep emotions just as you are—why would you do more to him? There is nothing more. The greatest agony is there. So what if you cut his throat there? Those cuttings and murders are just because people cannot touch there. The person has cut himself thousands of times; he has a body. He feels all the pain the body suffers. He is in the event.

My daughter lives abroad. She came here three years ago and stayed for two whole months for the first time. She could have stayed longer, but she preferred to go because she missed her friends, and I took her to the airport. I came home, and I started to cry. You should have seen me crying! I wanted to get out of that state, but I could not, and when I got up in the morning, I started vomiting.

Vomiting is the surfacing of the resistance you have to that feeling.

I went to a psychologist, and he gave me drugs. I did not experience this again for three years, but when I woke up this morning, I vomited. I thought I was cleansing, but it stopped there. If I was not in this consciousness ...

All I can say after this is that you have no chance but to let this happen. There is no other way. You cannot go around it. You have to go deep.

Is going deep like what we do in the sessions?

Oh no. You only let in the sessions. After all those talks and this seminar, it is bound to come out at some point. Something will happen when you are listening to a song or sitting next to someone, and you will enter a depth for no reason, and maybe you will want to cry and be alone, and something will happen. When you let it and when you go out of it, you will have an incredible mercy because it is automatically the exit of entering here. You go deep here, but do you know the exit of this place? Here. When you go deep here, you have to accept humanity. When you accept humanity at that level, an incredible mercy starts to rise—an incredible love, an incredible understanding. From that moment on, you cannot get angry at anyone, and you cannot say anything to anyone, because you know what humanity is in.

At the last session yesterday, we talked about many things. We said, "I am actually not Elif; I am me." That felt good. Then, when I felt bad in the session, the coaches said, "This is your self in the body," and when I went home at night, my head became somehow. On one hand, I was trying to understand the nonexistence of that body, and on the other hand, I was trying to understand my self in this body. But I've got the answer now.

But this is a dream, and that is it. It starts here in that magma, that fire, and it stays inside you. Then, as I said, when you come down here, that energy automatically goes to the heart. There is no other way. As long as you do not enter those deep emotions, no matter what you do, even if you meditate your heart 1,500 times, it will not make a difference. That is why we want the breathing to start from the stomach in the breathing sessions. Unless it opens there and unless an understanding is established, we cannot get anyone to come up here. You need that to happen here, and you need to connect to your human side. Then the energy jumps to the heart, and it happens automatically. There the love and mercy are in the heart. Let me put it this way: the miracle consciousness I have chosen allows me to accept everything, remember the truth, and look at this body from outside. But this is not real, and I am not even here. I am not the one who created the dream. I can only be the one watching it. I am not the Nevşah inside the dream. But even if I am in a dream, I am here since I am everywhere. When you remember the truth, you can look at this body. When you look at this body, you can face saying, "Let's look at what is there."

First of all, there is something. The blood is flowing to the veins. The heart is beating with this energy. There is an organism moving within that burning fire. All you can do is be a human, accept it, and come down here. After you come down here, the awakening starts. The energy jumps first to the heart, then to the third eye, and then to the whole information. In the breathing session, you need to make the effort required to breathe from the stomach. If you cannot do this, nothing happens in the breathing session; the energy does not go down here. You need to make the energy go down here in the breathing session. Exhaling should happen naturally. The jump is the gift of your huge effort. In a sense, you go down to the depths of the earth, to the fire, to the energy of the life from here. You connect to that place. As a gift of connecting to that place, first, a great love begins automatically. It is about giving—how much you can let this place be. However much you can accept and forgive, it goes up here, and then the jump automatically comes up to here. The descending is about me; the escalation is about the system itself. Therefore, the path to awakening goes from here because there is no direct escalation here, and I am not doing the escalation. This escalation is made by the nature of the self, God's truth, because this is my journey back home, and I cannot do this. But I need to go deep in the world.

The way back is guaranteed because it is the reflection of God's plan. This is Adam; this is Eva. One is my choice; the other is God's plan. One is my will; the other is God's will. Therefore, if I rise by myself, if I intend for the information, it will not work. That is why awakening is downward. Of course, awakening is upward, but the way up goes from the way down. It is the direction. You cannot exhale before inhaling. There is no award without effort: inhaling and the effort there and exhaling and the devotion there.

The most successful people in the world are the ones who have done everything, the ones at the top of their career. And not being able to find anything …

There is something I always say. I hope you participating in the miracles course will have everything you want and see that this has nothing to do with the big picture—all your material and moral wishes, including your soul mates and twin spirits. I hope you will see that the truth is not about any of these. My will and God's will are a whole. I am writing the purpose of this place now. Here my will and God's will are a whole. Even in the dream, my power is the reflection of His power.

I do not know if this is a resistance. This my sixteenth or twenty-seventh breathing exercise. The miracle has started. I feel something close to fear and hate because I can breathe in 80 percent.

You are afraid to enter here, and you realize this. All the games of the ego are to keep you away from this place, from your humanity. The ego consciousness is making you fear your humanity by making you believe this is it; everything in the body is yours. Now you can remember the miracle consciousness and say, "This is a vehicle; this is not me. Therefore, her feelings have no effect on me. I can go as deep as it gets." This fire has nothing to do with my core. This is my human side, and that human is a dream. Okay then, I can go as deep as it gets. I can feel the emotions as deep as they go, and I can do what I am supposed to do in the world. I do not need to run away from the life in the world, from the action here, from doing. When you look from the miracle consciousness, you wake up to the fact that you can live anything, and you will do everything you are supposed to do.

While breathing, especially in the beginning, I got really tired. Like a whining child, I wanted to quit.

Not connecting to a feature coming from childhood. This develops from childhood.

Does it pass in time?

The mind does this. You need to be determined; it is not about time. You need to decide where you will stand. If you are in the miracle consciousness, nothing will scare you. You can go deep into pain; it does not matter. You are not associating yourself.

Oh, I think like I should let the breathing to enter by itself. "Do not do it; let it be."

Then there is an effort. You need to make some effort at this level. It means you have too much effort.

Should I be mad at this?

No. Do it with a little effortless effort. Something happens there automatically. But that is the next point. You need to make some effort until there.

You might say, "I am confused. You said there was neither emotions nor thought."

There is not. The things I am telling you are not feelings. The thoughts in the mind are not feelings. An emotion creates. It is emotion—the energy motion, the moving energy. Therefore, I meant his when I said I cannot label those emotions as emotions. It is moving, burning energy. You are talking about anger and ambition, but they are creations of the mind. There are two states: one is your natural energy, and the other is your thought of sabotaging that energy, along with the feelings produced by that thought. These feelings are not suitable for your nature, and if there is a feeling in your system, you need to be freed from it. If you feel messed up or bad, this is not a feeling. This is burning fire. I can say *ambition*, *fear*, and *pain*, but at the same time, it is none of them. All intense energies have nothing to do with the feelings produced by the thought. The feeling created by the thought is a pain that should not be in your system—a pain that messes with you and disconnects you from the world. For example, the depth I have mentioned is not a bad thing. The fact that you call that depth *bad* creates that feeling. Meltem just said, "Fear starts before the breathing session." The thought *This place is a scary place* puts fear there. There is no fear here. There is something truer here. Yes, it is similar to fear and panic, but it is not. Since you ascribe too much meaning, I am intentionally using words such as *fear*, *anger*, and *panic*. You need to ache for feeling them to connect. The mind has ascribed too much meaning here—here and the world. The mind ascribes meaning to the world, and the world is here in your body. All that burning energy, the blood, and the body symbolize the world. The mind has ascribed so much meaning to the world—and, therefore, to the burning fire in your body—that it thinks this place is a horrible place. It associates this place with pain and despair. If you associate that burning fire with fear and despair, you can connect to that place.

I started doing yoga. My third eye opened. My blinds have gone up.

I am not understanding these concepts. All I know is that an energy rises when you enter here—probably to the third eye. There is ascending. But only the opening of the third eye does not mean anything to me.

I experienced the thing I feared most in Çeşme. I was really afraid of losing my control and going mad, but during a session in Çeşme, I went deep, and I came out. After I came out, there was a huge love and need to tell. I am telling everyone. I felt my heart had expanded, and I started writing. I always want to tell because I cannot stay like this. That feeling came again. I will go deep again. I came to this advanced-level miracle because I want to live it. I need to enter there again to continue.

Of course, you need to ache for it. The expressions "My third eye is open" "My chakras are open," and "It has happened" are not relevant. This happens all the time. There is no opening and closing and then reopening and reclosing; there is no ending. This is about your breath. This may be better: I keep my breath and my system so open and am so careful about this and so committed to this that I can keep all my chakras, all my energy centers, open. It does not end when it is open. This is the world of action. When you stop doing, you are doomed. This is the law of the world. If I stopped the miracles courses, training, and sessions for a year, you would not even recognize me. I am not at a level that will allow me to stop—in the sense of consciousness, of course. It is not possible. I know what is what. Or if I stopped for a year and did it by myself, you would not recognize me, because doing the exercise myself and devoting myself here are different. I keep myself at this level because I continue giving. There is a law of giving in the world. Nothing you do not do happens. Yes, it happens at the level of truth, but this about myself, not about Nevşah. If I think I need to do something about myself, I will be wrong because the true me is the light itself. Let me tell you the mistake made by everyone: The true self is already the place remembering the truth, the light. It is the reflection of perfection and God. The true self says, "I am love and light; I am perfect." Why? Because it is His representative, like God's arm. He incorporates all of His features, and nothing is required for this.

I am in the perfect way as God created me. Here it is the physical mind-body of Nevşah. This mind-body, which operates as a simple electrical device and which contains this burning fire, has nothing like that. If you say, "Nevşah is who, and she does not need to do anything," then you are in an illusion. You understand the message like that because you still associate yourself with Nevşah. You have not realized that you are not Nevşah. If you mean Nevşah when you say, "I am whole and perfect," you have not understood yet. I have nothing to do with Nevşah. What is whole and perfect about Nevşah? As I remember that I am whole and perfect, I direct Nevşah to stay whole and perfect as she remembers the truth. I am the one who is directing Nevşah. I am the one who knows what wholeness, or perfection, is. I am the one who recognizes the wholeness and perfection in this world. I am also the one who recognizes the opposite.

I remember myself so well that when there is a mistake here, I would not say that mistake is whole and perfect, because it is not. When this body does not look as I want it to look, I am not so naive as to say, "But it is whole and perfect as it is." Why? Because I remember the truth. I am the one who knows wholeness and perfection. I know the whole and perfect state of this body. Why would I fool myself? I know when my life seems whole and perfect. Why would I fool myself? If you remember what wholeness and perfection are, you know this also here. You know the whole and perfect state of a relationship.

What happens if you do not make it whole? Your nature does not allow it. If I am in this body, this body will be whole and perfect, and I will always have her do something for this. I will make her do sports. I will be careful about her diet. I will do whatever is necessary because this body is in the world of doing. This body is not in the world of being. This body is whole and perfect. It is me. I am whole and perfect, and I am the one who can make this distinction. This is the light and miracle consciousness.

When you make this distinction, everything becomes clear. The world of bodies is the world of doing. I and my core are the world of being. These two have nothing to do with each other. I am the light itself. But it is impossible for my body to stay in the light by itself. This body needs to do something to stay in the light—to stay in the breath, to give training. Saying, "I am the light itself," does not interest the body. What does Nevşah have to do with this? It matters only if I am in the ego consciousness. When I say, "I am the light," you think Nevşah is saying this. No, I do not mean Nevşah here, but I make her say, "I am light," a hundred times a day to make her feel. Then Nevşah also becomes the light, and she can look like the light always in the world of doing. When I stop saying, "I am light," it will be all over. The most beautiful game of the ego is to say this: "I am whole and perfect. I do not need to do anything." You think Nevşah does not need to do anything because you see yourself as whole and perfect, because you are in the ego consciousness. If I can see that I am not Nevşah and can see from outside, I will see that I need to do plenty. The person needs to stay in action. You cannot leave it alone. Otherwise, it will turn into garbage; it does not have such a skill. I am the light itself, love and truth. Therefore, shouldn't I wake up? No. I reflect the awakening—me, the light itself, the self as the reflection of God. He never slept. Therefore, he does not need to wake up. Will this mind-body, Nevşah, wake up? No. She never will. Because she never slept. She is the role in this scenario. Will Romeo come out of the book and become a real man? This is nonsense; the man playing Romeo, his impersonation, is a player. This is a role. Why would a role wake up and revive? It will never understand and never know. It cannot know and understand within the story, within the spiderweb. It is not possible for it to know or understand love. Therefore, you need to let it be somewhere along the way.

When Meltem wants Öznur to understand, she does not. This limits you. But she will never understand and never know. Leave her alone. She does not have such a capacity. You do not need to wake up either. All you need to do is leave her alone. You cannot be the light because you cannot do this. You cannot understand you are the light because you deal with being the light while struggling to make the one that is not the light understand, while dealing with the role—which will never change—you have forgotten that you only play. For most people, this can be summarized as follows: An actor is only playing Romeo in the state. He goes home, and he still thinks he is Romeo. All you need to do is distinguish between these two.

It seems to me there is a dilemma here. The core, in a way, will not meddle with the mind-body. On the other side, it always has to force it to do something.

Let me put it this way: it's like a play. Now I am playing Juliet in *Romeo and Juliet*. As an actress, there are places I can interfere with, and there are places I cannot. For example, have you ever watched the same play with different actors and actresses? I have. Everything is the same—only the actor is different—but it looks as if something else is happening. While the actor is saying the same things, it looks as if something else is happening. This is where you interfere. As an actor, you can only interfere with how and where that role will be played. Another scared actor may say the same words, but it is about the energy.

He can say the same sentences, but you will not understand. Or an actor says such a thing that you will understand everything. Actually, the scenario does not change while everything else changes. There are certain concepts in the scenario: where you will be on which day, what will you wear, whom you will run into, and the speeches. You do not have any effect on these—not on a horizontal level but on a vertical level. The scenario is ideal. Two actresses will play it. One of them is professional; she does not associate herself with the scenario. So that she really understands Juliet, she is the same weight as Juliet, has the same hair, and mimics Juliet's hand movements. She is an awesome actress, and she never associates herself with the role; that is why she can act so well. She is so free from the role that she becomes Juliet. Then there is another actress. Juliet weights fifty-five kilos, and she weighs fifty kilos. Juliet has long hair, and she has short hair. She did not pay any attention. She did not practice the role; she did not understand it. The reason she cannot act is that she keeps criticizing the role. She missed the details of her role while saying, "How did Shakespeare write this play? Juliet should not have said that. She should have done this." She cannot act.

The scenario is such that you cannot make any changes that will affect it. It is not allowed. If you are a decathlon racer in the scenario, you cannot weight one hundred kilos. You cannot. But if you are behind a desk, it is possible. You can weight fifty or a hundred kilos. If there is a decathlon racer in the scenario, your primary concern will not be your weight. That is dealt with within the scenario. If you are a model in the scenario, that is also done; that is your type. There are things in everyone's scenario that will not change, and there are things that can change. Those are about how well you play your role. When you look as Coşkun remembering the truth, remembering your wholeness and perfection, how much does Coşkun reflect this—100 percent, 80 percent, or 50 percent? You need to work there. That is it. I know what perfect, or whole, is. Therefore, when I look at Nevşah, I know where she will be more loving. But Nevşah cannot see this. If I think I am Nevşah, I will not be able to see either. This is one of the places we must understand well.

When I am in the miracle consciousness, I can see when Nevşah is full of love in that light. Then I say, "She must be like this here, and Nevşah is doing something about it." This happens automatically. I am not telling anything to Nevşah. The existence of this self shows something here. You are looking from the outside while the role is being played. But if you have chosen the ego consciousness and if you see yourself as the role, you cannot see what you are doing since you are inside. If you think you are really Juliet, you miss how well you play the role. You need to remember she is just a role. You shouldn't say, "You should have said this. She should have moved her hand like that." If I forget this, something stupid happens: even I raise my hand.

"I am whole and perfect"—I started to memorize this like a prayer. But the way you work Nevşah and the way I work Arzu in the world of doing are not the same. Our human designs are different. But are our perceptions of whole and perfect different?

The wholeness and perfection of Nevşah and the wholeness and perfection of Arzu are different.

We are not the same.

We are the same. Let me put it this way: For example, when Nevşah sits like this, at this moment, she feels whole and perfect. Arzu feels whole and perfect when she sits another way. Now, is sitting like Nevşah or Arzu whole and perfect? Whatever we choose in our consciousness is reflected here. If I choose wholeness and perfection in my consciousness, I am whole and perfect no matter if I did this or that, because this has nothing to do with the scenario. The problem begins because we cannot make this distinction. If the actress is perfect, she can play either Romeo or Juliet or Ayşe. If the actress knows herself, I am in the miracle consciousness, and when I look at the actress, I will be perfect even if I am playing a singer with eight kids who got married five times. I will be perfect even if I am playing a man living alone who never got married or had kids. This place has nothing to do with these. The consciousness here is continuously reflected here if you remember this place is light and if you do everything with light and love.

In my own experience, sometimes I do or say things that people would not tolerate if it were not me. But they see that I do or say it out of love. For example, you are an actress, and you say to the other actress, "You are a fool." This is in the scenario. When you say, "You are a fool"—what you say never matters—while remembering the truth and the love, the truth and love go to the other actress, and nothing but love is perceived. But when you say, "You are a fool," and forget you are love and think you are a body, the other actress gets offended. Has the event changed? No. You said the same thing. But everything changed according to how and with

AWAKENING

which consciousness you said it. When you say, "I love you," to someone from your heart, looking deep into his eyes, he will not leave your side for the rest of his life. You can repeat this sentence because it is in the scenario, but if it is not in the consciousness, it will not work. Therefore, the things in the scenario do not matter; what matters is what there is in that depth. Whom I have in my life is not important; the point where I found my relationship is important. You get satisfied with the play then. Ali, Veli, or Ayşe does not satisfy you. You are satisfied because there is love. Therefore, the scenario can stay as it is.

You will marry whom you are supposed to marry, and you will be friends with whomever you are supposed to be friends with. They can all stay the same. It will not matter when you are love. Or when you are not love, would it matter if you are with Ali or Veli? How you feel and who you are have nothing to do with this place. Who you are matters to you. This is the area you need to work on. You are responsible for holding yourself here. You need to stay in the miracle consciousness. The scenario is not under your responsibility; it happens automatically. However, because you confuse the two, you cannot stay where you need to stay due to dealing with the scenario and due to thinking about what to say to Ali. What you will say is already determined in the scenario. You forget that you are an actress and who you actually are. However, if you forget this place and use your time to remember who you are, this place will be a totally different place. The scenario is the same, and the role is the same but the highest possibility. There is great satisfaction there. There is the highest possibility in every scenario and every role. You are such a loving person that even your slap becomes lovely.

For two days, I have the same dilemma when I leave here. I have accepted the core. I have accepted the mind-body. It has a scenario, and it is playing that. But the core—where does it play?

I remember the thing you said. If I do not wash her, she will smell. If I make her eat fat, she will gain weight. Then I need to interfere.

The interference regarding this comes, Coşkun. You just need to step aside. As I have said, this is the discovery of the neurologists, thank God. I was expecting something like this. There is a reflex in the brain called the readiness potential. What you will do is determined eight seconds before you do it. Coşkun already gets these. "Get up. Take a shower.

Get up and do this." The vibration of those incoming messages changes according to what you choose in the brain. That incoming message is an electric circuit, and when you choose the miracle consciousness, the vibration changes. For example, it starts to say, "Shower twice." If you choose in your consciousness, the incoming message needs to be adapted because Coşkun has a high possibility and a low possibility. Coşkun is still Coşkun. Those messages come automatically according to the high or low possibility to a person in the miracle consciousness. For example, there is a scene in the role in which you are laughing. A person in the low vibration gets the message "Do not push yourself too much; laughing a little will be enough." There is still the message to laugh because the scenario has laughing. If you are in the miracle consciousness, the message will be "Laugh so beautifully that your whole face lights up." You laugh either way, but everything changes.

We look at physical examples, not physical ones—for example, Buddha.

Let me put it this way: do not get hung up on Buddha.

You and I are the same. We are perfect. For example, should a person who has finished this course quit smoking?

You are seeing the highest possibility. Do you think smoking can be in your highest possibility? The highest possibility of a body does not have to treat itself badly, but the low possibility in the scenario will. Therefore, you do not need to deal with the scenario.

The automatic messages are coming. There is automatic programming according to what you have chosen in your consciousness. For example, the next moment, because this is the world of possibilities. For example, Coşkun will take a step. But whether it is slow or fast, there are infinite possibilities regarding it. When you choose the ego consciousness, the lowest of these possibilities comes to you, and you do it. For example, you take a step, and your foot falls into a hole. But when you choose the miracle consciousness, you get another message, and you meet the love of your life. The system organizes one according to your choice and the other automatically. The scenario here does not change but gets modified according to your consciousness. But this happens automatically. Whatever happens, the point you need to work on is your choice because you only have power in this world of consciousness. Why? Because you are consciousness itself.

You are not this place, and your choice here causes an automatic change. You do not need to deal with it. Electricity from different dimensions comes. You go to a bookshop; there are infinite possibilities. The fact that you will go to a bookshop is in the scenario. It does not change. You choose one book in the low possibilities and another in the highest possibility. For example, your hand goes to one of the books of one of the miracles course writers because life changes automatically according to where you are. But when I say, "It is what it is," I am not saying that it will never change. Change happens automatically and as it is. I have no effect on this. The only place I have any effect is in what I choose in my consciousness. If I choose the miracle consciousness, the brain gets such messages that I live my highest possibility. I live a scenario like a dream. If I choose the ego consciousness, I automatically live a scenario in the low vibration.

Now it is clear. From the beginning, you have been saying, "The scenario never changes." When you say that, it looks as if the scenario will not change according to the possibilities.

The thing that does not change is that there is no interference with the infinite possibility. The automatic system determines it. Therefore, after a decision is made, after your decisions regarding the consciousness are made, change is hard. Because at that moment, something is changed.

I had nausea when I left here yesterday. I wanted to lie down, but I remembered what you said: "I am here. This place must be perfect. I must do the best." For example, my daughter is one month old, and she needed a bath, so I gave her a bath.

At the point of "I am perfect, and everything is perfect," the brain automatically gets the message "Give your daughter a bath." You cannot stop it. "Go there. Do this. Do sports"—these messages come. Changes happen according to your choice. The possibilities have changed. Your possibilities are rising. Maybe the person you run into in the scenario does not change, but the relationship changes. Maybe you speak about the same subject, but the worlds change. But you are still with that person. In one possibility, you fight, and in another, you are honeys.

The hardest thing to live is communicating.

In what sense? If you cannot communicate, you are in the ego consciousness. If the person across from you cannot understand you, you are in the ego consciousness. If I remember my wholeness, I understand them, and they understand me. It is always like this. All misunderstandings show that you are still dealing with the scenario, as do all hardships. Hardship is relative. For some, breaking their leg is hard; for others, a lack of money is hard; and for others, being stuck in traffic is hard. Whatever they are, those hardships are a reflection of your choice of consciousness. For example, I sprained my leg at the hotel. At that moment, Nevşah saw what it was. I said, "I need to rest; this happened because I did not rest." If that had happened in a lower consciousness, I would have slipped so hard that I cracked my head. This is a grace. I already wanted to rest, so I gave my training sitting down.

At home, they tell me, "You were good when you came back from Çeşme."

Then you would more in the miracle consciousness there. When you came back, you started to fall into the ego consciousness because you need to continue the action in the world of doing. You can only leave it empty when you are in the ego consciousness. When you associate yourself with this place, the problems start. For example, if had chosen the ego consciousness and thought I was Nevşah—I am whole and perfect; I am the miracle, the light itself—I would have started by saying, "Nevşah does not need to do anything." However, when I separate myself from Nevşah, Nevşah has to do always. Why? She is neither whole nor perfect. She is neither love nor light. I am all these. I made the distinction. What comes after: "Work on the miracles course, your lesson, and your role, and give breathing sessions." Just do.

One of the most important notes of today was the chapter of the energy of life. I have a problem with the activation and doing there. Since I am still in the ego consciousness, I know something is supposed to be, but I cannot act. You said that one method of activating this energy of life is adrenaline—sports. But since our human designs are different, I am heavier. To solve this, am I supposed to look at the human design in more detail and find ways to activate this?

I think the whole thing is living according to the human design, because it is the core of your scenario. For example, it was important for me to be able to look from my human design. Something will come out of there; it will be clear.

I confuse the world of being and doing. I was trying to ring being to the world, and it did not work.

It does not work with anybody. At the point of truth, the thought *I am whole and perfect* is a great thought. It works. It is the only way to be peaceful, especially by staying calm, but it does not work in this world.

Knowing *doing* really calmed me. In the first session, I was abruptly on the floor like the monkeys in *Tarzan*. I said, "There is so much to do."

That is what happened to me in my first session. Yes, there is much to do. This place is like that.

I thought if I told someone on the street, he would understand. It excited me. Not I worked for so long with my mind. Now there is no past or future. I want to live in the moment.

You are saying, "I am here."

I felt the things my friends told me. But I know human relations are not easy. Why do divorces happen, for example?

Because the scenario has a divorce. Let's look at an example. It might be an irrelevant example, but that's okay. You buy a cake on your birthday and eat it with a couple of friends. You eat more the next day. Someday it's gone. Some relationships end. It is what it is, like the cake that ends. That is it. Relationships end because you argue and cannot get along, or sometimes they end just because they end. One of the best examples is my separation from transformal breathing. I was originally a transformal breathing trainer. I was Turkey representative. While I was representing Judith's trend, one day my path with them came to an end. We were still good friends, though; we loved each other. Only that road came to an end. That is it. We were both in the truth and the miracle consciousness, and we both felt it as it happened. One day, when I said, "I want to talk to you," she looked into my eyes and said, "I know what you will say." This is what happens in the miracle consciousness. We are still friends, but that road came to an end. Now I see that it was a huge step.

Transformal breathing cannot reach NFS. In my vision, I saw the place I reached today and even ten years later. This is a start even for us; we are still going with baby steps. I see where we are ten years later. For example, transformal breathing will not come with me ten years later. Similarly, some come with you at one point, and then they cannot. They go somewhere else. Only paths are separated. It is the ego that ascribes pain to the separation. Many people experience pain when they go to the bathroom; you are also separated from something there. Many people ascribe meaning to death. Death is not something painful. You are separated from something every day. I left my husband and my daughter in the morning; I am here now. It does not matter. This is life. You get separated, and you unite or not.

I think happiness is also nonsense.

If you associate happiness with life, then it is. There is too much nonsense in the foundation of life. That foundation does not exist. The word does not even have a foundation. It is meaningless and nonsense. It is meaningful because I am here. I am here; therefore, nothing is nonsense. The times you call meaningless and nonsense are all the times you are not here. We must see right there. All the periods in which I saw nonsense and meaninglessness in life were the ones when I was not there. If the self is there, there is no nonsense, meaninglessness, or unhappiness. Everything is meaningful. Everything is meaningful because you know yourself. Everything is God's reflection. The most powerful saying possible is "I am here. As long as I am here, everything is my reflection."

When we speak, we speak from our mind. Therefore, maybe we should not speak but just meditate.

Everyone sees others as himself. What you say is new to me because the words come from your mouth from a point I never experienced: the mind. What you said—talking from the mind, planning, saying after thinking—is a far edge for me. There is no mind at the moment and the consciousness.

Don't we create duality by separating the body and spirit?

Did you work on these enough? Did you do the work? Did you embrace the mind?

Yes. We need to own our minds. We need to love the mind to unite.

I will say this: no thought that is questioned enough can be claimed. Therefore, I would have listened to you if you had told me, "Maybe it is like that." But you are saying, "We need to do it like that." These need-tos are the extension of a cycle of mind that was not questioned. Therefore, I am telling you to first question these, and then let's look at those thoughts with *maybe*.

Let me put it this way: when I look at the mind and the body as separate beings, the duality ...

Does Yonca think that this duality does not exist, even after this training of three days?

I think it does not exist because, for example, you are talking about a role. The person acts the best if you cannot understand he is acting. When you see him as a role, the duality comes. You need to integrate the scenario.

This is personal. But do you really want feedback? You are so mad at the duality that you cannot get out of it and look from there.

I feel the opposite.

You have an angry voice. I understand the side that does not want duality to exist.

No, I am not saying what I want to. If we are going to do something here, since there is nothing out there, there is only me. Everything I see is a reflection of me. The things that bother me in the scenario are the ones I need to fix. When I see that thing, I will fix it, and when I fix it in me, I will be satisfied with myself.

Please, will the ones who have understood what Yonca said raise your hands? Look carefully, Yonca. Are the things you have said true? These are your personal illusions. You need to let it go. Take a deep breath. Nobody can understand you now because you are in your mind, and it is your dream. You can wake up. It is time. You are disconnected from everyone when you are there. We do not even understand what you are doing. You shut yourself to the whole world. Do you want to be here with us? We all get you; we are all mad at the duality here when we look at it from the point of truth, from singularity. But as a thought, it does not exist; it is totally different. Another illusion. When you see this, you accept.

If you change, the person across from you changes also. He says, "It takes one to know one." You see yourself in that person, striking a happy medium instead of conflicting. Everything will be okay then—not doing what he says but knowing yourself.

For example, I am saying I am not the old Selvan.

It is my understanding that you need to continue working so as not to be the old Selvan. You are not saying, "I went to the miracle, it happened, and now it is over."

But I am getting really mad at something.

But you need to continue working. Work never ends. You are in the world of doing. You have to continue doing.

In constantly questioning life, going back, and questioning the future, I have understood that they are totally empty. The right thing is living in the moment.

I am in the moment not because it is the right thing but naturally. What else did you see?

I have a heart. I saw that. My heart really started to beat. I did not feel anything before I came here. It was a period when I thought what I was living was not meaningful.

You are in love. You are in love!

From time to time, I used to feel as if my heart would jump out of my chest during presentations at work. I lived that today. Totally different. Something about me.

You have started to be impatient, right? About being in life. Has it started in all of you? Super. And what else?

I have been in the miracle consciousness only in the last month. I am aware of the truth, and I am trying to take it here. I will go crazy. This place does not seem real to me.

You have woken up to the fact that you need to bring the meaning. That point is the point where people really go mad. If you cannot turn this place into the reflection of the truth—if you cannot turn this place, this body, this hall, and everything you meet into the representation of the magnificence, holiness, and light of the core—you will go mad. You will not rest until you look here and see the meaning, including this glass you are touching. When you see meaning everywhere you look, you are here. This is not information from the mind; these are firsthand experiences. When I am in the miracle consciousness for twenty-four hours, when I remember the truth in every second, this place becomes a reflection of the truth. If this place is meaningless, if it is nonsense, then I was not in the miracle consciousness. I do not remember. If had remembered, I would not have left this child, humanity, alone here. I would have done something. I would have held her. I would have illuminated her path. This Nevşah is in the dark. This Nevşah cannot see ahead. This Nevşah is limited and restricted, and she cannot produce love. She cannot produce light either. Since I am the love and light, I have to support Nevşah in her journey. If I leave her alone, she will not see ahead. Everything will seem meaningless. All she sees will be duality, and she will be lost in it. I am the one who brings the whole and the meaning, and I am here. Therefore, wholeness and meaning are here.

The miracles course does not say, "I ascribe meaning to everything." It says, "I am the one who brings meaning to everything." Understanding this like this is regarding the ego consciousness. It does not want me to be here and to turn this place into heaven. The miracles course says, "If I am not here, there is no meaning; there is nothing. But if I am here, even this glass is God's reflection."

After the miracle, something started to get better inside me. My husband, whom I used to see as a monster. I came to a point where I was hospitalized. But until then, I always held on to him. I was afraid of separation. At that point, I said, "It is over. Why am I afraid? I am strong. I can survive." But something happened to me.

The self supported Emel. The self backed Emel. What happened? This happened. The self sided with Emel. This is the same for everyone. The self gripped Emel's whole system, and it reflected its power on Emel. I am the one making it strong.

Later, my husband's behavior changed. I did not understand how it happened. He was the same man. I was just where I was. I stopped saying, "So be it."

This has nothing to do with Emel. That self came here. It is only about that. When the self comes here, it touches everything; it changes everyone. Emel cannot do this.

Since my childhood, my head has worked in a complicated manner. I was hung up on concepts once. I felt as if none of them had any meaning. "What is a lie?" I would ask myself. "What is?" My life was a mess. Then I went adrift. I stopped asking these questions. Then the second voice started talking again. This time, I started asking other questions, such as "What is time?" Then there was a third voice. I was already in a bad period. I started hearing voices all over. It was weird. "Which one of them will I listen to?" I asked.

Do you want me to say what exactly is happening? You cannot decide which consciousness to choose. There are different messages from different consciousnesses.

Then, with breathing, I left the miracles course. Then there was another voice, saying, "I exist. I exist." I said, "Let it be; you will do whatever you want to." Now there are constant voices. In this training, I better understood what I tell to stop, who the voices are, and who I am. Therefore, I am pretty comfortable. I am living in the moment. The machine is working. I even play with her. I say, "Come on. You have work to do. Go. Do this." While she does it, I sit as if I am on holiday.

This is the miracle consciousness. While all of this happens, I also wander around. You have separated yourself from Volkan. There is nothing better. Already your message is coming: "Get up at these hours. You have to pee. You are hungry." It continues automatically, and you are in the background."

I said, "I think this will never end. You need to do it again and again every single day."

There is a better idea: have it done. The next level is having it done.

I wanted to give breathing sessions to the men I saw on the street after the sessions. But then I said, "Why are you telling so much information to everyone? They cannot see!" But now I want to have my colleagues do.

You can only come to a certain point in your own process. It is not possible without touching someone else, without supporting. After the miracles course, you need to train others right away, even if it is just one person. When the teacher is ready, the student will also be ready. When you start training, you will see that is when you can stay in the miracle consciousness.

In summary, the only true relationship is our relationship with God. He is the Creator and the teacher in the relationship, and we are His students. The only relationship in the world is between the teacher and the student. Actually, nothing happens in this world. I am not sure if any of you have read the stories of Merlin and Arthur, a holy being and a human, and the dialogues between them. That is it. When am I a human and when a holy being? It always changes. Little Arthur is the child inside us, and Merlin is the holy self called the Son of God, the Holy Spirit, the core self, the side searching for the truth.

Who is Adam, and who is Eva? These are really intertwined. This is what we call a relationship. The human knows nothing, is helpless in the dark, and feels alone, burning desperately within those deep feelings. The holy self is the side that remembers that all these things are not real. It is the side that remembers the truth, light, and love. One is burning, and the other one is putting water on the fire. The little child keeps crying, and the self says, "None of this is real," and it embraces him with all his love. That is the whole thing. Nothing other than that happens. It does not even happen here. But this happens for us.

Actually, we all have had examples of not being totally disconnected from the self.

You cannot. The body and the spirit are not the same.

We actually had miracles in our lives. Is it because we are so disconnected nowadays?

You eventually need to make a distinction between the two. In your journey starting with the miracles course, your human side started the journey of learning from your spirit, that wise and holy self. In this course, I am Merlin, and you are the little Arthur. Merlin is a holy being, and Ebru is a little child. This goes on like this. For example, this information can come because Nevşah is ready to learn everything from the holy being. Since I do not let Nevşah go, nobody lets me go. I have many experiences like this. They are all intertwined. But this is the only relationship. It is actually a reflection of the relationship of God with Himself and with me. This happens here like this. In other words, the world is the place of relationships. Normally, there is no relationship. A human and a divine being are required for a relationship.

Is doomsday real?

Let's not go there. It is the subject of the miracles course. Doomsday already happened a few times in this course—the revolt.

When you understand what the scenario really is, you feel comfortable with all those voices. Now I understand.

This is a huge gift. I know all our systems in NFS are a gift to us—a real gift, a savior, the reflection of our salvation. Yes, and?

I have been going through the processes you told about—the crying, not leaving the bed if I am allowed, and getting up to do whatever you need to and then going to bed again. Everything seems meaningless. I would be relieved if I slept and never woke up again.

The answer is hidden here: "Everything seems meaningless. Then why do I exist?" Look how simple and how meaningless it is. "Why do I exist?"

To give meaning. "Everything is empty. What will I do?" I will fill them. That is all. There is no love—what will happen? You will bring love. It's that simple.

A doctor I went to said, "You are depressed; you need medication." But on my fourth day, I started saying, "I do not want to take the medication." I am surprised this happened only in four days. One part of me says, "You need the medication."

Lilya needed medication because the self was not by her side. As long as the self is with her, she will not need anything. "I am here"—this is the answer to all your questions. Will the self leave something? Nothing stays outside infinity. You are already in it.

I was writing stories when I started coming to NFS. In one story, there was I and myself. I and myself were trying to kill each other. Should I kill me or myself? After the sessions, I said, "We will live like this."

In summary, that little child needs the self, and he will do anything for it. That is why the little child is in the world of doing. He has the capacity to do anything for it. Anyway, the one who remembers he is everything does nothing. He has the capacity of doing nothing. Do not confuse these two. Existence does not need anything. It is already whole and full. He needs nobody; he needs to neither go somewhere nor come from somewhere. He just stays there. But in that little child, in the human, there is nothing. Because he is nothing. He does not exist. There is nothing—an alone cloud of dust. He needs everything. Since he needs everything, that little child will do anything to get the love, light, nutrition, and power he desperately needs from that holy being, from existence. Since he does everything, he is in the world of action and doing. You need to understand and see this. That is the place where he is limitless. He will do anything to meet his needs. That is why he is in the world of doing. But the self that is part of existence wants to do nothing. Then who will execute the work of doing? Nevşah. The self does not want to do anything. The whole responsibility is in the self. It just stays there and erupts. You need to do something to take from it. You are an expert in doing anything.

I am sure this is becoming clear: the human and the Son of God. The human is Nevşah, born from a human, and there is the life, the Son of God, which is not born from Him but a part of Him. The Son of God is by the side of the human. The human needs to do something to remember this. The Son of God does no need to do anything to remember.

Is the distinction clearer now? Do you see the integrity in that distinction? Do you see the perfection in the background of that distinction? Do you see that the flow in that relationship is the energy of life? That communication is a huge deal.

I want to ask something. I have seen this movie. I feel like this. The mission is here. They laid it before me and told me to do it, and I said I would, and I started to give. But I did not know how that system worked in the world. I think that then I did not fulfill the mission; I took a step back and turned into my state in this world. I am here now; the mission is being assigned again. But my past failure causes me to doubt whether I will be able to achieve this. I wonder if it was a mistake to take on that mission when I was not ready.

You actually know the answer to that. That is why I will not respond.

Maybe I do know, but I feel such huge remorse. I have a second question: Was it a mistake to leave it then?

First of all, there is no mistake in the scenario. It is the scenario. It starts with the big bang, a failure. Since the scenario comes from that seed, if you look at the world in the ego consciousness, everything is erroneous or faulty. The core is this when there is no truth. It is my miracle consciousness who will fix that error and failure. There is a mistake here. What will I do? I will fix it. There is a failure, a problem. What will I do? I will solve it. The Son of God talks like this to the human. These things happened because you probably did not allow the fix or because you did not look at the thing to be fixed. When you took over that mission, when it was working here, it came here to fix something. Now you are more aware on the subject. The mission is changing here. Your mission is remembering that you are here and transforming this place into what you want. The enjoyment and the joy are there. Like in old cartoons, everywhere is dark, and there are trees with horns in the place where the witch is. Out of nowhere, an angel, a representative of the miracle consciousness, comes. When she takes a step, everywhere blooms with flowers and grass, and the birds start to sing. When we take a step, everything and everywhere changes. Remember, at the end, everywhere freezes in *The Snow Queen*. It actually tells it really well. When you are in the ego consciousness, you let the world be. The reflections of the ego consciousness are letting it be, not caring, and horns.

The human mind may operate with fear now, but when it starts to operate with love, the human mind becomes one with God's mind and disappears. Then the spirit and the mind unite.

We call this consciousness, and we call it the mind cycle of past and future.

What I mean is the thinking mind. When it becomes one with God, there will be only God's thoughts. There will be a moment when the mind unites with God's mind, and there will be no humans.

I am telling this, but we call the mind the consciousness. We call that union "I am here." I tell the state when it happened, and you are telling it as if it is in the future. This is the problem.

4

Final Messages

You cannot lose yourself.

The only thing you cannot lose is yourself.

It is not true that you do not know yourself. You do not know a mortal mind-body. You know yourself well. You know that you are an infinite spirit, and you know what that means. That is why you cannot understand death and why you feel as if you will never die.

Because you will not. You are a representation of the Creator, but your body is not. When I say this, I do not mean a person. I mean the truth, the reality of the infinite spirit. This body is a temporary vehicle given to you so you can travel in a temporary world.

You do not need to know yourself, your spirit, your core, but you need to know your body and mind. You need to learn what is good for your body and mind. Why? Because you do not know.

An infinite being cannot know or understand something mortal within a temporary dream. It can only learn what it is.

An infinite being, a representation of the Creator, the one who was never born and never will be and who never died and never will, does not know this mortal body, this mortal world, and the temporary. That is why the world is a place you learn—not because you need to learn but because you inherently know nothing.

5

WHAT HAVE WE LEARNED?

None of the people perceive the truth as I do, as known by the core. The reason for this is their not choosing the core self and their caring about the world and the human.

Even when I, as a reflection of my true self, am sure about my identity and stand undoubtedly before the people, they might not believe me, because as long as they do not choose the core inside them, they cannot see *I*. The minds that choose to be human cannot connect to the core self; therefore, they can neither write a book like this one nor be an inspiration for thousands of people or serve the single purpose. They are preoccupied with being a good and right person. Their minds want to know how to be a good, right person, not the truth.

Even if I am sure of myself and my true identity, the people—the human side—might doubt that I am me. They cannot perceive the possibility that I can always be a reflection of the infinite self.

That is the test of the human. They cannot know the self even if they see it right in front of them. They judge, criticize, and defame the ones they do not recognize, know, or understand. The person who has chosen the true identity refuses the human identity; he is no longer like the other people because he did not accept being a human.

It is not possible for the human to understand the point of self-confidence. At that point, when we are connected to the core at all times, the human consciousness can do anything to prove the contrary.

The miracle consciousness—the truth—says, "I will not talk to the human because even if I did, it would not understand," and the ego consciousness gets angry at this because it feels humiliated. When I say,

"You cannot reach this information," it says, "If you could, I will too," because it perceives me as human. However, the ones in the miracle consciousness can say, "Yes, you are right. I cannot reach that information because it is only you who can." The information comes from a single channel. The ones who know that channel shut up and listen when it is open.

You cannot understand the core with the human consciousness.

Therefore, people who chose the human side cannot understand the people reflecting the self.

A person who is aligned with his true self and remembers his true identity will not ever care about the humans, let alone criticize or judge them. His presence says, "Who the hell are you?" to the ego. That is why people who have chosen the ego and the human feel humiliated, not appreciated, in the presence of people who have chosen the truth.

Look at the world and the humans with the light of the truth. What do we see? What happens in the realms below?

Humans cannot keep their promises. Most people are not aware of how effective their promises are. A promise is magic; when you give it, the whole life shapes around it. Unfortunately, since most people are not aware of this, they give various promises every day, which take their lives in different directions, and then they wonder the reason for the unbalance in their lives.

We learned that most people pretend to be a good person. Even they do not know what good it does, but I guess they have this belief in their minds: *If I become a good person, then things will follow their course.* Pretending to be a good person makes people sick; I also learned this. The human is within a duality, just like the world, which means the human is both good and bad, healthy and unhealthy, calm and crazy. Only strong people, the people who have made peace with themselves, are able to accept this duality. The rest are busy with being good, and unfortunately, this can be nothing but an empty dream. When they do this, they cannot realize how much they hurt themselves. The only way for a human to be healthy, happy, and strong is to be himself, both good and bad, healthy and unhealthy, calm and crazy. However, the ones trying to be only good or only calm have a huge war inside them since they are not totally at peace with themselves. They die off and enter into some weird feelings.

The human does what he does to himself. The ones who do not make peace with themselves—the ones who try to be only good, successful, and beautiful; try to different from others; and try to be ahead of others with the features they try to have—are the ones in the back. As long as they do this, as long as they crush one part of themselves, they make themselves smaller. The loser human model is formed, and they are always crushed in society.

Imagine a person who has accepted his existence, including all his features—good and bad, beautiful and ugly, polite and rude, calm and nervous—and uses his full potential at all times. Whatever he needs to be and whatever he needs to do, he is and does—not caring about whether it is good or bad. He just lives 100 percent. However, a person trying to be good, successful, polite, or whatever is always on tenterhooks. He tries too hard to reveal a feature of himself and to conceal another feature. Here is the result: first feeling stress and anxiety, then being a loser, then feeling anger in the awareness of this, and then probably cancer. Naturally, being yourself is the best. Humankind, there is no need to try so hard. We all are everything. Take it easy!

A group of people cannot find the time to live life by interpreting it. This is hilarious. They cannot find the time to just live life as it is freely and do what they want to because they are too busy to interpret it. They waste so much time on interpretations—rights, wrongs, shoulds, and meanings; who did what with whom; and who is where—that they cannot even feel the life flowing.

A few days ago, while sitting on the beach, I overheard someone talking, and I burst into laughter. She said, "I cannot understand people. They share every moment on Instagram and Facebook. I think they are not enjoying the moment. They cannot enjoy life while taking pictures." I wanted to go ask, "Honey, are you aware of the fact that we are at the beach right now?" She was so caught up in her thoughts and comments that I am sure she did not realize the sea and the beach. These people talk about not being able to seize the moment and how people miss life. I've learned that people think everyone is in their situation. Who knows? Maybe the person who posts pictures on Instagram enjoys life when she does this. Maybe at that moment, she feels like it, and she does whatever she wants to do unconditionally and without asking questions. If she wants to post a picture, she does it, and she enjoys posting a picture on Instagram at the moment. Then she turns and drinks a glass of water. Who knows? Comments, judgments, and thoughts, not actions, take us away from the moment.

People think they can conceal themselves. This is also hilarious because this never happens. Every person carries his though structure, belief system, breathing habits, past, and point of view wherever he goes. People affect every environment with these, with their inner state. All around you have experienced the times when you are with them and the times when you are not, so they know how it feels and who you are. I find people thinking they can conceal themselves funny. I experience without you; I experience with you; and between my experience of being alone and my experience of being with you, there is your experience, you. I want to say to everyone I meet, "I know you better than you know yourself." I want to wake everyone up. Everyone sees and knows everyone; nobody can conceal himself. I want everyone to wake up and stop claiming to be someone other than himself. It's a waste of energy and a pity.

Humans have forgotten the truth of the spirit and His pureness and beauty. Otherwise, when they saw the self, they would recognize since they would know themselves. Recognition aside, they cannot even understand what they see.

The people who are closest to us are the people who reflect us the best and show us who we are and where our consciousness is: our partners, children, and friends. Someone married to a politician is also a politician. Someone married to an athlete is also an athlete. The partners of the people show everything about them because a partner is a reflection of the person's mental choices.

In the world, spiritually, women are stronger than men. A woman can destroy anyone when she wants to. Every woman is half wizard and half witch. The female body contains the creative and changing features of the Creator. The woman who is aware of this manages the world and changes the world with every thought, and yes, when she wants to, when she is in her dark side, she can destroy someone and even wipe someone from the earth just by thinking. The woman has such a power. Every woman knows this but cannot say. Therefore, you would not want to hurt a woman, especially a powerful woman who is aware of herself. When a woman is sad, the angels run to help and say, "Mother, your wish is my command." Whatever the woman wants, it happens. That is how babies happen—with the will of the woman. Men should be careful about this. If they hurt a woman or if they cannot get the heart and permission of a woman, life may be hard for them. Many men get sick, fail, and fall materially and morally because of this. Heaven lies at the feet of the mother. If you want heaven, you need to be more careful around women. When you have understood this, then you have understood the universe.

A person who crushes himself in his mind; does not let himself do what he wants to do; thinks like society, his partner, his friends, the rules, and the system; and feels the need to be approved becomes a loser individual. Loser individuals criticize the people who express themselves and have the freedom and power to do anything, good or bad. Actually, loser individuals see what they want to be and criticize because they cannot be like those who are free. If you are criticized, you must have done something good, and if someone is picking on you, it is because you are in a higher place. Never look down. Continue living as you want to your heart's content, limitlessly, and let them admire you. Maybe one day they will take your example and rise to your level.

I have learned that the more you have, the more you fear losing. However big the thing you own is, it becomes impossible to lose it, because you stick your heart and soul to it.

The things people ascribe meaning to shape their lives. People meet the point of the things they ascribe meaning to. Because of the order of the universe, humans can only be together with people with the same values. Similar values bring similar people together. Therefore, be careful about what you value in life. Your values will determine your path in life.

Love is the only truth. However, the human cannot know true love. People say, "I am full of love," but they are actually full of judgment. Love and judgment cannot be together. Love and limit cannot be together either. At that moment, they must wake up. They must say, "Love does not exist in the world," and they must let their human sides go. However, most cannot do this.

The bigger a light you are in the world, the harder it is for people to understand you. None of the enlightened spirits were understood in their centuries. They were all understood later. In every age, there were people who ascribed meanings to the enlightened people and criticized, judged, and stoned them because they could not understand. The light and love are a dimension the human cannot understand. Since the light and the love are a state in which you cannot know how to flow and what to do, they come differently in every period. Love gave its messages through wars in one period, meditation in another period, and self-expression in another period.

Now we are in a process wherein enlightenment is freedom, and as in every period, there are people who are not enlightened and cannot see, understand, or realize because of their darkness. The sentences "I am different from you. I am the one bringing the light. I am the one who has chosen God" echoed differently in the ears of people in each century. In each period, the messenger seemed different to the people. The messenger always told the people there was a messenger, someone carrying God's message, but they never believed that messenger. This is the classic story. Every messenger encountered believers and nonbelievers. Most could not see the truth, purity, freedom, wisdom, and greatness the messenger's body and humanity had. Because they chose to be human and to stay tiny, they could not see. This greatness scared them; it was never credible since they thought they could never be that great. Then the jealousy came, and they could not see that they were delaying their own awakening with the comments "Do you see yourself as enlightened and over everything? I think you should question yourself. If you say these things, then you are not there." This has been the case for centuries.

The human is lost within the human.

The human is lost within his humanity—his emotions, thoughts, points of view, and perceptions.

The human cannot turn to himself while wasting time in analyzing himself and, therefore, others.

The human is lost in the earthly choices and behaviors.

There is still hope because you still have the chance to leave the human; your humanity; and the loss, boundaries, limits, and mistakes.

Why not now?

Epilogue

The truth stays where the true self is, and it is waiting for you.

The way to reach this place is simple but singular.

You have woken up to the fact that you have two identities because of the duality of the world. One is your concrete identity, the one with a name and shape. The other one is your abstract identity—your spirit, your breath, your self.

The truth is connected to your abstract identity by your spirit, and it is where you are.

First, the state of doing must end in order for you to reach that place in the world, the state of being.

In other words, you need to do and finish whatever you need to do in the world to switch to the state of being.

If you do the requirements of your role in the world, do whatever you are supposed to do, say whatever you are supposed to say, and stop limiting yourself with your concrete identity, then you live touching your abstract identity.

You can reach the state of being only when you finish the state of doing—when you finish what you are supposed to do.

Therefore, a person who is limiting himself can never reach the truth. Only the persons who express themselves 100 percent can reach the truth—their core, their spirit, the state of being.

The truth starts when the ego ends.

The ego ends with the end of the state of being—when you only play your role and do what you are supposed to do.

Love starts where it ends.

Live whatever you came to the world to live. Stop limiting yourself.

Finish what you need to finish, do what you need to do, and say what you need to say. Just allow everything your role requires.

When you do this, you will see that your ego ends in the moment, and you become connected to your core.

Finish it. End the ego.

End the world. End your life in the world.

Live whatever you are supposed to live, and finish the road.

Otherwise, you will be in the way to reach the truth but can never reach it.

You cannot take the world to the afterlife, the place where you are connected to the truth.

If you want to wake up and stay awake, first finish the world. You will have wishes, desires, targets, things you came to the world to do, things you came to say, and things you will chase, just like everyone else.

Again, just like everyone else, you will need to go after those wishes, desires, and targets.

However, as you and I both know, you will go after them not because they are valuable but because you want to finish the world and end the world and the ego.

Good boy! Keep on walking on the earth. Whatever happens, whatever the obstacle is, keep walking. Do not look back, right, or left. Do not care what people say or do. Do what you know. Walk on your path, and finish what you are supposed to live.

There is no other way.

You need to turn your back to the ones who do not understand you, do not know you, and see the body, not you. Turn your back to all of them. This will be your final test.

Final Test

There is a final test the consciousness who has chosen the truth must take in the world.

Most people call this the last temptation or the last seduction.

The world is trying to tempt the ones whose golden eye is open, the ones who have known since the day we were born. It brings millions of traps in front of us to make us give up on ourselves, go out of our path, give up on being ourselves, be political, and live moderately. Unfortunately, many people live by giving up on themselves now. They chase after the things they have ascribed meaning to and the things that dazzle them, and they sell themselves, their core, their true wishes, the things they want to say, and the things they want to do for those things.

Many people give up on themselves to be loved and liked and to have a good social environment. They have ascribed so much meaning to the human that they are busy buying more humans by selling themselves; their core; and their true wishes, words, and thoughts. The more they are liked the better. The more people like them the better. It is obvious they will be disappointed when they understand that the human is just a void and a cloud of dust, just as this universe is, because they have invested in the void. They have sold themselves, and they bought void in return. They gave up on themselves for the void—for nothing. Every day I see people who have made this choice and sold themselves to be loved or liked by humans—clouds of dust—face what they have done with the pain they suffered by giving up on their cores for nothing as their breathing opens. I work with these people. I understand them and know them well.

The ones who do not know themselves are the ones who have chosen fear. They ascribe meaning to the world, and they are scared of dying, being without any friends, not being loved or liked, having their social environment collapse, failing, and being broke. In summary, they are afraid of the shape of their status in the world. Thus, they cannot live as they want to, and they sell their core for the position they obtain in the world.

The ones who know themselves know this.

They know "I am a human. I am different from the other humans. Not everybody has to like me. There may be people who do not like me and who criticize me in my path, but it does not matter. Humans and thoughts are just clouds of dust, and they cannot stop me." They say, "Living my core brings such great pleasure and life energy that I do not need the world to honor me. I do not need to be applauded." Because they know.

Because of what you know; because you know yourself and cannot stop yourself when others are political, limit themselves from saying what they want to say, and stop themselves; and because you will never give up on knowing yourself, experiencing your core, and doing whatever you feel like doing, even in the world, you must stay away from the ones who do not know themselves.

This will be your last choice.

I know this is a tough choice. But you know that this is your final choice.

This is your final decision.

If you know yourself, you have to stop being friends with a place you know not to be true: the world.

The world has done everything to dazzle you, take your mind away, and make you forget the truth you have known since birth. You faced test after test, trap after trap, and obstacle after obstacle, but you were never fooled. You always left. You always left the world. You did not touch it, and you have passed the test.

Now there is one final test: the world will test you with the truth you know and are sure of.

It will test the teacher with what she has taught.

The things told by people will not happen.

The prophecies of people will not come true.

They just guess, and none of them come true, because the ones who have chosen humanity, who have chosen to be asleep, do not know.

What they say will never happen.

Life will never flow as they say. They are always nervous and angry because of this. They are actually angry at their limited perceptions. They do not want to admit how little they know. They do not want to see what their choice has done to them, and when they see true power in you (in me), they want to sıp it with the traps they have implemented for themselves. They can never be successful.

The world is neither a friend nor an enemy for the ones who know themselves; it does not exist. Therefore, they do not go after it. It's that simple.

When the final test is close, the person who knows herself is tested for the truth. She knows the truth is distributed to the world through her mouth, but in the world, humans twist her truth with their own perceptions and reflect that back to her. This is the last trap of the world. It is put there to make you doubt the truth and question yourself.

In my experience, people who came to my courses in a total state of sleep and then entered the path of awakening through breath and the secrets of the golden book confused the roles, even though they were just in the beginning, and tried to teach the one who knew. If I had accepted the earthly lessons they were trying to teach, I would have fallen into the trap. But I did not do that. I said, "I know that I know, and I know that I know that I know," and I let them be.

It must be a tough test for the ego consciousness—for a consciousness who came here to wake up and learn—to meet a consciousness who knows and also knows that she knows.

For me, it was hard to confirm that I was the one who knew. Whatever you say to people, however you perceive the truth, it is a hard test to stay at the point where you say, "I am the one who knows the truth, and the truth is as I know it and will not change with your comments."

As I said in the beginning, there are awake consciousnesses in the world, the ones who know. They come here knowing; they are here to teach. They are the ones who always know the truth, the true teachers. In the same way, there are sleeping consciousnesses, the ones who came here to sleep. They have chosen to sleep and get lost in the world. They will never run across this book.

There are consciousnesses who come as a test to the awake. They are in the beginning of their journey of awakening and are still asleep but think they are awake. These are the real tests of the ones who know themselves, the awake consciousnesses. They are the ones who interpret the truth. They deal with the truth because they do not know. They deal with me because they want to learn from me. As long as they are with me, they can learn, but since their learning has not completely happened, they are on the road, and they still interpret what they learn with the human consciousness. They say to the one who knows, "The truth says this; you are wrong."

Oh, I swear to God, I love those types.

They learned and heard that the world is an illusion from me, and they dare to think they know better than I do just because they went to two courses, two breathing sessions.

I want to say to them, "Honey, look, the one who knows the truth knows it, and the one who does not knows it like herself. What are you trying to teach or tell to the one who was born knowing, who was actually never born?" I say this to the ones who understand.

This is the road map the one who knows herself chose for herself.

I could write a book about how the ones in the path wake up to the one truth and twist the truth as they want just because they are not the ones who know the truth, but it is not necessary. Why not? Because they have a long path. They will misunderstand a lot; then they will wake up.

There are people who wake up to what I say ten years later.

The truth is one. It stays where it is. The ones who have it and know it will know; therefore, they are patient to the ones who cannot yet comprehend the truth, the ones who are on their path to awakening.

One who knows the me knows me; the one who does not knows it like herself.

You know that you are far away from the ones who do not know. You will not even meet them in the journey of the world. But you will meet the ones on the path to awakening, the students.

Never forget your role.

Do not confuse your mission.

You are the one who knows and sees; they are the ones who do not know or see.

You are born to be a teacher, and you know this. Even your parents were trained since the day you were born. Everyone you meet is in training. Never forget this.

If you enter the path of learning even for a second, you will lose. That is a place you will never be able to enter, a place that does not exist in your choice, your experience. Let it be.

It took me years to accept that I learn nothing new about the truth and that I already know everything. The only thing the one who knows herself should do is accept that she knows herself, acknowledge how much she knows, and accept that she already knows the truth. When you do this, your students will line up before you.

The final test of the one who knows himself is love. The final test is the only thing he is required to be free from: love for the world.

Since He is the one who loves everything, He also loves the world. However, neither the world nor humans are worthy of His love. The worst part is that the whole world lives with His love.

If there were not that love, if He had not wished for a place where His love flowed, the world would not be.

The one who knows himself is in the world to give up on love and knowing himself.

Everything fits now, right?

The sleeping ones came to sleep, the ones on the path to awakening came to wake up, and the awake ones came to sleep again.

The world is a trap, a simple game to pull the one who knows himself.

That is such a huge attraction, such a huge magnetic field, that it can throw a creature in heaven into hell, inside the fire.

That creature needs to give up on the things he does for love, on throwing himself into the fire.

When he does this, he will only stay for a moment.

Everything will happen as it is supposed to.

Then there will be only God.

The final test of the one who knows himself will do this.

Then the final test is passed, and doomsday will come.

That doomsday already happened in my world.

Actually, doomsday was my birthday, the day when the trend of the secrets of the golden book descended into the world. In my world, humanity started to wake up as of March 17, 1975, and this awakening still continues.

I want to thank God, who gave me the courage to write all these things; my core; and my healthy body, the vehicle that ensured this information came to the world. I come from a long journey. I was tested with the ones who misunderstood me and the ones who do not know me. Every word coming from the truth and every look was a slap in the face of the people. They judged, criticized, got mad, did not like me or love me, loved me or liked me very much, adored me, came after me, and left me. It did not matter. The truth I know did not change. Irrelevant to the things happening in the world, it stayed there and waited for its time.

The time has come.

This is the time.

The trend of the secrets of the golden book contains great information of truth, whatever you think about it. The fact that you cannot understand it will not change the truth. The fact that you criticize what I have written or judge me will not change the truth either. Nothing done by humans affects the truth. They will eventually understand this.

Doomsday will ensure this.

Here is the first sign of doomsday: the final test.

It is an experience that will dazzle you in the world and may end with you forgetting yourself and the truth.

Your meeting with your twin spirit.

11:11.

It is, of course, not a coincidence that the day of the meeting is 11:11. The spirits split in half will meet in the days with the number 11:11, which symbolizes duality.

I have written the experience we have with our twin spirit, with the brother of our spirit.

The first deterioration, the big bang, the destruction of singularity, switching to duality, and the split of the spirit and the truth.

The formation of the sleeping and awake sides.

The meeting of two points at the beginning and end of the universe. The one at the beginning wants to end, and the one at the end wants to go back to the beginning. The moment when the angel in heaven fell in love with the world and descended. The attraction, the purpose, the reason.

Dark emotions deep in the world.

The attraction formed because of divine order.

One part of the spirit or the consciousness wants to sleep, and the other wants to stay awake. There is a constant union between these two. One looks to the right, and the other looks to the left. One perceives the world, and the other perceives the spirit. One is turned to the core, and the other is turned to the world.

They can never fully understand each other, but they know that they are a whole somewhere—at the moment of the destruction of humanity and the universe.

The earthly attraction between twin spirits is the last temptation.

The sleeping side looks at the awake side, and it wants to wake up. Meanwhile, the awake one wants to fall asleep immediately. They are like the two face of a medal.

You want to be him, and he wants to be you.

It's an endless dilemma.

The twin spirit will run away from you the more you try to reach him and will take you deep inside the world.

That fire. The fire itself.

Death.

The moment we meet our other half, we start to feel the agony of separation in our hearts at the deepest level.

We meet our twin spirit because we want this.

We meet our twin spirit, the last point that holds us in the world, because we have chosen the divine love experience. The twin spirit is the opposite pole, the person we will never reach.

Finding our twin spirit is our meeting with our part we are separated from. From the moment the separation started, the thought structure under the universe resulted in our touching the deepest pain of humanity, the pain of separation.

The human is separated from the Creator. He always feels like this because this is in his experience. Yes, you can live as one, as a whole with the Creator. You can live feeling His presence and constantly thinking about Him. But at the point of the start of humanity, we must mention the divinity, the Creator.

Where there are two, there is no one.

Where the human starts, where the spirit is split in half, and where one is turned into duality, into two spirits, the Creator is just a memory.

Facing this truth takes great courage.

You will not even want to breathe because of the pain. Your heart burns in a fire, and you wake up to the fact that you will never heal.

That heart is for burning.

The human is deep in the fire, deep in hell. He misses the Creator, heaven, and true life every single day, but he cannot reach Him. He cries inside. He bleeds inside.

Your twin spirit faces you with this.

As you look at him, you face the separation with your first idea of separation from the Creator.

He and you—you are not one.

Your spirits are in the same place because they remember the one and only truth, but none of us, in either spirit or body, is God.

He is where we are not.

The Creator starts when the human ends.

Our twin spirit is the last point where we wake up and get freed from this world.

We suffer as we look at him.

Our heart bleeds as we look at him.

Most people confuse this with love, but we cannot call the love in the world true love. It is fire.

Falling in love with the world is throwing yourself inside the fire.

Your twin spirit is this earthly love, the burning fire. You think you are in love, and your heart burns, but this burning is not actually love; it is the fire—hellfire, the true world.

If you go there, you will burn. You will be alone. You will lose your mind, your feet will be swept away, you will lose yourself, you will forget yourself, and you will forget the truth.

The wise ones will never do this to themselves.

The wise ones will fall in love with nothing in the world.

The wise ones are the ones who are done with earthly love. They are the ones who do not chase after this love.

To be wise, you are given someone you cannot stop loving: your twin spirit. He dazzles you, and you want to go to him, hold his hand, and be with him. If you intend for the love of God, you will wake up one day totally and completely.

You say, "I will never hold those hands," because you see. "He will burn me."

You know.

Your golden eye is opened.

I threw myself into that fire many times. I fell in love with the world or something in the world many times. I was naive like a child; I was fooled. First, I jumped, then I lost myself, then I came back, and then I threw myself again. Each time, I burned a little more. I did not give up. I burned and burned, until I was forty.

The day I entered my fortieth year, I was finished because of all that burning. I was not left enough to fall in love with the world. I was nothing.

When I did not reach my hand to the fire again, when I was not fooled by the world again, doomsday came.

The ego played its last card. It tried to fool me with love. It tried to pull me to the world by making me fall in love.

I said no to the only reason I am in the world: love. I said no to my humanity.

Since then, I have been saying no.

This is the final test.

Leaving the love of the world for the love of God will be the final test for all of us.

You will have this test whether willingly or not. The ego thought, *The one who knows herself can say no to anything, but she cannot say no to the commitment to her brother, to a part of herself, to her twin, to the need to be one with him.*

It was wrong.

The world and the ego will test you with the final love. Remember.

Your love will burn you, but you will not go there this time. You will say, "No. The love of the world will burn me. I do not want it."

Then your heart will burn always, not for a moment. Then you will reject everything that pulls you—everything you want to reach in the world willingly—and your heart will always burn.

Then there will come a day when you think you are dying.

At that moment, you will end. You will be destroyed. Only love will remain.

This is your final test, a moment in which you will need to choose the Creator, not your earthling brother.

You will not go after the world; you will disregard the desire of your humanity; and willingly, you will throw yourself into the true fire. That fire will be the place where you end.

You will leave human love for the love of God. This will be your final test.

If you can pass this test—if you can leave the world you chase for the love you feel for your brother and can give up on choosing him—you will bring the start of doomsday.

I had the final test in my world.

I passed that final test.

I resisted the final temptation.

I stayed in myself.

There is nothing in the world that can tempt me or end with my losing myself.

My golden eye is open.

The secrets of the golden book have started to spread.

In my presence, the world ended, and He began.

Doomsday came.

It is your turn now.

That is all I know.

I know that.

I do not know that you know that you will not know.

I know what I know, and one day, when I die, you will know what I know just as you know what you know.

When you stop chasing the love you feel for the world, your heart is filled with true love. If you can leave your most beloved brother for the love of God, then your human side cries every day, she burns every day, and your ego will be destroyed every day because you disregarded it.

Your human side becomes nothing.

You disappear.

Doomsday comes.

The moment when your humanity ends comes.

Then love happens.

And anyway, there was only love.